Why Most Investors
Are Mostly Wrong
Most of the Time

WHY MOST INVESTORS ARE MOSTLY WRONG MOST OF THE TIME /

William X. Scheinman

The reader should keep in mind that any discussion of the
financial markets is of necessity a discussion of constantly
changing statistics and other data. Therefore, while both the
original and supplemental data used in this book were
current at the time they were originally furnished, such data
applied to any specific situation described may no longer be
applicable.

For the other Bill in my life

CONTENTS

LIST OF
1970 EDITION CHARTS

NOTE

The source of each of the charts used in this book is credited below it. Where possible, standard sources which are available to the average investor have been used. In certain instances it has been necessary to modify the original charts by deletions or additions. In a few other cases special charts have been created. The full identification of the standard sources used in this book follows.

Chartcraft, Inc., Larchmont, N.Y. 10538
Chestnutt Corporation, Greenwich, Conn.
Comparative Market Indicators, P.O. Box 1557, Bellevue, Wash. 98009
Current Market Perspectives. Published by Trendline, 345 Hudson Street, New York, N.Y. 10014
M. C. Horsey & Company, Inc., Salisbury, Md. 21801
Securities Research Company, 208 Newbury Street, Boston, Mass. 02116
Time chart copyright 1969 by Time Inc.; reprinted by permission.
Daily Basis Stock Charts by Trendline, 345 Hudson Street, New York, N.Y. 10014

LIST OF
1991 EDITION CHARTS

All 1991 edition charts created by the author and computer drawn.

PREFACE
TO THE 1970 EDITION

There is perhaps no activity in which human behavior with all of its contradictions reveals itself more intensely than it does in investing in the stock market. Past books have commented upon certain aspects of this behavior, but virtually no attempt has been made to measure that behavior and use the results as a working tool to assist in timing the purchases and sales of common stocks. It is this task that I have undertaken through the *divergence analysis* of sophisticated and unsophisticated investment actions.

To effectively use the insights gained from a study of crowd behavior in the stock market, familiarity with fundamental and technical considerations is required. Unfortunately, none of the existing books on fundamental or technical analysis of securities—excellent though many of them are for the specialist—are of much use to the average investor. My examination of the habitual wrongness of investment experts as a group (Chapter 2), of fundamental considerations (Chapters 3 and 4), and of technical analysis (Chapter 5) should enable the reader to integrate these factors into a practical approach to stock selection, market timing, portfolio management, selling strategies and the measurement of performance—whether he does it himself or uses professional services.

I have no magic answer for beating the market; indeed, I do not believe there is one. This book tells about investor behavior like it is—what investors, sophisticated and unsophisticated, are doing (in contrast to what they are saying) and how to evaluate it. Having evaluated it, I then attempt to show how most investors can use this knowledge to get out of the rut indicated by the title of this book and become instead mostly right most of the time.

PREFACE
TO THE 1991 EDITION

When I learned that a new edition of my book, written more than 20 years ago, was to be published, I felt challenged in several ways, though I was pleasantly surprised that so many of the theories discussed then have stood the test of time. After rereading my original book, I thought it would be worthwhile to provide certain new material and charts, not only to emphasize those new tools which I feel are worth using but also to show specific examples of how most of the *yardsticks, techniques, theories* and *concepts* seem as relevant today as they were then.

Since I continue to feel that the key to investment success is the correct evaluation of investor psychology in any given investment situation, specific examples from today's financial markets of *unit counts, resistance line measurement, the cut-in-half rules, double trouble* and the *Rule of Three* are provided. For the reader's convenience, this new material is placed at the end of each of the chapters to which it relates so one may easily compare then and "now".

In light of the 1990s' overload of investment information—especially the widespread dissemination of almost infinite varieties of technical market analysis—it seems even more timely now than then to learn *what data to focus on, where to get it and—most importantly—how to evaluate investment information for yourself.* I hope these new comments and computer-drawn charts will be a positive step in that direction. Where I've not referred to 1970 material, this means that I feel I have nothing new to add, although the statistics have necessarily changed with the years. An Appendix is now furnished beginning on page 255 to serve as a check list on which to focus, prior to making investment decisions. The opinions expressed herein are those of the writer, who provides market timing services for institutional clients based on his theory of Divergence Analysis. The application of Divergence Analysis as a tool for forecasting stock, bond, commodity and currency prices attempts to measure investment psychology and integrate these measurements with fundamental and technical analysis into a complete system of investment selections and market timing. These opinions are based primarily on psychological-statistical gaugings of crowd behavior as distinguished from fundamental investment factors. This book should be considered in the light of the limitations inherent in the approach employed and the caution required in its application. Investors and their advisors are further cautioned that investment is not a science; hypotheses and theories are not facts and should be applied, modified, or disregarded, on a case-by-case basis; and investment decisions, in the final analysis, should be based on a synthesis of possibilities or probabilities.

Reno, Nevada
January 9, 1991

ACKNOWLEDGMENTS TO THE 1970 EDITION

All research builds on and borrows from the work of others. During the four years I have been engaged in the research and application of divergence analysis and in the writing of this book, certain persons have so materially assisted me that without their help and encouragement I never would have completed my work. First of all I must thank my dear friend Arthur M. Borden, who first suggested the idea for the book and who, together with our mutual friend, his law partner John H. Ball, has assisted me without stint for many years. Joseph A. Alvarez worked with me at every stage of the writing, editing and final revision of the manuscript; I am indebted to him.

I also am grateful to my brother Robert, one of the most sophisticated of all investors for the past twenty years, whose advice and help enabled me to overcome some major obstacles. I am indebted to Robert M. Bleiberg, the courageous editor of *Barron's*, and Gerald Loeb, one of Wall Street's few authentic wise men, for their encouragement from the very beginning. My friend Hugh C. Paulk helped me in countless ways I can't begin to enumerate.

Finally, I owe special thanks to two persons without whose inspiration and cooperation the enormous investment of time in this book would not have been possible. One is my wife, Nadine, who also contributed importantly to the physical preparation of the manuscript, in particular much of the art work for the charts. The other is my son, Billy, who sacrificed many weekends of fishing and other such important activities to give me the time to write.

ACKNOWLEDGMENTS TO THE 1991 EDITION

Many people have helped me develop my stock market career over the past 21 years. Those whom I owe special thanks to for their valuable lessons are: Peter Bernstein, the distinguished economist, for helping me learn that the "big picture" fundamentals really matter, especially at major turning points; Jim Birmingham of Lincoln Partners who's shown how steady, active management without exciting stories can produce consistently superior returns; Arthur Borden of Rosenman & Colin for teaching me what "intricate merchandise" means and why it's important for those offering investment advice to qualify their opinions and separate those from facts, so that the public is not misled; Brad Goldberg of Jennison Associates for demonstrating that being big is no excuse for not trying to excel; Peter Griffiths of Denver for illustrating why modesty [the virtue the Chinese prized above all others] in money management works better than grandiosity; Allan Grolimund of Delaware Management, a keen student of technical market analysis, whose cycle analyses, together with strong selling and buying disciplines, have helped a large manager produce superior returns for more than two decades; Gian Klainguti of Bank Adler, Zurich, whose early and concentrated attention on Far Eastern stock markets has led to my interest in that part of the world; Jerry Levine, partner at the boutique, Weiss Peck & Greer, whose ability to handle volatility, in small stocks and large, and beat the market consistently, has always challenged me; Joe McNay, whose discernment in distinguishing between those technology stocks which are on the leading edge and those which are followers, ever-changing universes, is outstanding; Don Pitti, my former boss at Arthur Wiesenberger, who gave me my first real job on Wall Street and with it the opportunity to go as far as I could; Chuck Royce of Quest Advisors whose example of persistence, patience and consistency in the search for value is one I've often needed, and, my good friend, Herbert Schober of Girozentrale Vienna, who not only has helped me develop a world view about investments but also shares my interest in C.G. Jung.

Why Most Investors Are Mostly Wrong Most of the Time

1 / The Market and Its Players

> Trit trot to market to buy a penny doll;
> Trit trot back again, the market's sold
> them all.
>
> —MOTHER GOOSE

"There is nothing so disastrous as a rational investment policy in an irrational world," said J. M. Keynes, who made a fortune in the market while sipping his morning tea.

How else explain why an obscure stock with no earnings and no dividends soars 100 percent or more in a matter of days while some blue chips with yields of more than 5 percent plod along for months selling at less than ten times earnings? There is no self-evident explanation because the price-action of the stock market has no apparent logic.

Most investors attempt to beat the market with information. They read the financial press; they subscribe to one or more investment advisory services; they seek "inside" tips from their brokers or from those said to be close to corporate officers. But information is worthless unless it can be related to stock prices, and this is where a vital operational gap exists. Investors, even the so-called experts, often confuse the quality of a company with the price of its stock—with disastrous consequences. For example, who doubts that Du Pont is a great company? Yet for years it has been a pathetic stock.

After carefully studying the information they get, most investors try to draw logical conclusions from it. That is

1

one reason why they are mostly wrong most of the time. The very nature of the stock market precludes the probability of making successful investments based on the obvious logic of business information. "I don't care whether the company makes women's sweaters or atom bombs, just if the stock is going up," says the manager of a high-flying investment fund. "*Why* is for others to figure out. A stock that has tripled will keep going up because so many people think it's too high. *The market always does what it has to do to make the majority wrong.*"

Most investors, being human, are incapable of acting logically anyway. For example, although the closing hour of trading is usually the weakest, many investors wait until then to sell. Hoping against hope that their stock will go up before they sell, these investors crowd the exits at the last minute—which, of course, further depresses prices.

Logical? No. Emotional? Yes.

The deep roots of human emotion play a powerful role in market action. Investors are not machines that calculate price-earnings ratios and print out buy and sell orders but vulnerable people, usually at odds with themselves, who act out their emotions, often unconsciously.

"It is important," Freud lectured to a Vienna lay audience more than fifty years ago, "to begin early to reckon with the fact that the mind is an arena, a sort of tumbling-ground, for the struggles of antagonistic impulses; or, to express it in non-dynamic terms, that the mind is made up of contradictions and pairs of opposites. Evidence of one particular tendency does not in the least preclude its opposite; there is room for both of them. The material questions are: How do these opposites stand to one another and what effects proceed from one of them and what from the other?"

Almost everyone who has been whipsawed in the market has felt "the struggles of antagonistic impulses"—to buy, to wait, to sell, to hold on—and then made the wrong decision most of the time. Their fault lay in relying on reason alone. "The gift of reason and critical reflection," wrote Freud's one-time collaborator Carl Jung, "is not one of man's outstanding peculiarities, and even where it exists it proves to be wavering and inconstant. . . . Rational argument can be conducted with some prospect of success only so long as the emotionality of a given situation does not exceed a certain critical degree."

It is well known that investor psychology is a major—if not *the* major—cause of the dramatic rise and fall of stock prices. Investment professionals have made some rudimentary attempts to define and measure this psychological influence on the market; the study of the patterns of odd-lot buyers and sellers, investors who purchase or sell stocks in less than 100-share quantities, is one example. But little has been done to analyze definitively the emotional factors in investing and to construct a theory of human behavior in the stock market that can be applied practically to the selection, buying and selling of securities.

Instead, the investment community spends millions of dollars researching new applications of the conventional "fundamental" and "technical" analytical approaches to the market. But fundamentalists, calculating price-earnings ratios and interest rates, must wait for their choices to "work out," thus tying up capital as if time were of little importance. And technicians, studying the trends of market-action, must chase stocks, hoping to be not quite the last ones in and out of a situation. Besides, the fact that these approaches are so widely used by the myriad advisory services and brokerage houses dilutes their effectiveness, for in the market an investment policy depreciates the more widely it is adopted.

That is not to say that the fundamental and technical approaches do not have their uses; they do. The first gives us some evaluation of the economic factors that affect the market, and the second provides some indications of possible trends in market activity. But neither approach attempts to *predict* the timing of price-action. Even the

3

newer lines of research utilizing modern computer technology are essentially mechanistic; they look for price trends *once they become established and, again, after they have been broken,* an ultimately self-defeating approach as more and more investors adopt it.

The initial success of the widely heralded "performance" funds has prompted many investors—as well as the more conservative institutions and insurance companies —to question the traditional approaches to the market. If the performers have done nothing else, says *Forbes,* they "have exposed the shallowness of so much conventional money management: the old idea that the money manager's job was to play it safe, to diversify, to pick a list of blue chips and spread his accounts over them almost by a formula. This was, after all, not much *management.*"

The performers achieved their most dramatic successes in precisely those stocks that appear to defy all of the conventional investment wisdom, glamour stocks such as IBM, Polaroid and Xerox *before* they had gone up their last 1,000 percent. Not only do the performers buy these stocks but they trade them back and forth to catch the market's up and down swings, with the newer hedge funds able to profit from *short* selling as well. While the conventional mutual fund may turn over a small percent of its holdings in a year, replacing them with new stocks, the performers' turnover may be better than 100 percent —as may be, sometimes, their growth rate. Of course, you have to be a very astute manager to do this without getting caught going up the down staircase. And that, indeed, is the key to the successful performers: Their managers have insight into the psychology of the market, the kind of insight into human behavior that made millionaires of such loners as Bernard Baruch and Joe Kennedy.

When we look into the psychology of the market we find that hope and fear are its predominant emotions. That is not surprising. In our society, the hope of making money and the fear of losing it probably motivate more people than any other drive, except perhaps sex—and only perhaps. What better arena for the acting out of these drives than the market? In this context the stock price averages, and particularly the Dow Jones Industrial Average (DJIA), are as much psychological indicators as financial measurements.

"Money doesn't bring happiness but it calms the nerves," says a French proverb. But that depends upon how it is acquired. The stock market is not noted for its soothing influence, even upon relatively successful investors. There is always the problem of when to get out of a stock. If it goes up, the temptation is to hold it for more profit; if it goes down, the compulsion is to hold it in the hope that it will turn around. Selling always involves psychological stress for the ordinary investor. Indeed, the psychology of selling is completely different from that of buying. The buyer is optimistic: he hopes his stock will go up. The seller is either greedy for more profit or fearful of further loss. And unless he sells at the absolute top—which is as statistically probable as hitting the Daily Double twice in one week—he will berate himself for not making more, or for losing more.

Greed and fear tend to paralyze sellers. That is why people are quick to buy but procrastinate when it comes to selling, despite the necessity of moving decisively in and out of situations. That is why most investors sell at the last minute, even though it is the period of weakest prices.

A thorough understanding of the psychologies of buying and selling is part of the psychological insight into the market which produces more profit than loss in one's portfolio balance sheet. The fear that paralyzes most investors enables others to make money from it. In fact, as we shall see, the greater the fear in a given situation, the greater the financial opportunity.

Few traits more clearly mark the average investor than his unwillingness to change a poor position in a stock. He will go from bad to worse rather than get out, because to cut his losses would be to admit to himself—and perhaps to his wife—that he made a mistake. And that hurts the ego. To get out, he also has to call his broker—another admission of error, another blow to the ego. It is all very painful.

Lord Keynes was aware of the crucial role of the ego in the making of stock market decisions, even among the professionals. In 1935 he wrote in his *General Theory*:

> It might have been supposed that competition between expert professionals, possessing judgment and knowledge beyond that of the average private investor, would correct the vagaries of the ignorant individual left to himself. . . . [But] most of these persons are, in fact, largely concerned, not with making superior long-term forecasts of the probable yield of an investment over its whole life, but with foreseeing changes in the conventional basis of valuation a short time ahead of the general public. . . .
> This battle of wits . . . can be played by the professionals amongst themselves. . . . For it is, so to speak, a game of . . . Musical Chairs—a pastime in which he is victor who . . . secures a chair for himself when the music stops.

Large and growing numbers of Americans are plunging into the emotional cross-currents of the market; they watch their stocks morning, noon and night and measure their success or failure against their neighbors', much as 20 years ago they compared the tail fins of their cars. More than 25 million Americans, about one in eight, now hold stock, compared to less than one-sixth that number in 1945. According to Robert Haack, president of the New York Stock Exchange, an additional 100 million people have an indirect interest in the market through pension funds or through other institutions owning stocks.

In 1945 there were 880 companies on the NYSE, with 1.5 billion listed shares outstanding; today there are more than 50 percent more companies and almost 15 billion shares. The market value of all NYSE stocks at January 2, 1970, was $629.5 billion, of which the institutions owned

6

24.1 percent. The "Big Board" accounts for about three-fourths of all trading values, the remaining shares either being listed on the American Stock Exchange, regional exchanges or available over-the-counter. With the increasing activity of the institutions, a "third market" has developed in NYSE stocks traded over-the-counter as institutions and specialized brokerage houses do business with each other directly at more advantageous terms than can be secured on the floor of the Exchange.

The ratio of shares traded annually to shares listed (turnover) also continues to rise. The present average level approaches 25 percent; but this conceals a wide variance in turnover. For individuals it ranges from nil to several hundred percent; for major institutions, from 20 percent recently for private non-insured pension funds (almost double their rate of 1964) to well over 50 percent for mutual funds, about three times greater than five years ago. More investors, more shares and more turnover have led to soaring volume in recent years. On the NYSE volume rose above 15 million shares on more than one-fifth of all trading days in 1968, creating a paperwork crisis in the back offices that resulted in the failure of some of the best-known brokerage houses.

Despite a more than 20-percent drop in the DJIA during 1969 (the third largest decline in the past twenty years), and despite the decline in trading activity during the down market, the ranks of investors continue to swell both through direct investments and through the proliferating mutual funds and other institutions seeking new ways and means to attract investors' dollars.

The challenge to the ego is irresistible. Smith sees that Jones makes some money in the market and reasons that Jones is not smarter (maybe dumber) than he is, so he should be able to do as well or better. Grabowski, who was Phi Beta Kappa at a fashionable eastern university and *knows* he is smarter than either Smith or Jones, decides he can top them both. And so it goes.

In the market one can both play a game and make money. It's a real-life version of Monopoly, the most American of board games. Win or lose, everybody loves the game. In one of his serio-comic nightclub routines, Joe E. Lewis has well characterized the attitude of many of the players: "There is only one thing worse than losing—not to have played at all!"

Still, it is more fun to win, most of us will agree. Successful investing, however, demands more skill, insight and discipline than most investors bring to it. Most intelligent people, especially successful businessmen or professionals, assume that applying the abilities and judgment that made them successful in their own fields will enable them to beat the market. These people frequently are the biggest losers. They delude themselves. Even after losing, they delude themselves that they can recoup their losses by more persistent application of their intelligence; by then, of course, ego justification also is involved.

The relatively few investors who are fairly consistently right in the market are right because they do not delude themselves. Knowing themselves, they are better able to understand others and to apply the insights they gain to interpreting the psychology of the market. The reason there are relatively few such investors is that the human animal is very adept at self-delusion. Most people are afraid to learn the hidden truths about themselves— ignorance is comfortable as well as blissful. Fear of the unconscious psyche often is so great, said Jung, "that one dares not admit it even to oneself." That is why most investors continue to make the same mistakes: They are afraid to learn *why* they err. Their fear is so deep that they prefer to take repeated losses in the market rather than confront themselves.

Some investors even have a psychological *need* to lose money. "Our losses are often voluntary sacrifices," Freud pointed out. "Losing may equally well serve the impulses of spite or of self punishment; in short, the more remote

8

forms of motivation behind the impulse to do away with something by losing cannot easily be exhausted."

But assuming a will to win and a modicum of self-awareness, how can a person not blessed with intuitive insight into the psychology of the market improve his investment performance? There is no magic formula of the kind that unsophisticated investors constantly seek, but I believe that investors of average intelligence who are prepared to be reasonably honest with themselves can materially improve their performance. Indeed, my own experience is a case in point.

As a young man of thirty-eight, recently retired as president of a publicly owned corporation which I had founded at age twenty-four, I thought I knew a little about the market—and that the experts, some of whom were personal friends, knew the rest. My disillusionment was expensive. On the advice of some of the most respected names in Wall Street, I bought heavily in Chrysler in 1964 and lost when the stock unexpectedly plummeted. When I recovered from the shock, I asked myself two questions: Why were the experts wrong? Could anything be done to avoid such miscalculations?

I devoted two years, with time out for an economic study for the government of Kenya, to detailed historical research of selected data generated by each day's stock market trading to determine whether statistical evidence could provide a means of reliably measuring prevailing investor psychology. I found some interesting relationships and analyzed them against the background of some basic psychological observations to ascertain whether they could be utilized for forecasting stock price-change with any degree of accuracy. After finding what appeared to me to be confirmation of my thesis that investor behavior *could* be measured, I tested my theoretical conclusions with hundreds of historical tests of specific stocks. Then I made the final test: current stock selections. Selecting a total of 81 stocks from late 1966 to mid-1967, I was able to verify my conclusions

9

in actual practice. Since then I have been advising selected institutions and individual investors. This book, then, is a distillation of both theory and practice.

Despite all the advances of modern psychology, individual behavior is still mostly unpredictable; one cannot foretell with certainty how a particular person will react to fear of punishment (loss in the market) or the prospect of reward (gain). Given adequate data, however, *mass* behavior can be predicted with a high degree of accuracy. Crowds, wrote Gustave le Bon in his classic study of mass behavior, *Psychologie des Foules,* are influenced mainly by images produced by "the judicious employment of words and formulas." If one knows what images influence a crowd—for instance those produced by the words "war," "peace," "depression," "inflation," etc.—and if these words have produced a particular reaction in the past, one can predict with reasonable certainty how the crowd will behave again. Nine times out of ten if anyone yells *Fire!* in a packed theater, the crowd will panic and bolt for the exits, even though an orderly withdrawal would be safer.

In the market, of course, there is the problem of ascertaining what factors are influencing the players at any given time in order to determine what their reaction might be. The stock exchanges do not now provide sufficiently timely statistical data on which to base highly accurate day-to-day predictions. But they do furnish directly to the public and through governmental agencies some data arising from daily market transactions from which certain deductions can be drawn. These are the raw materials of my work. I apply this data as scientifically as I can, but my interpretation of it is necessarily subjective and dependent upon my own skills and insights.

The problem of measuring the psychology of the market is formidable. It cannot be done directly, unless one psychoanalyzes daily the thousands of investors who may act on any given day, a clearly impossible task. But much can be done, I am convinced, indirectly, if we accept a basic preconception. That preconception is: There are many different kinds of investment actions in the market, but almost all of them can be classified into two broad groups—relatively *sophisticated*, or informed; and relatively *unsophisticated*, or uninformed. And further: Each of these groups acts on the basis of either a different set of facts or a different psychology—perhaps both. For example, at the outbreak of the Six-Day War in the Middle East in 1967, unsophisticated investors panicked and sold, while sophisticated investors, regarding this panic as creating an opportunity, bought at good prices.

Many emotions may be involved in stock transactions. Essentially, however, unsophisticated investors tend to react emotionally; sophisticated investors, with psychological insight into (and control over) their own emotions, evaluate the emotional reaction of the first group and turn it to their own advantage. It is superior psychological insight which, on balance, enables sophisticated investors to win consistently in the game of Musical Chairs.

Is it difficult to classify investment actions as relatively sophisticated or unsophisticated? Not at all. The use of the word "relatively" should be noted. For example, there is no doubt that a NYSE specialist is a relatively more sophisticated investor than an odd-lotter. Specialists may be well or poorly informed, but compared with odd-lotters, their actions are sophisticated. After all, specialists make the market—that is, buy and sell individual stocks from exchange members, the stocks which the rest of us buy and sell through brokers—and unless the specialists are almost consistently right they don't last very long.

Similarly, if two investors buy or sell stock of the same company, one in the amount of 100 shares and the other in the amount of 1,000, the smaller transaction is construed to be relatively unsophisticated compared with the larger. In any particular case the smaller transaction may prove wiser than the larger one; but for analytical purposes in evaluating all such transactions (which in the aggregate make up one class) it arbitrarily must be considered relatively unsophisticated.

In a general sense there are only two categories in the stock market, buyers and sellers; but there are in addition to these two groups many others that cut across the buying-selling line. For example, how do the actions of stock exchange members as floor traders compare with those of other members with respect to purchases, sales or short sales? What is the behavior of dealer round lots for odd-lot accounts, compared with customers' odd-lot transactions? The comparisons that can be made are almost endless. In other words, there exist many segregated classes of transactions, the data for which is available from public sources.

In my research I measured and recorded hundreds of such categorized investment actions, analyzing the sophisticated and unsophisticated buying and selling patterns in each case against different price-action backgrounds. The categories were derived from the market as a whole and from certain individual stocks and groups of stocks such as steels, computers, airlines, the Dow Jones Industrials, the glamour issues and the like. I found that stock price-changes—minor, intermediate and long-term—were frequently (if not usually) preceded by contrasting changes in the prevailing behavior of the sophisticated and unsophisticated investment categories.

These psychological changes can be measured to some extent, at least with respect to contrasting or diverging behavior patterns of the two groups. The investment behavior of the two groups frequently runs parallel or fluctuates randomly for considerable periods of time. But *at key market turning points*—tops, bottoms and breakout areas —the groups' behavior frequently tends to diverge vis-à-vis each other: one will on balance buy more and the other will sell more. My theory of "divergence analysis" is based upon this phenomenon, which appears with remarkable consistency in every week's market action.

In a later chapter I will discuss further the mechanics of divergence analysis; before that would be profitable, much related material requires clarification. The key questions divergence analysis attempts to answer are how investors, sophisticated and unsophisticated, *are behaving* and how they *will behave* as new price-action circumstances unfold. I have found that by measuring investor psychology through divergence analysis, and by integrating the results with conventional fundamental and technical analyses, it frequently is possible, as we shall see, to forecast market prices for individual stocks, for groups of stocks and for the market as a whole. Divergence analysis, however, is not a mechanical, sure-fire formula for stock market profits. Anyone who claims to have such a formula is either a fool or a liar. Rather, it should be seen as a new tool which, when integrated with fundamental and technical analyses and effective money management, can lead to improved, more timely stock selection and selling decisions.

The human behavior of investors, unlike the ever-changing economic factors and price-action of the market, is essentially constant—as constant as human nature. Since human nature in the mass tends to operate in predictable patterns, insight into these patterns and measurement of them should enable us to anticipate to some extent the direction of future price-action.

Divergence analysis measures investors' human behavior —not in the abstract but in actual buying and selling situations. It can be especially useful during periods of crisis, particularly at climactic tops and bottoms, when people's conflicting impulses operate most intensely. At these times it can help us to measure the hopes and fears of different groups of investors as expressed by their buying and selling activities. All the careful fundamental research and expert opinions—however authoritative—do not have as much force and effect on stock prices as a single 100-share transaction. Research and opinion are outside the market; in the last analysis it is what investors *do* that directly determines stock prices.

My aim for divergence analysis as applied to the market is no less than Freud's aim for psychology:

Our purpose is not merely to describe and classify the phenomena but to conceive them as brought about by the play of forces in the mind, as expressions of tendencies striving towards a goal, which work together or against one another. We are endeavouring to attain a *dynamic conception* of mental phenomena. In this conception the trends we merely infer are more prominent than the phenomena we perceive.

1991 ADDENDUM

One of the wisest discussions that I've read in the past 21 years, yet concise, articulate and scientifically based, "on the kinks in human nature that lead to irrational decisions in such important areas of finance as dividend policy, asset allocation, stock selection, and sell strategies," is an article entitled, *Cognitive Biases and Investment Practice.* This article was written by Professors Meir Statman and Hersh Shefrin of the Leavey School of Business and Administration at the University of Santa Clara, California. It was published on April 1, 1989 by Peter L. Bernstein, Inc., 75 Rockefeller Plaza, New York City 10019. I was particularly fascinated by their evaluation of what constituted *growth stocks.* I strongly recommend reading it.

2 / The Experts: Tower of Babble

War, it has been said, is too serious a matter to be left to the military. Recent American experience attests to the wisdom of this observation. It can be said also that one's investments are too important to be left in the hands of Wall Street's experts without continuous monitoring and evaluation. One proof of this can be demonstrated by measuring what the market does against what the experts predict it will do.

The difference, shown on Chart No. 1, is considerable. Indeed, this divergence is so significant that I include it as a guideline in my analysis and evaluation of market trends. It is consistent. If the experts predict bull, the likelihood is that the market will turn bear, and vice versa. There are, of course, *individual* investment experts who are mostly right most of the time; but as a group they are mostly wrong most of the time—no better nor worse in their collective judgment than the uninformed, unsophisticated investor.

Since the early 1960's, Investors Intelligence, a statistical service in Larchmont, New York, has maintained a continuous record of the sentiments of more than 65 leading investment advisory services*, categorizing their opinions as bullish, bearish or undecided. The thin curve on Chart No. 1 shows the opinion of these services against the background of the daily price-range of the DJIA; it was constructed on the basis of the percentage of bearish to bullish opinion every other week. (When the curve *peaks* the experts are pessimistic; when the curve *valleys* they are optimistic.)

Note the experts' wrongness at the market's major turning points:

In January 1966, shortly before the market began a 265-point decline, the experts were bullish by better than 10 to 1—52 percent bulls to 5 percent bears. The October low that year then found the experts bearish by 61 to 24 percent, at which point the market rose 216 points by September 1967 to 951.57. The experts had, by then, become bullish again—and remained so even as the decline set in from that high and continued downward 134 points. By April 1968, bearishness had reached a ratio of better than 6 to 1 when the market rose more than 100 points. The December 1968 high of 994.65 coincided with bullish sentiment of 44.8 to 22.4 percent. And, of course, there was a decline into 1969 from that high of almost 100 points. Again, at the February bottom of 895.39, this group of experts reverted to bearishness by more than 2½ to 1; then the market made another sharp advance to the May high of 974.92. By this time the experts became bullish again by better than 1½ to 1. The experts' optimism provided an excellent sell signal to sophisticated investors, and the market plunged 187 points to the July 30 bottom of 788.07 (a de-

* There are perhaps thousands of services, but these are the principal ones with the widest circulations. The others are a mixed bag with smaller, specialized audiences. A few are excellent but others, such as *Zolar's Stock Market Horoscope,* an astrological analysis of the stock market, may be of lesser utility to the realistic investor.

CHART 1. HABITUAL WRONGNESS OF ADVISORY SERVICES AS A GROUP

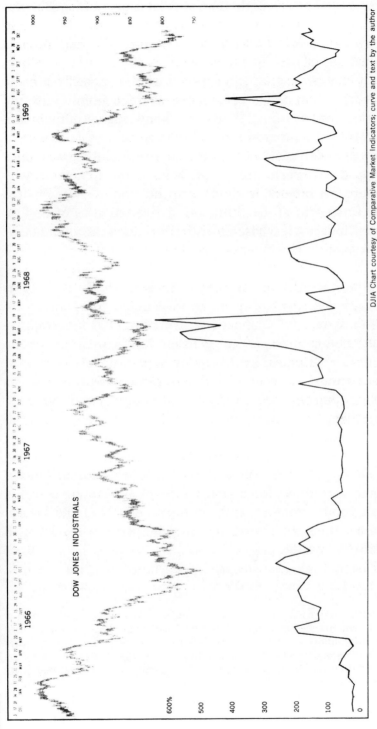

DJIA Chart courtesy of Comparative Market Indicators; curve and text by the author

The vertical lines represent the daily price ranges of the DJIA. The curve represents the percentage of bearish opinion to bullish opinion of leading investment advisory services. Note how the services' pessimism coincides with market bottoms and their optimism with market peaks.

17

cline of greater length than any of those of 1966). But by the summer bottom the experts had reversed to extreme pessimism more than 4 to 1; of course, the market then rallied sharply.

So it appears that the experts, who supposedly are the authorities on what constitutes average opinion in the market, and presumably use that knowledge profitably, are themselves, as a group, more average than not. As one of the Street's best-known technicians, Bill Jiler, once quipped: "Experts are people who know tomorrow why yesterday's prediction didn't turn out today." We can see this further in an examination of the activities of institutional investors, whose stock transactions are directed by professional investment managers.

Who are the institutional investors? Mutual funds (legally described as open-end investment companies) are the most widely publicized. But institutional investors include non-insured private pension funds, insurance companies of all types, banks, foundations, university endowment funds, state and local government trust funds, as well as personal trust funds* and holdings of foreigners. Together the institutions hold about 33 percent of all stock in the country, up from less than 25 percent a decade ago and steadily increasing. The estimated market value of all stock at the end of 1968 was 761.3 billion. Mutual funds accounted for about a fifth of this total. Personal trust funds (mainly bank-administered) held the largest share, almost one-third, followed by pension funds, with almost a quarter.

The growth of pension funds, however, over the last

---

* Personal trust funds, with $80 billion of common and preferred stock, command the largest portion of institutional stockholdings; they are individually owned but institutionally managed. (In many calculations, personal trust-fund stockholdings are included in the individual rather than the institutional sector, thus greatly altering the ownership ratios.)

twenty years has been extraordinary, and it is expected to continue. Almost 30 million employees now are covered by private pension plans, up from under 10 million twenty years ago. By 1980 this figure will rise to 45 million, and the combined assets of the funds should exceed $220 billion. This growing pool of invested assets can be expected to exert increasing influence on the security markets of the future.

Institutions, which in 1960 accounted for 24 percent of the volume of trading on the NYSE, now account for more than 50 percent of that volume—and the percentage continues to rise. All this activity is a direct outgrowth of the initial success of the performers, which showed that astute, aggressive trading of a fund's assets could maximize profits and increase those assets much more rapidly and dramatically than carefully nurturing them in the traditional manner.

Inspired by the performers, mutual funds have proliferated at a pace unforeseen just a few years ago, and the future promises more of the same. New mutual funds increased almost 20 percent in 1968, closer to 30 percent in 1969. The Investment Company Institute expects these funds to grow to $150 billion in assets by 1980—almost triple the industry's current size. The fastest-growing segment of the mutual-fund industry are the "no load" funds, sold without charge to investors by those funds themselves. (Load funds are sold by salesmen or brokers who charge a commission, a load.) While no-load funds hold less than 10 percent of all fund assets at present, they are growing at twice the rate of other funds. Their extremely rapid growth rates have undoubtedly been stimulated by the fact that no-loads have led the performance race in recent years, with two of them, the Neuwirth Fund up 90 percent and the Gibraltar Fund up almost 73 percent in 1968 alone. But, as we shall see, the "go-go" no-load funds may be under the greatest pressure to produce spectacular performance results often at the cost of accepting what any prudent fiduciary would regard as unacceptable risks. As the industry journal *FundScope* explained recently:

This pressure is induced by severe competition from load funds in the area of distribution. Load funds have salesmen who "push" their shares, regardless of performance. Indeed, some load funds with consistently mediocre performance have become big precisely because their salesmen are top performers and not because their portfolio managers are top performers.

Institutions now hold ten times the percentage of their own assets in mutual funds than they held a decade ago. And this figure is rising. The life-insurance industry, with assets of close to $200 billion (and only a small percentage of them in stocks), is moving rapidly into the mutual-fund business in an effort to recapture its once dominant share of the public's savings dollar, a share that in the past twenty years has dropped from almost 50 percent to somewhat over 10 percent.

The banking industry, too, is anxious to get into the mutual-fund race despite objections that such activity could cause unwarranted conflicts of interest, inclining a bank to favor companies whose stock is held by its fund and to invest in stocks of companies the bank is lender to irrespective of their investment merits. Every bank teller a mutual-fund salesman? The idea would be funny if it weren't so dangerous.

From time immemorial insurance companies said they were selling peace of mind, security, whereas the funds were selling speculation in the stock market. But, as every neophyte life-insurance salesman knows, the major part of the life-insurance dollar is really a form of savings—not true insurance; the mutual-fund salesman was tapping an ever-wider market as the two competed for many of the same dollars. More and more people bought protection through the much cheaper *term* insurance, putting their savings dollars in mutual funds and directly in stocks. The present rush by the insurance industry to buy, merge with or start their own mutual funds reflects a late recognition of the competitive need to go "where the action is."

But training agents to sell fund shares may present some interesting ethical problems. "Life insurance," says Connecticut General's president Henry R. Roberts, "is a set of guarantees. A mutual fund is a hope, an expression of confidence."

The most basic of all ethical and legal standards governing conduct in the securities business is that success in the market *cannot* be guaranteed. What will happen if the life-insurance salesman gets the two products confused? This also may become a problem for mutual-fund management companies, which in increasing number are now going into the insurance business to fight the entry of the insurance giants into their own industry.*

The potential ramifications of the insurance industry's impact upon the market are awesome to contemplate. About 60,000 salesmen and brokerage representatives are now licensed by the National Association of Security Dealers (NASD) to sell mutual-fund shares to the public. The insurance companies add a potential sales force of 500,000 to this total—there are 450,000 licensed life-insurance salesmen alone—and they have access to 130 million policyholders. By comparison, only 5 million Americans out of the more than 25 million who own stock now own mutual-fund shares.

The proliferation of funds and other increased institutional activity prompted NYSE president Robert W. Haack to ask recently: "What happens as public savings become increasingly institutionalized? What happens to the present balance of individual and institutional investors, and how might this affect market depth and liquidity?"

---

* On November 5, 1969, the Midwest Stock Exchange announced that it was permitting its member firms to sell life insurance. This was the first time any securities exchange had authorized life insurance sales by brokerage house members.

Haack had no answers to these questions, but the experience of the shareholders of the Mates Fund suggests how preponderantly institutional investment might affect market liquidity. Mates was the top performing fund when the SEC, discovering that inaccurate information had been circulated about Omega Equities Corporation, suspended trading in its stock, leaving Mates, with 300,000 shares of Omega, or about 15 percent of its assets, high and dry. To avoid a stampede by shareholders out of the fund, Mates obtained permission from the SEC to suspend the shareholders' redemption privilege.

Traditionally, the redemption privilege—which allows mutual investors to cash in their shares at any time for their current market value—has been the cornerstone of the mutual-fund business because it gives the investor instant liquidity. It is the same as being able to draw your money out of the savings bank whenever you wish. Mates' action, however, froze its 3,300 shareholders into the fund and left them at the mercy of the market—a declining market at that. Not surprisingly, some shareholders filed suit against Mates in federal court.*

They contended that Mates improperly evaluated Omega, a "letter" stock—that is, a security not registered with the SEC and which can be sold only to a buyer who supplies an agreement binding him not to resell his purchase on the market for some years, under penalty of law. Letter stock commonly is sold at a large discount from the market price. But many funds, after buying these stocks at a discount, habitually evaluate them at more than the purchase price. Four other funds besides Mates had bought Omega letter stock. The five funds had paid slightly more than $1.7 million for the stock, then had valued it at better than six times its purchase price, more than $10 million.

Such practices give a fund "instant performance"—the true value of which, however, is indicated by Mates' experience. When the SEC suspended trading in Omega, the

---

* In his reply to the lawsuit, which is still pending, Mr. Mates denied the material allegations of the complaint.

stock was selling at $25 a share. Four months later, when the ban was lifted, the stock was down to $5—and, with Omega besieged by the SEC and by lawsuits totaling more than $2.5 million, nobody was buying Mates' 300,000 shares. The Mates shares themselves were quoted at $8.63, down from $15.51 before the Omega disaster. As the 1969 market declined further, the Omega shares dropped to $1 a share and Mates' to about $4. Near the bottom of the decline Omega filed a registration statement for 2,600,000 shares (including Mates' Omega shares) but by then there no longer were any eager buyers.

While Mates' was the first widely publicized case it certainly is not the exception. Soon after the Mates case broke, Norman F. Dacey, an attorney, filed lawsuits against the $1-billion Enterprise Fund and three other mutual funds charging them with improperly purchasing and valuing restricted stocks.* At the annual meeting of Enterprise Fund shareholders, Dacey said** that on June 28, 1967, Enterprise had paid $743,000 for 50,000 shares of Wellington Electronics and had listed them as being worth $1,263,938 in its June 30 report—an appreciation of 59 percent in 48 hours; that on December 22, 1967, the fund had bought 80,000 shares of AITS Inc. for $2,081,000 and had put a value of $2,718,000 on those shares in its December 31 report—up 30.6 percent; and that on December 22, 1967, Enterprise had picked up 21,000 shares of Larson Industries for $2,101,000 and had valued them five days later at $2,473,000—an 18-percent increase.

Mutual fund holdings of letter stock exceeded $3 billion by the beginning of 1970. Almost half the leading funds— including seven of the top ten—held restricted stocks, which may help to explain the funds' exaggerated performance swings. "You don't see the garbage until the tide goes out," one leading analyst explained. "And when the market drops, suddenly these letter stocks seem to be dogs that can't be sold at any price."

* Commenting on the lawsuits, which are still pending, Enterprise said in its annual report: "In the opinion of the Corporation's legal counsel these suits can be successfully defended and are without merit."
** As reported in the New York *Daily News*.

Another path to instant performance favored by some fund managers is buying thinly capitalized issues, principally traded either over-the-counter or on the American Stock Exchange, which lists stocks not widely enough held or seasoned enough to be listed on the NYSE. Block purchases of such stocks almost can make a market in them; and as the price goes up the fund looks good. The company, however, which often had few realistic prospects to begin with in relation to the price paid for it, looks no better. And who will buy it if the market weakens? "The question is not can you sell the stock," says one fund head, "but can you support it?" One such stock, favored by many go-go funds, was National Patent Development, a company that never earned a nickel. It once reached almost 200 but by early 1969 had declined to 62. By then funds owned a fifth of the 760,000 shares outstanding. One fund manager who still had a paper profit on it because he had bought it at 50 said: "The only trouble is, we couldn't sell it now without breaking the market. I wish to hell we had lightened our position while it was going up."

Probably the biggest collector of such thinly capitalized stocks is the same Enterprise Fund mentioned above. At the beginning of 1969 its almost $1 billion in assets were in some 400 issues, most of them small companies. Twenty percent of them were unlisted, 7 percent were letter stock. The former manager of Enterprise, Fred Carr, said he concentrated on "emerging growth situations" and vigorously defended his practices. In 1967, when Carr had only $100 million to play with, Enterprise rose over 100 percent and led the go-go derby; in 1968 the fund started with $250 million and gained 44 percent by year's end in assets value per share. But in 1969, starting with the almost $1 billion, Enterprise was down over 25 percent by year end, and buyers at the beginning of the year, with the 8.5-percent load charge they must pay, had one-third less dollar value than they had started with.

With the added burden of handling ten times as much money as only two years before, the downside leverage inherent in any situation of self-fulfilled prices became all too apparent. The enterprising (excuse the pun) financial writer Robert Metz of *The New York Times* asked Carr during the 1969 summer decline why the newspapers hadn't quoted the price of Enterprise Fund the previous few days. Metz was told this was because Enterprise couldn't get reliable quotes on many of its stocks. It takes no genius to figure out that when one is unable to get quotes on even 100 shares, the holder of huge blocks has what is, in effect, almost unmarketable securities, not much better than restricted stock. This raises, of course, the most interesting question of all: What happens if, during a major market decline, fund holders of this kind of fund demand redemptions in excess of the fund's cash reserves? This is more possible than it may seem; for example on June 30, 1969, the liquidity ratio of all funds as a group was 8 percent while the redemption ratio was 8.2 percent. If funds converted into even 10 percent cash— a very high ratio by historical standards: the funds' *raison d'être,* of course, is to invest money, not to sit on it— redemptions just as easily could soar even higher.

A third method of achieving instant performance is through the hot new issues market, the psychology of which reflects the desire of the crowd to get something for nothing operating within the framework of a legitimate need by new companies to obtain equity capital.

Because the issue is "new"—that is, no market previously existed for the equity—theoretically the price can rise to the sky. Price-earnings ratios of publicly owned companies of similar size in the same industries do provide some guidelines, but basically the price is set between the company and the underwriter based on a combination of what they think may be in their respective best interests. The company, and the insiders who are bailing out, naturally seek the highest price, and the underwriter naturally seeks the largest compensation. But, where the company and insiders may not ordinarily be as concerned about the "after" market—how the original price will stand up after the offering has been completed—the astute underwriter must consider this factor, since the issue is being marketed to his customers, to whom he will want to return in the future with other offerings. To satisfy them he needs an offering price low enough to command a premium in the after market.

Underwriters who understand the game and are concerned with the welfare of their customers, refuse deals where companies insist on excessive pricing, accepting only those that in their opinion clients will do well with both over the longer term and, ideally, immediately. Such underwriters, especially during periods of rising markets, rapidly build a following, and invariably the demand for the stock that they underwrite exceeds the supply of it. Consequently, it is parceled out in quotas to favored clients. Indeed, for the ordinary investor without special connections, the rule on new issues should be: "If they're any good you can't get them, and if you can get them at the offering price they won't be any good."

The 1967–69 new-issues spree, which included, for example, a well-known delicatessen in New York, was fueled by huge injections of investment by the mutual funds. These injections have produced essentially the same results as for the listed issues with thin capitalizations discussed above: an early upward bulge followed by a later collapse for those equities whose original bases were not ground in reality.

Fund managers themselves are quite realistic about the new-issues market: "They use their brokerage power to force underwriters to give them a good chunk of a new underwriting," explains one money manager. "Then they start buying the stock in the open market, which is a thin market, and thus force the stock up. With a relatively small amount of buying they thus produce a nice gain in their portfolio. This makes their performance look good and it brings in more public money and they repeat the whole process." But not too long ago when a particular fund decided to take profits in a new issue bought at an average cost near $20 per share—the market price then was $60—the fund, being realistic, tried to get $50 per share. When word got around, however, who was selling and how *big* the block was, bids vanished at once. "The next thing we knew," said the fund manager, "the market disappeared. The stock was being quoted at 40, then 35. We had no choice but to pull back." Sometime later the stock was being quoted at 75 and the fund's portfolio looked better than ever—on paper.

The value of new stock issues in 1969 was $7.7 billion compared with $3.9 billion in 1968; at the SEC's 1969 fiscal year ending June 30 new registrations were at an all-time peak with 4,700 new filings vs. 2,900 the year before. More than half were from virgin companies—those being offered to the public for the first time—vs. less than one-third virgins the prior year.

Stripped of its glitter, the new-issues market is a creature of the crowd's deep-seated desire to be fooled, the desire of Wall Street—essentially a retailing business—to give the public what it wants and the need for performance funds to show performance on paper. Speculation in 1929 was in the blue chips; today it is in hamburger stands, nursing homes and other new "concepts." As one of the partners of a conservative brokerage house quipped: "Mutual funds are supposed to be the prayer rug in the temple of investment, but some people are using them as knee-pads at a crap game."

What has turned institutional investment into a crap game is the "cult of performance" among investment managers. "This cult," says SEC chairman Hamer H. Budge, "focuses attention on gains in market value over the previous year." Traditionally, the institutional investor has sought to conserve capital; it was the individual investor who speculated. But, with increasing competition for the management of money, institutions are being forced to play the performance game or lose business. Their decision to play is understandable, but it raises some thorny questions. If, for example, the managers of a pension fund get caught in the revolving door of the market, will the fund be able to meet its liabilities to the beneficiaries? Conversely, if the fund does perform, will benefits increase, or company contributions decrease? Similar questions can be raised about any large institutional fund which must meet a collective responsibility. Craps is a high-risk game.

"There is much to be said in favor of the recent revolution in asset management," Amex president Ralph S. Saul said recently. "Certainly performance has produced results. . . . But competitive pressures on portfolio managers to perform will, if not balanced against other considerations, lead to results which may be ultimately self-defeating." Howard Stein, president of the Dreyfus Corporation, put it more starkly. "If the performance cult becomes the continuing objective of fiduciaries," he warned, "the future excessive adjustments could make the market a wasteland."

Retrenchment already may be in sight. The funds' generally inferior performance in the past few years may prompt a re-examination of the true meaning of performance. It has never been measured properly anyway. The advance or decline in fund prices calculated in the abstract is at best a misleading yardstick. It implies that alternative utilization of the shareholders' money would produce no return. This, of course, is not true; even savings banks pay 5 percent—and at no risk. There are only two realistic yardsticks: one, current fund price compared with the cost price, with the *rate* of that advance or decline measured against the alternative utilization of the same money; and two, the advance or decline of a particular fund's shares compared with that of other funds or investment managers and with that of various market indexes. And even these comparisons may be meaningless without taking into account the risk factors already cited.

Measured by these yardsticks, mutual funds have not performed so spectacularly over the past few years. A study in *Fortune* magazine showed that over a period from 1966 to 1967 the stocks *sold* by most of the leading performers did better than the ones they purchased. Statistics for 1968 show that the ten largest funds had an average gain of only 5.5 percent, less than the 9.4 percent advance of the NYSE composite common-stock index. While 237 of 307 funds outperformed the NYSE index, the seventy funds that lagged behind accounted for 43 percent of the assets under fund management. Finally, the 1968 leaders, almost without exception, in 1969 were drastically down from their own 1968 performances. During the sharp sell-off in late February 1969 the "go-go" contingent was particularly hard hit, with thirty-five such funds down between 7 to 11 percent compared with a 2.2-percent loss by the DJIA. One fund officer wailed: "Our portfolio stocks got hit by selling from all sides. For a couple of days I felt like the bird that wandered into a badminton game."

So poor was the record of most funds during the first half of 1969 that the list of "best performers" is really a list of those that lost the least. Only one of 327 funds with assets in excess of $1 million managed a gain, according to statistics compiled by the Nuveen Corporation; the 326 other funds all declined, and of these, only fifty-one lost less than the 7.5 percent decline of the DJIA. Of 369 funds ranked by the Arthur Lipper Corporation, the average decline was 12 percent, 1½ times as much as the DJIA.

By the end of 1969 only 12 of the 307 funds in existence at the beginning of the year wound up on the plus side. About two thirds of them—195—were down more than the worst performing market average—the DJIA, which lost more than 15 percent. About 60 funds lost one quarter of their assets. One had the distinction of losing 52.17 percent! Of course, fund critics long have maintained that it is difficult for fund managers to put two good performance years back to back. In fact, said one observer recently:

"There are those who believe that a mutual-fund manager is like a ballplayer. Last year's .300 hitter may be this year's trade."

Experts that inconsistent are hardly better than amateurs. And, with some 1,000 funds now in existence and new ones pouring out daily, there may soon be more funds than there are stocks listed on the New York Stock Exchange. Even now the sheer number and variety of funds have made the choices for the individual investor almost as complex as selecting stocks for himself. A relatively new company, First Multifund of America, invests only in other mutual funds. Its sponsor says that with the vast multiplication of mutual funds there is need for professional guidance in investing in other funds. But First Multifund itself declined in 1969, losing 50 percent more than the average loss of all funds.

The redemption privilege no doubt has been a factor in accelerating these funds' poor performance. "Good performance," says Allan B. Hunter, president of the One William Street Fund, "leads to net cash inflow and poor performance tends to do the opposite. When you have net redemptions, you have to think of your first obligation— the one to your shareholders to buy them out." In a serious decline, concludes Hunter, "you might be forced to sell things on balance that you might not want to, and how can you be 98 percent invested with redemptions running at 14 percent?"

One observer attributes the funds' failures to the fact that the best money-management talent in the mutual-fund business is being drawn to the private funds because the managers there get a big part of the action. Where the public-fund manager may get a fee of 1 percent of the money under management, the private hedge-fund manager may get 20 percent or more of the *profits*.

Whatever the reason for the fund's poor performance record in 1969, the record itself indicates that the funds essentially are bull-market creatures. It is widely rationalized that the market *must* keep going up as mutual funds and other institutions keep pouring cash into it, that this continual demand will always exceed the supply of stocks. This spurious theory confuses cause with effect, as funds can only continue to attract new money—sales exceeding redemptions—so long as the market (and the value of fund shares) keeps going up. When the market goes down for an extended period of time the reverse takes place.

The professional money manager's place in the overall mutual-fund scheme of things is curiously anomalous. Almost all mutual-fund sales literature emphasizes heavily the fact that one's money will be *professionally* managed, the inference being that the investor will do better with the fund than he could himself. All funds, both load and no-load, charge management fees; the more money under management the bigger the fee. But, as we shall see later, the successful management of money requires a great deal more than simply selecting stocks; for example, one of the best decisions most investors could have made at the beginning of 1969 would have been to withdraw from the market completely—an action several of the most astute investors I know did take, including my Uncle Jesse, who also sold at the 1929 top and was an active buyer of stocks during the lows of the 1930's. But this kind of basic decision-making is rarely made by any fund, however much in the shareholders' interest it might be, because it conflicts with the funds' basic interest of maximizing the amount of money under management. To have withdrawn from the market entirely would have left the funds' money unmanaged and therefore subject to withdrawals by investors, who prefer to collect their own interest at the savings bank; and withdrawals would have left the funds without any marbles to play with and hence no management fees.

Not long ago Henry C. Wallich, a member of President Eisenhower's Council of Economic Advisers, told a Senate Banking Committee: "The true value of investment advice is, on average, virtually zero." Recent studies, he explained, had shown that "mutual funds, on average, do not do better and usually do worse" for their investors than a random selection of stocks would do, *particularly when the element of risk is considered.*

An amusing experiment conducted by three top executives of *Forbes* underscores Wallich's contention. Each executive "selected" ten stocks by throwing darts against *The New York Times* stock tables. When they measured the performances of their "selections" over the past five years, they found that one dart thrower's portfolio outperformed 69 percent of all stock funds, another's outgained 64 percent of them, the third's did better than 46 percent!

So much for the record, on the whole, of professional investment managers. At the very least it suggests that a reasonably alert individual with insight into investor psychology can do better. Indeed, I think there is no question that individuals, because they can get in and out of stock positions more easily than institutions, *can* outperform most institutional investors. Because of their size, institutions necessarily must deal in large blocks of stock, and they easily can get frozen into a position. "Even in the most liquid stocks," notes analyst and editor Charles D. Ellis, "a $1-billion fund has trouble cutting in and out of positions that may average $15 million (300,000 shares of a $50 stock). That much stock is hard to buy and hard to sell."

If individuals can outperform the performers, why don't they do it more often than they do? One reason is that most investors lock themselves into one or more of five popular approaches to investment, thus assuring themselves of being mostly wrong most of the time. I call the first approach the "chase-the-rainbow" strategy. Its adherents spend their time and money looking for another Xerox. Since there are not that many Xeroxes around, this approach is tantamount to playing the 100-to-1 shots at the racetrack. And about as profitable.

The second approach I call the "shotgun" method: participation in as many stocks in as many groups as possible on the theory that some of them eventually will work out. This is what most institutions use and what most investment advisory services, in their noncommittal reports, in essence recommend. But its rate of return is low and it requires huge capital to practice.

The third approach is pure story-buying—superficial analysis combined with information from presumably dependable sources. But every time we go into a down market many story-buyers return quickly to the fundamentals.

And the fourth approach is sole reliance on technical analysis. The best characterization of it is Sam Steadman's saying: "When you go hunting, you take your hound dog along, but you don't give the dog the gun."

Finally, there is the "long-pull" approach, grounded in the fundamentalists' "value concept" preferred by most unsophisticated investors. This is used by most brokerage houses, investment advisers and managers to evade responsibility to their customers and by investors to justify to themselves their generally wrong investment decisions. The long-pull approach, however, merely begs the question. The most incisive comment about it was that of Lord Keynes, who said that in the long run we'll all be dead.

A second reason for the poor performance of most investors is directly related to the market information they assimilate. The information upon which investors act ("react" would be more accurate for most investors; initiative being more characteristic of the sophisticated group) must be considered an adjunct to their investment approaches, for it influences the choice of tactics and, indeed, often determines the success or failure of their implementation. Information is not only the investor's intellectual input but the emotional stimulus to action as well. Since most of it emanates from so-called experts, it may be useful to study its value.

"The name of the game is to get information before anyone else," a prominent broker has said, "and there isn't one guy worth his salt on Wall Street who doesn't want to get it first." This perverted view of the brokerage function, and the illusory assumption of the value of "hot tips" to the average investor which it implies, indicates the usefulness of most information distributed by brokerage houses. "The longer I operated on Wall Street," Bernard Baruch wrote in his autobiography, "the more distrustful I became of tips and inside information of every kind. Given time, I believe that inside information can break the Bank of England."

Had the broker told it like it really is, he would have said something like: "The name of the game is making money, and there isn't one broker worth his salt on Wall Street who doesn't know that the sure way to do that is to stimulate trading because that generates commissions."

This is not an indictment—indeed, there are individual brokers who would never consciously even consider churning customers' accounts—just recognition of the facts of life on the Street. Brokers are in business to make money; they make money with no risk whatever through commissions; trading generates commissions—*ergo,* brokers have a vested interest in stimulating trading. This may be the only logic in the market.

As for the argument—often advanced by brokerage houses—that brokers are sincerely committed to the "little fellow's" financial welfare, we need only examine the SEC findings in the recent Merrill Lynch–Douglas Aircraft case to determine the depth of that commitment.

Said the SEC, Merrill Lynch, as underwriter for a $75-million issue of Douglas debentures, received

material non-public information from Douglas' management with respect to its earnings which it in turn . . . disclosed to certain of its institutional and other large customers. That information . . . revealed a significant deterioration in the prospects of Douglas.

Some of the selected customers thereafter sold from existing positions and effected short sales of more than 190,000 shares of Douglas stock on the NYSE and otherwise prior to public disclosure of the information and without any disclosure of such information being made to the purchasers. . . .

While this adverse information was being disclosed to various large customers, registrant did not disclose this information to other customers *for whom it effected purchases of Douglas stock.* [Italics added.]

These "other customers" included the small investors whom Merrill Lynch had long professed to champion. Of course, as soon as the adverse information was made public the stock plummeted more than 20 points from its pre-leak price. The favored institutional investors made millions; the small investor was left holding the bag. Merrill Lynch earned commissions all around.

Merrill Lynch's action eventually led to the firm being penalized for violating the Securities Exchange Act.*

There are dozens of ways to legally and unobtrusively mislead the average investor. For example, there are three operational aspects to the exchange of investment information: one, the *literal* meaning of the words used by the dispenser of the information—McDonnell Douglas Corporation earned $3.49 per share in 1968 compared with only $.03 in 1967; two, the *hidden* meaning the words may be intended to convey—that is, depending upon the context in which these statistics are cited they may imply approval of McDonnell's earnings gain or criticism that it wasn't greater; and three, the *reaction* of the recipient in the form of buying or selling or ignoring McDonnell stock.

The dispenser of information may not be consciously aware of the hidden meaning of his words; nor may be the recipient; but the words themselves, and the recipient's reaction to them, are no less real. A mother, for example, may nag her child to take his bath; the child may respond, "All right," but fail to do so. By repeatedly telling him to take a bath (the literal message) the mother is also unconsciously telling her child that she lacks confidence in him and that is why she keeps repeating herself. That is

*See note at end of chapter.

35

the hidden meaning. And the child, while he acknowledges the literal order by perfunctorily agreeing to comply with it, actually reacts (also unconsciously) to the hidden meaning of his mother's lack of confidence by resisting taking the bath.

The information subtly and systematically withheld from most investors may affect them even more adversely than the ambiguous communications they receive. There are more ways not to skin a cat than there are to skin one, and Wall Street knows them all. Common sense, for example, dictates that an investor quickly sell his stock in a faltering company, and that in a major market decline short selling is an investor's most profitable tool. Yet, one of the Street's unwritten laws is: If you don't have anything nice to say about a company, don't say anything. To which the corollary is that a corporation, like Caesar's wife, is above reproach. The result of this policy is that the analyst's negative research findings on a faltering company rarely reach the investor—for whom, presumably, the research is conducted in the first place. "Put a negative report on paper? You must be crazy," said one of the Street's most respected analysts. "Negative report?" exclaimed the head of research of a leading brokerage house. "We haven't tried one of those in a long time—this kind of activity doesn't seem to be very profitable."

And it's not profitable because the emphasis on the Street is on buying, not selling. Most brokerage houses refuse to recommend short sales regularly because they don't want their track records measured, and short selling makes that easier to do. Some friends in the brokerage business have told me candidly that recommending short sales is "bad for business," that they can build up their commissions better through long (buying) recommendations. And, of course, negative reports threaten a broker's underwriting and investment-banking business.

With the hedge funds' increasing demand for short sales, however, things are changing somewhat. The president of

Argus Research, a $500-per-month advisory service, stated recently: "Most people say it's un-American and speculative to short a stock. But to our research people it's not un-American, and in many cases it's the most prudent thing to do." And the partner of a large investment banking house added: "I feel short selling could be used a lot more extensively. I don't understand why most brokers fail to realize that you can get a commission for a sell idea as well as a buy idea."

The corporations themselves, of course, place negative reports in the same category as *Das Kapital*. Some of them threaten to sue, others resort to public indignation. In 1967 Argus Research concluded that American Motors' automotive business had "deteriorated too far to be salvaged by the limited resources available to the company," despite the fact that AMC stock was rising. Argus, predicting AMC would lose $60 million in 1967, suggested that the stock's rising price was a "speculative flurry" that investors should seize as a "selling opportunity." AMC's president promptly branded the report as "absolutely ridiculous," adding, "I just can't understand how they can say these things. It's most unusual and totally unwarranted." AMC, however, closed out that year with a net loss of $75.8 million.

A corporate official's evaluation of his own company's stock simply is not to be taken seriously, even when he is sincere. The average investor places great stock (forgive the pun) on inside information from corporate officers. As a former corporation president, I can assure you it is usually worthless or, like the Douglas Aircraft and Texas Gulf Sulphur* tips, illegal. Businessmen, however able they may be in managing their business, are notoriously poor judges of stock market timing. This is demonstrated

* Certain officers, directors and employees of Texas Gulf Sulphur, on the basis of their confidential knowledge of a significant ore strike by the company in Timmons, Ontario, bought company stock, and tipped others to buy it, before news of the strike was publicly disclosed. They were found guilty of violating the Securities Exchange Act by trading and tipping on the basis of inside information.

continually, but my two favorite examples of it in recent years are those of Polaroid and Control Data:

Throughout 1966, officers and directors of Control Data Corporation bought 700 shares of the company's common stock and sold 175,643 shares, including 9,375 shares in December. The prices ranged from 23 to 39. Within nine months, Control Data had risen past 160. The officers and directors' sales cost them more than $20 million.

Again, on June 29, 1965, Edwin H. Land, the president of Polaroid, and James P. Warburg, the noted banker and a director of Polaroid, each sold 300,000 shares of the company's stock at about $30 a share. The stock began to move up a few days later; by the end of the year it had more than doubled; the next year it reached about 90, and the following year it went over 120. Messrs. Land and Warburg's poor timing cost them $54 million.

These examples are not atypical of what I found when I studied the SEC's monthly summary of insiders' stock transactions and researched subsequent price-actions. Why, then, look to corporate officers for inside information even about their own companies? The information the average investor may get, if it is not illegal, is likely to be misleading, inaccurate or, at best, too late to be of use.

The same can be said for most newspaper and market-report commentary. Most of it is confined to describing *ex post facto* what happened and why, instead of what investors would really like to know, which is: What is likely to happen and how can I handle it? Few commentators, however, regard the function of attempting to predict market behavior as a professional responsibility. For example, one of *Forbes'* regular columnists (he is also associated with a NYSE firm) some time ago disclaimed any responsibility for meaningful prediction. "No attempt is ever made in these columns," he wrote, "to guess the short-term behavior of any stock."

Perhaps it is just as well. When the experts do take the

plunge, most of them seem to dive into empty pools. Or perhaps they have been diving into empty pools too long. For example, on December 10, 1968, just as the market topped out and the DJIA headed downward 100 points, the first leg of 1969's major decline, the readers of the financial section of a major New York newspaper were fed the following commentary under the headline "Downturn in Stocks? The Experts Say NO":

It is suggested by [one analyst]* that the market action has left it with good chances to close out the year with all of the price indexes in new high ground. "Certainly," he says, "the momentum and all the technical indications point in that direction. Moreover, the news background is providing sufficient fuel for a continued advance."

And:

[One technician] foresees newspaper headlines hailing a close by the Dow Jones Industrial Average above 1,000 for the first time in history. "The market's strong underlying technical foundation remains intact," he maintains. "All of these factors combine to enhance [the] probabilities for the appearance of such headlines in the not too distant future."

This story was no better nor worse than those run in most other publications, even though the experts had all the odds on their side because the traditional year-end rally had taken place in twenty-three out of the preceding twenty-six years.

Again, on May 1, 1969, just a few weeks before the market made another top at 974.92 and began a decline of 187 points, *The Wall Street Journal* in a feature story quoted some of the most respected names on Wall Street on why the market was likely soon to soar to all-time highs. No one can say, of course, how many investors are

* I feel it would be unfair to cite by name just a few errant experts and their firms who are, after all, merely representative of a group failing.

encouraged by such stories to buy into markets about to top and decline, but we can assume the number is not insignificant.

As bad as advice on the general market is, however, that on individual securities is even worse. A typical example is the recommendation on May 19, 1969, of Goodyear as the "Stock of the Month" in one of the most widely circulated advisory-service publications in the country. Goodyear then was trading near 32. The service, in the usual style of services, stated that "at roughly 14 times estimated 1969 profits, the stock of this diversified company offers attractive value." The stock immediately moved to 34, the rise undoubtedly caused by the press of buying created by this very recommendation. Then, slowly but steadily, Goodyear dropped off to 25 in the next two months, a loss of almost 30 percent for those unsophisticated buyers at the top.

What this nationally known advisory service failed to emphasize was that Goodyear already had risen some 25 percent from early in the year, a substantial rise in such a short period of time for a cyclical blue chip; and that, with the stock recently split 2 for 1, buying activity in it was likely to be of the most unsophisticated kind, as we shall see later.

So much for the quality of most information reaching most investors. The fundamental problem remains not getting it but evaluating it. A plethora of fact and opinion is available, but does it have any meaningful relationship to the decision to buy (or sell) a given stock at a given price at a given time? One investment manager labels as "useless" much of what emerges from Wall Street research departments. "As documents with conclusions designed for action, research reports are plain failures," he adds. Indeed, the mass of information that is ground out by most large brokerage firms probably is more confusing than enlightening to most investors. John R. Hayes, the author of *Human Data Processing Limits in Decision Making*, has found that giving a decision-maker more than four facts reduces both the quality and speed of his decision.

It does not follow from this, however, that illiterates are the best decision-makers. What follows is that one must look only for essential information. There will always be far more research available on a given stock, or on the economy, or on the market as a whole, than one can utilize effectively.

The idea is not only to cover the field but also to get "lateral thinking," which produces a heightened sense of awareness. For this I find the following publications useful: *The New York Times* and *The Wall Street Journal,* for daily news coverage; *Barron's, Economist* and *Business Week,* for both general and specific business news; *The Institutional Investor* and *Financial Analysts Journal,* both of which are penetrating, incisively written monthlies; monthly periodicals of the St. Louis Federal Reserve Bank, *Monetary Trends* and the *Review,* the First National City Bank and Mellon Bank newsletters, for succinct monetary and economic analyses; important SEC releases; Standard & Poor's *Earnings Forecaster* (weekly), which carries brokerage-house and services' earnings estimates for leading companies; *The Wall Street Transcript* (weekly), which carries reprints of brokerage-house reports and speeches to analysts; Horsey's long-term monthly chartbook, the Chartcraft monthly (and annual) point-and-figure chartbooks, the Trendline chartbooks, *Daily Basis Stock Charts* (weekly) and *Current Market Perspectives* (monthly), and *Comparative Market Indicators,* a weekly graphical summary of market barometers.

Of course, I read other publications as well, but I believe that any serious investor who confined his reading to the publications cited above, as well as to in-depth data on individual companies being considered for investment, would have at his fingertips 95 percent of what he needs to make more informed investment decisions.

Unfortunately, for most investors, this doesn't seem to

be enough. Lacking confidence in their own judgment, they insist upon seeking "professional" advice. Like everyone else, they want an authority to which they can turn for reassurance and support in moments of insecurity and doubt and, if necessary, for self-justification after the fact. Basically apprehensive, most investors suffer from what Freud called a "free-floating anxiety . . . ready to attach itself to any thought which is at all appropriate, affecting judgments, inducing expectations, lying in wait for any opportunity to find a justification for itself."

Of course, a good investment professional is better equipped to handle day-to-day portfolio management decisions than the average investor. But since, as we have seen, professional opinion en masse is no better nor worse than average opinion, the selection of the particular professional becomes a crucial task. The professional must have the necessary insight and knowledge to play the game successfully. So the investor himself must acquire enough understanding of the game to be able to judge the performance of any professional service he may engage. No football fan, for example, has to be told of Dick Butkus's star quality.

One of the principal problems investors face today is surviving modern philosophical and technological innovations which provide new investment opportunities yet threaten traditional investment concepts and institutions. The money game, like everything else, has become increasingly complex. Yet it still is played by people (even institutions are managed by people), and the behavior of people in the mass is predictable, which makes a concept like divergence analysis a valuable tool. The search for information, I hope I have demonstrated, is essentially self-defeating. Information *about* the market and the behavior *of* the market rarely coincide. That is why divergence analysis concentrates on measuring the data that reflects what sophisticated and unsophisticated investors are *doing*, not what they are saying. What investors do, of course, they often do out of motives as complex as the market itself. In the next three chapters we will examine some of the forces, fundamental and technical, that play upon investor psychology. A knowledge of these factors will sharpen our interpretation of the trends, discussed in Chapter Six, which divergence analysis reveals.

*In these proceedings (SEC Findings, Opinion and Order in the Matters of Merrill Lynch, Pierce, Fenner & Smith, Inc., et al.) pursuant to Sections 15(b), 15A and 19(a)(3) of the Securities Exchange Act of 1934 and Section 203 of the Investment Advisers Act of 1940, an offer of settlement was submitted by Merrill Lynch (and others). Said the SEC, under the terms "of the offer . . . respondents waived a hearing and post-hearing procedures and, solely for the purpose of these proceedings and without admitting the allegations in the order for proceedings, consented to findings of violations of anti-fraud provisions of the Securities Act of 1933 and the Exchange Act and rules thereunder by registrant. . . . Respondents further consented to the entry of an order imposing, in our discretion, certain sanctions as specified in the offer of settlement."

1991 ADDENDUM

It is hardly surprising that one of the major proponents of *letter stock* in 1969 is the very same Fred Carr [page 24] who is the chairman and chief executive officer of First Executive Corporation. This is the insurance company whose enormous investment in *junk bonds,* many of which were purchased through, or upon the advice of, Carr's good friend, Mike Milken, has brought disaster upon it, not to mention the potential exposure by the insurance company's innocent policy-holders. The stock which peaked in 1986 at 23 ended 1990 at 37-1/2 cents!

I still feel that so-called *expert opinion,* as a group, is generally wrong and I still use the data provided in the chart on page 17 [Habitual Wrongness of Advisory Services as a Group]. A current version is on page 43B. However, these data have become so widely followed that I also use certain other series to try to stay in tune with *investor sentiment.* For example, one of the best of today's sentiment indicators, in my opinion, is the 10-week moving average of the CBOE Put/Call Ratio on page 43C. The sentiment *rounding peak* in early-1990 defined an important stock market low as did the mid-year *valley* help define a major selling juncture. In fourth quarter 1990 a new and higher bearish peak was consistent with the emergence of a classic 4-year market cycle low in 1990-1, I believe.

Other data related to *option* activity, which is of shorter term importance, includes the 20-day moving average of Put Premiums Less Calls [CBOE] on page 43D. Note, especially, the valleyed *sell* indication of year end-1989/new year-1990, the February 1990 buying peak, the mid-1990 selling valley, as well as what I believe to have been the important buying juncture of fourth quarter 1990. On the way down at year end 1990, I would be surprised if this series, together with others, doesn't help decide another desirable time to get out.

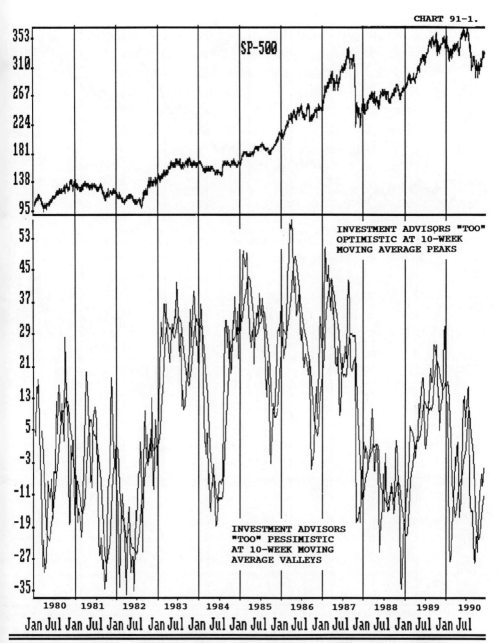

CHART 91-1.

INVESTMENT ADVISORS "TOO" OPTIMISTIC AT 10-WEEK MOVING AVERAGE PEAKS

INVESTMENT ADVISORS "TOO" PESSIMISTIC AT 10-WEEK MOVING AVERAGE VALLEYS

INVESTMENT ADVISORS, PERCENTAGE BULLS LESS BEARS & 10-WEEK MOVING AVERAGE

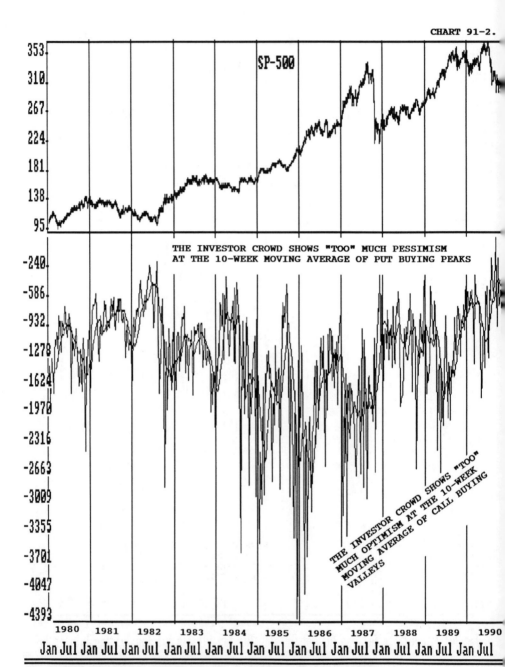

CHART 91-2.

SP-500

THE INVESTOR CROWD SHOWS "TOO" MUCH PESSIMISM
AT THE 10-WEEK MOVING AVERAGE OF PUT BUYING PEAKS

THE INVESTOR CROWD SHOWS "TOO" MUCH OPTIMISM AT THE 10-WEEK MOVING AVERAGE OF CALL BUYING VALLEYS

PUT VOLUME LESS CALL VOLUME [CBOE] & 10-WEEK MOVING AVERAGE

43C

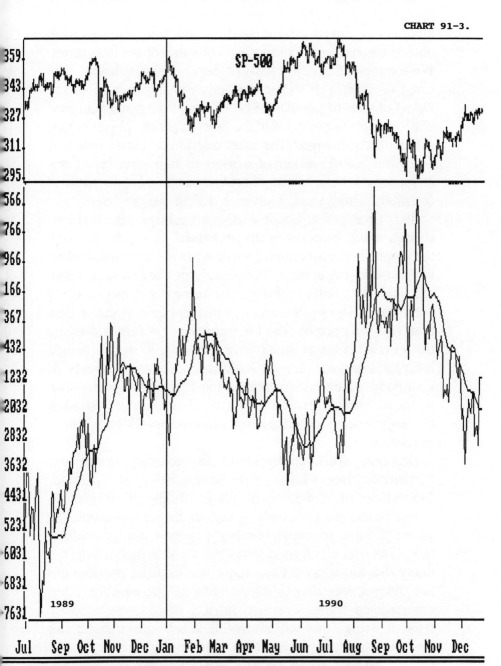

CHART 91-3.

SP-500

359
343
327
311
295

566
766
966
166
367
432
1232
2032
2832
3632
4431
5231
6031
6831
7631

1989   1990

Jul Sep Oct Nov Dec Jan Feb Mar Apr May Jun Jul Aug Sep Oct Nov Dec

PUT PREMIUMS LESS CALL PREMIUMS [CBOE] & 20-DAY MOVING AVERAGE

43D

Other sentiment series mentioned in 1970 continue to be useful today, in my opinion, even though the advent of huge amounts of option-related trading and stock futures have altered the statistical composition of some of the data series. For example, I believe Odd-Lot data remains valuable. The chart on page 43F shows a 10-day moving average of the Odd-Lot sales-to-purchase ratio. Whereas the peaking in late-1988 was consistent with the low in stock prices which subsequently emerged, the unusually low levels at year end 1989 was an indication of a short-term market top. Consequently, I believe the soaring year end 1990 ratio is consistent with a market advance in first quarter 1991.

Two final points about *expert investment advice*. First, though many investors seem impressed by insider activity, the record of insiders in recent years has just as often worked in reverse, in my opinion. Particularly on the buy side. There are many examples to match the record of Citicorp CEO John Reed who in late-1990 owned 100,000 shares at less than half the price he paid for them a year before, according to *Barron's*. Others stuck in a big way in 1990 include leveraged buyout artists Kohlberg, Kravis, Roberts & Company, along with some of the legendary Tisches, not to forget Donald Trump. Look at *Value Line* if you want to see hundreds of additional examples of flawed insider purchases.

Secondly, don't blindly follow any advisory service and particularly those who claim to be number 1, or *top rated*. Many, if not most of those, including virtually all who provide *testimonials*, are invariably going to be disappointing, or worse. Claims to being number 1 almost always are due to *selective recall* of good decisions without mentioning the many disastrous ones. Even more unethical, in my opinion, are those services providing *hot line* advice which is often contradicted by their written advice. In this way, whether right or wrong, they will always be able to quote something they said or wrote which makes them appear right.

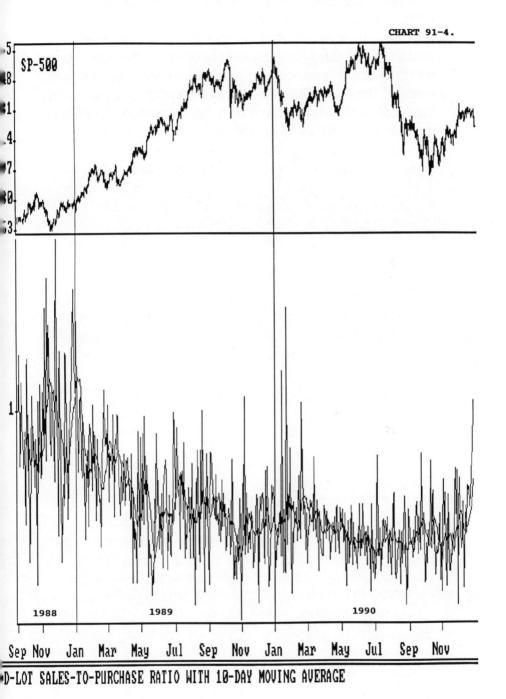

CHART 91-4.

SP-500

1988   1989   1990

Sep Nov   Jan Mar May   Jul Sep Nov   Jan Mar May   Jul Sep Nov

D-LOT SALES-TO-PURCHASE RATIO WITH 10-DAY MOVING AVERAGE

43F

Whereas on page 41 I mentioned some of the investment publications I read two decades ago, I now think it more useful to provide the various categories of information I examine and the specific data series in them [with their sources] which I use as an investment check list. Though some of these are illustrated in the new charts, all of them are listed in the Appendix. I then use a computer to collect the data and graphically portray it.

This page intentionally left blank.

3 / Profits and Politics

Things are seldom what they seem,
Skim milk masquerades as cream.
—GILBERT & SULLIVAN
in H.M.S. PINAFORE

Carlyle called economics "the dismal science." But in practice it appears less of a science than an art, and more deceptive than dismal. We have seen how unreliable investment experts are. If we examine the record of economic experts, we find a matching reliability gap. Indeed, the one characteristic shared by investment and economic experts as groups is the habitual wrongness of their predictions. For example, two of the most prestigious economic organizations, the Federal Reserve Bank of Philadelphia (FRB-P) and the National Industrial Conference Board (NICB), regularly present consensus forecasts of economic conditions, specifically estimates of the gross national product; comparison of these forecasts of the GNP with the actual figures since 1960 shows that the economists were consistently off in their estimates—at times by as much as 40 percent. This differential raises the question, observed economist Pierre A. Rinfret recently, "of whether economists forecast reality or the statistics that are purported to represent reality."

Rinfret's question is a good one, particularly as it applies to the impact of economic forces on the market. There usually is little *direct* connection between a given set of economic facts and the movement of stock prices. Stock prices essentially reflect *futures*—that is, they usually rise or fall in anticipation of future business success or failure.

Earnings per share—more specifically, the expectation of future share earnings—is the bedrock from which stock prices are projected; but current earnings, and consequently, price-earnings ratios based on the past year's earnings, have little relevance to current stock prices, as was shown by the general stock market decline in 1966 despite the reporting of sharply higher corporate earnings.

Yet some investors, sophisticated and unsophisticated, devote considerable time to the study of economic and financial statistics to help them evaluate the "intrinsic" worth of a company's stock. In the market this is known as fundamental analysis. Taken undiluted, it can be misleading. But taken *cum grano salis*, it can add to our knowledge of the factors that affect investor psychology and, therefore, investor behavior.

Without question, investor behavior is affected by both the general economic environment and by the financial outlook for a specific company or industry. For example, when discretionary income (income beyond one's basic needs) rises, people not only feel optimistic economically but they have the money to invest in the stock market. Certain industries—the automotive and travel industries, to name two—themselves are affected directly by the amount of discretionary income available to the consumer. If people have the money, they buy cars and take trips; if they don't have the money, they buy cars and take trips anyway, but not as many.

Investors who take the trouble to compare investment opportunities are quick to note that the earning potential of a relatively small firm in a rapidly growing industry is greater than that of a huge firm (such as General Motors) in a relatively static industry. Both companies may prosper, but the smaller company's growth *rate* will be substantially higher. And, of course, any company's dividend is of interest to an investor, who must compare the risks and the

45

rate of return on a stock investment with what he might realize from alternate disposition of his funds—for example, in bonds or in a savings account.

The emphasis on the Street always has been, and is now, primarily on fundamental factors—that is, economic and monetary conditions. Few money managers will take a major position in a stock without an appropriate "story," one that is always related to the expectation of future earnings. This is inevitable since common stock is property, and people always are concerned about the property they own. I have discovered, however, that even if a person knows what corporate profits will be, has an intimate knowledge of tax structure, is completely abreast of all the latest technologies, has expert knowledge about the effects of inflation, knows the latest world-trade figures and knows what expert opinion is on the outlook for a change in the price of gold—even with all this knowledge at his command, his performance in the stock market may still be well below par.

Indeed, some investors, including some professionals, entirely ignore fundamentals. They rely solely on technical analysis, the subject discussed in Chapter Five. One active trader using this approach once told me that the only times he ever made serious mistakes in the market were when he had some fundamental knowledge of the company, that as far as he was concerned the less he knew the better, and all that counted was a stock's price-action—which he claimed to be able to anticipate through his charts.

As ill-conceived as such an approach is, it does raise the question of the value of fundamentals.

One reason, of course, why an investor must have certain fundamental knowledge, apart from its own value, is to be able to assess the mass of economic data with which he is bombarded by the media and the experts. If one is surrounded by water, one must learn to swim.

How fundamental factors affect stock prices and how the crowd *thinks* they affect stock prices, however, may be quite different. One always must bear in mind the incestuous relationship between economics and politics, especially in an industrial democracy. "The fact of the matter is that politics and economics are one," notes Pierre Rinfret. "Today we live with and deal with political economics. The economist proposes and the politician disposes."

Under these circumstances, it is no wonder that economic policy is seldom clear-cut, usually ambiguous and invariably confusing.

So, although investor psychology is the principal cause of the wide fluctuation of stock prices, particularly in the short term, fundamental considerations affect both the range and the volatility of these fluctuations. That is why even the stocks of companies that show constant rates of growth may decline in price—often precipitously—when the outlook for the economy as a whole is negative. And why the stocks of companies with no individual prospects rise when the general economic outlook is rosy.

In short, the fundamental factors which either enhance or inhibit the growth prospects for a particular company, an industry or the economy are key elements in formulating any individual stock market decision. The effect of these factors is often clear in retrospect but murky at the time of their impact. One of the reasons for this is that emotion clouds the eye as events unfold; another reason is the lack of insight of most economists, who don't realize that economics is, in the words of the distinguished banker Paul M. Mazur, "basically sociological." With that insight in mind, and with the dispassionate eye of generalists, we will examine in this chapter some basic economic factors and how they affect the stock market.

The first of these factors is corporate success. "The engine which drives Enterprise is not Thrift but Profit," Lord Keynes pointed out. Most investors are insufficiently aware of the wide impact of corporate profits upon eco-

47

nomic policy and upon the stock market. Rising corporate profits create optimism among businessmen, which stimulates expanded capital spending; declining or static profits foster pessimism, which induces cutbacks and caution.

From 1961 through 1966 corporate profits rose consistently at a rate better than 10 percent annually. This encouraged businessmen to invest heavily in plant and equipment and to carry high inventories, both of which helped to power the economic boom of those years. Since 1966 the rise of corporate profits has slowed considerably, and while the commitment to capital spending has continued to increase, the increase has been due largely to inflationary expectations—to beat price rises—and to diminish labor content of manufactured products as wage costs also spiral. The GNP also continues to increase, but it does so principally because of an inflated dollar as well as certain built-in reasons—rising population, for example— therefore its expansion must not be confused with booming business. Booming business means booming profits.

Of course one of the investor's problems is how to determine a corporation's real profits, and, in particular, *earnings per share* (EPS). How many stockholders have been driven to astrologers trying to decipher an annual report? "Even a trained accountant cannot figure out an annual report in ten minutes," the president of the American Institute of Certified Public Accountants (AICPA) said recently. He added that unusual items often took prolonged study before the professional could grasp their meaning. What, then, are the chances of the average investor, even after exhaustive cryptography?

The three elements of corporate success which, for most money managers, form the backbone of a decision to buy or sell a stock are the *amount* of future earnings on a per-share basis (EPS), the *trend* of those earnings compared with the past and the price-earnings (PE) multiple to be placed on EPS. The relationship between the price of a share of stock and the earnings that underlie the share is usually expressed as a "price-earnings ratio." If a particular stock sells at $15 per share and the company earns $1 per share annually, the stock carries a price-earnings ratio of 15-to-1, or simply 15 in the jargon of the Street.

As we shall see, the mania for growth has produced a scandalous situation regarding the *reporting* of earnings to stockholders in an effort by certain companies to inflate the prices of their common stocks through "manufacturing" or otherwise manipulating earnings to show a growth trend.

Most security analysts tend to extrapolate the immediate past-earnings pattern into the future but they run into serious trouble with companies in cyclical industries when the cycle is about to reverse, when stocks in fashion go out of style and when high-fliers with high growth rates suddenly report a bad quarter. Individual PE ratios also are affected by those of the general market. For example, the PE ratio on the 30 DJIA stocks was as low as 7.7 during 1948–50 and as high as 20.9 by 1958. In the third quarter of 1961 it reached almost 25, about twice the level at the market's 1969 low.

The go-go "money-runners" ("running money" is how the gun-slingers refer to their work) have made *conceptual* investing quite an art. It's not enough to pick stocks whose earnings will go up; earnings must be expected to continue to rise. For example, a person buys a stock that has earned $1 per share during the last twelve months and is selling at $15, a PE ratio of 15. If the earnings increase during the current year to $2 EPS, will the stock sell at 30, that is, at the same multiple of 15? Given the right story, with the projection of a future that implies sharply rising earnings for many years to come, the PE multiple can quickly rise to 30, 40 or even 50. So, instead of a $30 stock, the person now owns a $60, $80 or even $100 stock.

This is what the money game as played in recent years has been all about: rising earnings accompanied by rising multiples. One problem—assuming one has been fortunate enough to buy a "new emerging growth" stock near its low—is where to get off the skyrocket. As earnings multiples grow, there is very little that fundamental analysis can do to forecast where a top is likely to be. I have found one useful yardstick, however, which is worth mentioning here. In my experience, stocks that rise in a period of six months or more to double the price at which they sold at their base lows often become the objects of sophisticated profit-taking. Apparently, sophisticated buyers at the bottom are willing to accept 100 percent profits, provided the gain is long-term for tax purposes.

With this "doubling" yardstick, I have been able to estimate some selling targets. For example, during the week of September 8, 1969, one fund manager asked my advice regarding a large block of Standard Oil of Ohio he was holding, the price at the time being 118⅜. I advised him that the logical sell target appeared to be the 120 area since that was double the previous year's base low near 60. (My advice was also based upon other considerations.) The stock reached 119⅞ later that week, then precipitously declined almost 30 points in the next two weeks.

Another method of estimating tops is the "unit" concept, which I discuss in Chapter Five. (This concept also confirmed the sell target for SOH.) At any rate, in a world of exploding or sharply contracting PE ratios it is apparent that other tools, along with fundamental analysis, are required to estimate tops and bottoms for stock prices. But first let us see what has happened to the other element in the equation, EPS itself, since it and its trend is at the heart of the PE ratio equation.

The scandalous situation I referred to earlier is the inflating of reported EPS to stockholders in an attempt by corporate managers to inflate stock prices by manipulating earnings to show a rising earnings trend and therefore command a rising PE ratio for their company's stock. This situation may be attributed to the performance-oriented money-runners who insist upon what they term *"high-*

earnings visibility." Management attains this visibility by selecting the kind of accounting treatment for certain transactions of the company's business. While the accounting profession at last is taking some steps to eliminate some of the most blatant abuses, even today all kinds of deceptive accounting methods may be lurking behind even the simplest figures.

During 1968 at least twenty-four major corporations, including most of the big steel companies, Allis-Chalmers, Brunswick, FMC, Howard Johnson and Johns-Manville, changed their methods of calculating depreciation from accelerated to straight line. This enabled them to boost their reported profits by 15 to 33 percent. For example, B. F. Goodrich, by switching from accelerated to straight-line depreciation, and by one other complicated change in the method of tabulating earnings, was able to report EPS of $3.25; without these accounting changes, reported EPS would have been only $2.76, according to *The New York Times.*

Armco's president, defending his company's switch, called it a defensive ploy designed to get the stock up and out of the reach of asset-hungry conglomerates and other acquisition-minded folk.* It succeeded—but at what price to the investor? "Investors paying high price-earnings multiples for companies using these methods of generating earnings growth may sustain losses when the manipulative techniques can no longer be applied," warned one CPA.

Some companies even go back to accelerated depreciation after a year of straight-line depreciation to achieve their ends. "This switching back and forth will work very nicely in cases where the spigot of extra earnings must be turned on and off," explains another CPA.

But there are many other ways besides playing with depreciation schedules to inflate a company's reported earnings. For example, many of the land companies that were among the hottest market performers in 1969 were really nothing more than conventional home builders

*According to *Barron's,* September 30, 1968.

whose reported EPS had been inflated by questionable accounting practices. Typical of these companies was the Deltona Corporation, a favorite of the go-go funds. Tripling in price in 1969 alone, DLT skyrocketed both as a vogue stock and under the impetus of its inflated reported earnings.

Accounting practices typical of the industry include: contractual land sales to consumers are taken into current income (as income reported in the year the sale is made) at the face amount of the contract even though the consumer pays for the land over a period of many years. This leaves the company with high reported earnings but in fact very little cash to finance its business. Indeed, some land companies are left with a negative cash flow—that is, they pay out more in cash than they receive in cash, despite their reporting of high earnings! In the event that consumer land sales falter and current reported income isn't sufficient to hypo the earnings any further, a company could sell large tracts of land it owned to other companies. This clearly would be a *non*recurring event, since it is from such tracts that subdivided lots are available for sale to consumers; but by lumping these sales in with its regular and recurring sales to consumers, a company could instantly inflate EPS.

According to an old Wall Street story once popular among brokers who were proud of the American Way, it was the habitual custom of foreign businessmen to keep three sets of books: one for the stockholders, one for the tax collector and a third set for themselves so they would know what really was going on. With the establishment of the SEC, it was commonly thought that this no longer was possible. But in recent years the conglomerates have shown that such things are still possible. Indeed, veterans of the Street say that conglomerates have broken new ground with their balance-sheet razzle-dazzle. Some conglomerates, says the vice-president of a leading brokerage house, have made acquisitions "for no other reason than to increase the flexibility in their financial reporting so they can manage their income." AMK Corporation, a diversified conglomerate, was able to boost its fiscal 1968 EPS 74¢ over the previous year through three accounting switches. Without these, AMK's EPS would have declined 25¢, says the *Wall Street Journal*.

As is well known, most conglomerates report a single earnings figure instead of separate earnings figures for their individual companies, leaving investors in the dark as to the true state of the union. Another way to inflate income is to allocate a major part of the cost of an acquisition to the long-depreciated production facilities of the subsidiary rather than warehouse inventories. Then, when the subsidiary begins selling its products, its production costs are low because its raw materials are undervalued.

For a long time the public and many of Wall Street's experts were fooled by clever promoters who generated huge paper values out of literally nothing, creating the image of enormous growth momentum. But by mid-1969, after exposure of the blatant practices of some companies, the conglomerate stocks went out of fashion in as spectacular a manner as they had come in. Gulf & Western declined from above 60 to below 20; Ling-Temco-Vought dropped from 135 to 20; and even Litton Industries went from above 100 to below 20.

Nevertheless, many conglomerates, either out of desperation or habit, continued to do their thing. For example, in a news release of mid-June 1969, Gulf & Western stated that its nine-month earnings (April 30) were $2.60 per share, up from the prior year's $2.29, based on net income of almost $60 million for 1969 vs. slightly more than $50 million for 1968. But near the bottom of page two of the release GW reported that 1969 income included gains on sales of securities of almost $20 million, or 91¢ a share, compared to slightly more than $2 million and only 11¢ per share a year earlier. What this meant, quite simply, was that earnings *from operations*—that is, the recurring

53

and regular business of the company—was $1.69 per share compared with $2.18 the previous year. But even these figures represented what are called "primary earnings"—that is, they did not allow for potential dilution by the conversion of debentures and warrants into common stock. Fully diluted operating earnings were only $1.51 per share for the current year vs. $2 a share the year before, actually *down* 25 percent.

Gulf & Western officials had said earlier they regarded security transactions as a regular business of the company—which was tantamount to saying that a non-recurring event could recur and therefore what is non-recurring might be recurring—but two years earlier the AICPA had published an opinion requiring that earnings before and after such extraordinary items be given equal prominence so that unsophisticated investors would not be misled.

The company's true inventiveness, however, was revealed in its 1969 news release, which stated that "amounts shown have not been reduced for the cost of carrying the securities portfolio, the primary cost of which is interest income." But when asked to comment on this, a company spokesman finally admitted: "By our best determination, our cost of carrying all securities in our portfolio exceeded the dividend and other income on these securities by about $8.5 million."

For years even the banks, the most respected members of the financial community, classified as "non-operating" transactions losses from bad debts and profits or losses from sales of securities, thus excluding these items from the calculation of "net operating earnings." One of the nation's most respected banking analysts estimates that from 1960 through 1968, twenty-five major banks overstated their profits by $437 million, or 5.7 percent. The SEC finally stopped this practice in July 1969.

The real price of everything may be, as the venerable

Adam Smith once said, "the toil and trouble of acquiring it." Where corporate mergers are concerned, however, modern "creative accounting" has changed all the rules. Indeed, in most corporate mergers, it is difficult to determine the real price of anything.

The AICPA defines two methods for treating business combinations, *purchase* and *pooling of interests.* Purchase is described as "a business combination of two or more corporations in which part of the ownership interest in the acquired corporation is eliminated. . . ." The key element here is the *changing ownership* of the acquired firm, which makes necessary a new basis of accounting. The net assets of the acquired firm are brought forward at their *present market value.* If the purchase price paid is greater than the market value, the excess over cost is known as "goodwill," which must be amortized over a period of time, that is, charged against current earnings. This, of course, has the effect of reducing reported current earnings.

In contrast, pooling of interests has the effect of dramatically increasing reported earnings of merged companies.* The stockholders of both companies are assumed to have pooled all their assets, including goodwill, into one big pot. In most cases, of course, one company simply buys another; but pooling of interests is described as a "business combination in which the holders of substantially all of the ownership interests in the constituent corporations become owners of a single corporation which owns the assets and businesses of the constituent corporations. . . ." The key fact here is that *no ownership change* has taken place; therefore, there is no new basis of accountability. More important, however, the net assets of the acquired firm are

* For example, Automatic Sprinkler Corporation of America reported that its after-tax earnings doubled from 1966 to 1967, rising from $4,425,000 to $9,193,000. But, if the earnings of companies acquired by Automatic Sprinkler in 1967 had been reported for the preceding year the actual trend in after-tax earnings would have shown a 15 percent decline.

brought forward into the combined business entity at existing *book value,* which usually is well below actual cost since such properties are depreciated each year for tax purposes and frequently are so far below actual current market value that there is little realistic relationship between their book and market value. As a result, despite the fact that the acquiring company may (and usually does) pay far in excess of book value, the question of goodwill never arises. So those acquiring companies choosing the pooling method of accounting treatment don't have the unpleasant problem of writing off goodwill against and to the detriment of current earnings. But beyond this advantage, there is an even greater one: the availability of a "bank of earnings" from which instant earnings can be created at will whenever the market value of assets acquired exceeds their book value—the usual case.

In a recent study of the reported earnings of twenty-six of the nation's leading corporations that had acquired 169 companies through the pooling method during the twelve-month period ended June 30, 1967, professors Ronald M. Copeland and Joseph F. Wojdak of Pennsylvania State University showed that those companies had ballooned their reported earnings from .03 to 98.15 percent of total income, the average being 31.5 percent.

Even the more conservative purchase method of accounting can be juggled by astute management to create instant income. The details are too technical to go into here, but Dr. Abraham J. Briloff, professor of accounting at the Baruch College of the City University of New York, writing in *Barron's,* noted that "the way purchase accounting is being applied we all too frequently are reminded of the Biblical reference to 'the voice of Jacob but the hand of Esau.' "

The basic problem is that there are few standardized accounting practices. "Generally accepted accounting principles," Professor Warren Law of the Harvard Business School recently noted, "now have a half-life of about ninety days." Furthermore, recent accounting changes, according to a top AICPA official, are "from a conservative method to a liberal method" and "have the effect of reporting higher asset values and higher current income."

The Accounting Principles Board, a rule-making arm of the AICPA, for years has been attempting to invoke more conservative accounting standards throughout the profession, without much success. Behind some of the accountants' resistance to reform is their reluctance to displease their clients. "Accountants are so tied to the corporations whose financial statements they audit," noted one observer, "that they're unable to bite the hand that feeds them."

AICPA did manage, however, at least to nip the corporate hand with a recent ruling requiring companies to include dilution factors—convertible debentures, preferred shares, warrants and options—in calculating their earnings. This gives the investor a somewhat more accurate picture of what he is buying and selling—but only somewhat. Professor Law, describing a recent exchange offer made by Ling-Temco-Vought, said of the 166-page prospectus: "I've read it twice and I still don't understand it. Of course, I only have a Ph.D. and teach at the Harvard Business School. I am sure a lot of widows and orphans out there do understand it."

It appears that accountants have developed a language that even their own colleagues have trouble understanding. For example, Scotland's Institute of Chartered Accountants, the Scottish equivalent of the AICPA, recently noted that there were twenty-four different interpretations of the word "depreciation" in their accounting literature. That is not unusual. The question of what "accounts receivable" are is likely to draw as many different answers as the number of accountants asked. Perhaps Rutgers University professor of economics Edward F. Williams was right when he said: "In an era of increased communicative and analytical skills, the professions of accountancy and security analysis remain as economic anachronisms."

Thornton O'Glove of the NYSE member firm Blair & Company suggests a few things investors might do in evaluating a company's earnings statement. These are:

1. Isolate capital-gains transactions from operating income.

2. Determine whether investment tax credits are being amortized or flowed through in reporting earnings. If the latter is the case, earnings are being inflated because the entire credit in a given year is offset against taxes.

3. Be alert to excessive deferrals of research and development expenditures. Such an accounting procedure can result in future earnings being severely penalized by the amounts deferred.

4. Try to determine whether a particular company has paid excessive amounts for acquisitions. This is difficult to determine, but some idea may be obtained by examining prospectuses for the amount of goodwill (the difference between book value and the cost of the acquisition) that may have been hidden via pooling-of-interests accounting.

5. Look for changes in inventory evaluation that would considerably boost profit in an inflationary environment.

6. Be aware of installment sales accounting which permits a company to include its entire profit on a particular transaction—even though the payment may be made over a period longer than twelve months.

7. Determine a company's true reporting policy concerning credit delinquencies in relation to outstanding receivables.

Since things are seldom what they seem on the balance sheet, it appears advisable to understand some of the other factors that affect corporate success. One of these is corporate management. In the opinion of John Westergaard, president of Equity Research Associates, "management is to the economy of the twentieth century what industrialization was to the nineteenth."

Westergaard divides management in American industry

into two "schools." The first he calls the traditional "General Motors school," formulated by long-time GM head Alfred P. Sloan, in which management has narrowly defined responsibilities within a tightly structured system of communications and decision-making. He calls the second the new-breed "Free-Form school," characterized by Litton Industries and Xerox Corporation, in which management demonstrates its capacity to anticipate change and to deal with it. In this school, flexibility, initiative, creativity and adaptability, rather than Sloan's "efficiency," are the principal criteria of sound management.

"In effect," adds Westergaard, "free-form management is a philosophy rather than a type of corporate structure. It is 'opportunity-oriented' toward the widest possible range of industries and products, whereas traditional management is 'industry-oriented' toward particular markets, customers or techniques."

I agree with much of what Westergaard says, particularly with respect to the importance of quality management. Yet, "free-form" management, operating without well-defined standards, values and goals, too often pastes together empty promotional conglomerates. Sophisticated investors may have been thinking somewhat along these lines when Xerox Corporation announced its intended merger with CIT Financial: Xerox's stock plunged almost 60 points before management called off the merger. The sellers felt that Xerox would dilute its earning growth potential by moving into the relatively prosaic (though solid) field of commercial financing. When SCM merged with Glidden, the market's reaction was similar: SCM's stock dropped 40 points as sophisticated investors began selling off their holdings. They were unwilling to accord paint (Glidden) as high a price-earnings multiple as business equipment (SCM).

Why should a company like Xerox seek to dilute the quality of its highly priced earnings with those of a business like CIT? Perhaps one explanation is that as Xerox grows larger its *relative* growth rate must decrease, and management, knowing that the high PE of Xerox stock is most vulnerable once it becomes common knowledge that the company is facing a declining growth rate, was seeking to acquire solid assets to substitute for some of the blue skies while it still could.

How does one distinguish outstanding management from the mediocre? One standard for measuring managerial performance is suggested by Douglas B. Fletcher, president of Shareholders Management Company:

We find that there is one common denominator that runs through all companies and which allows meaningful industry comparisons and company comparisons; and that is a company's earnings on invested capital. If we find companies which continuously earn a high rate on invested capital then we have found investments that will continuously perform well for us.

Superior management is committed to growth, particularly to growth in common-stock earnings and equity. Growth, indeed, is the Holy Grail of the market today; everyone is looking for another Xerox or Polaroid. But, as Gilbert & Sullivan pointed out in *The Gondoliers,* "when everybody's somebody, then no one's anybody," which translated suggests that when growth is no longer unique, perhaps it is overrated.

Most investors look for growth through companies with technological leverage—a potentially significant impact (as Xerox originally had) upon the economics of an industry or a business. But while a technological breakthrough can lead to a company's substantial growth over the long-term, as it did with Xerox, small companies that make such breakthroughs often lack the financial resources to exploit their advantages. And if they do exploit them, their stocks generally soar to levels out of all proportion to their realistic prospects.

As author and financier Gerald M. Loeb recently said of

growth: "You have to be careful what you pay for it." He added that "people tend to get obsessed with growth, and then if it fails they get bored with it." Furthermore, since glamour stocks are the most volatile issues on the market, investing in them carries the risk of incurring huge losses almost overnight. These days, a technological innovation by one company is matched quickly by its competitors. With industry spending more than $25 billion annually for research and development, the technological lead time that once protected an innovator for a decade or more has shrunk to a few years or even months. For example, shortly after Du Pont introduced Corfam, other companies were able to produce their own versions of it by juggling a few molecules in the laboratory. "Companies that run up because of something special that has come out of their laboratories," writer Peter Landau recently noted in *The Institutional Investor,* "are subject to an almost instant reversal if someone else comes up with something that is better."

In fundamental terms, the ideal company to invest in is well established, well managed and well financed, has a continuing high growth rate or pays a high dividend, is in a position to exploit a new market made available by a technological breakthrough and has a stock price still low. Such companies, of course, are rare. But they do exist. For example, Western Union, a solid, established company, in 1966 and 1967 sold for under 30, where it yielded almost 5 percent; yet even then it was becoming a different kind of company than it had been, developing what may be the most sophisticated real-time communications and information system in the country. This well-known change in the character of the company, however, was not really reflected in its stock price until 1969, when it rose to near 60. In the 1969–70 market decline, WU fell back to the 30's. Nevertheless, its rise (which could be repeated) indicates that there are opportunities in relatively low-risk situations with as much potential as some of the so-called glamour stocks. Ironically, some investors may have shied away from Western Union because they thought it was too conservative an investment.

It is perhaps as well that management is the most important factor in corporate success because it is the only one over which a company has complete internal control. Other factors, such as taxes and labor costs, are largely beyond corporate control. One of the implications of this trend for the investor is that companies with a relatively high labor content in their products or services will be more adversely affected economically than companies with a low labor commitment.

So much for the economics of corporate success. We have seen that some industries are affected by the amount of discretionary income available; others are affected by the costs of raw materials, by shifts in public taste or opinion, even by the birth rate. Different factors affect different companies or different segments of the economy. A few basic factors, however, affect the economy as a whole, and these we will examine separately, for together with corporate success, they make up the fundamental framework an investor should consider in any market transaction.

Perhaps the broadest of these factors is the degree of confidence that people have in their government. Its influence upon the business climate is not unlike the influence of investor psychology upon the stock market—intangible, but pervasive and potent.

In the United States this confidence, or lack of it, is focused upon presidential leadership. The President sets the pace, the policies and the tone of the government; the ripples of his influence, like those of a stone dropped in a pond, spread to the farthest shores of the nation and even across the seas.

A leader gains his followers' confidence by leading, and

he keeps it through the force of his abilities and integrity. Without these conditions there can be no confidence. Political manipulation and careful image-making may carry a President to the White House, but it won't keep him there. Lyndon Johnson demonstrated that, and Richard Nixon appears determined to confirm it, convinced, says one observer, that "Johnson's failure was not one of substance but of style."

There are some indications that public confidence in presidential leadership remains substantially at a low level. The cause appears to be the war in Vietnam, but while the war has played an important role economically, siphoning energy and funds from vital domestic programs —the cost so far has been 40,000 American lives and $150 billion—the root cause of the loss of confidence in American leadership lies even deeper than that. During the Second World War the DJIA more than doubled from a low of 92.7 in early 1942 to a high of 213.4 by mid-1946. People then had confidence both in the righteousness of the Allied cause and in the presidential leadership. That feeling is missing today.

A former Defense official claims that the government has "the right, indeed the duty, to lie if necessary to mislead an enemy and protect the people it represents." But we have seen that the government often deceives us; at other times, that it says one thing and does another. A former presidential assistant has cited Plato as precedent for this view: "The rulers of the state are the only ones who should have the privilege of lying, either at home or abroad; they may be allowed to lie for the good of the state." But Plato's Republic was ruled by philosophers, not politicians.

Indeed, the *raison d'être* for this kind of "protection" is open to interpretation, and when we examine individual incidents of the government's deceit we discover that the interpretation is conveniently broad. In addition, deception

often lurks behind the government's economic reports.*
The 1970 federal budget certified expenditures for health
and welfare of $55 billion, "more than double the level
prevailing in 1964." But a second look at the accounting
disclosed that $42.9 billion of this came from Social
Security and Medicare, trust funds supported solely by
joint contributions of employers and employees. "So almost
four-fifths of this benevolent munificence," noted one
observer, "was from the beneficiaries."

The immediate prospects for an improvement in the
government's credibility are not sanguine. As the ambiguity
and ambivalence which characterized his first year in
office revealed, Nixon has resurrected Eisenhower's "politics of postponement." But where Ike inspired confidence,
Nixon breeds insecurity. "Adjusting to competing demands," *The New York Times* noted, "he has devised for
nearly every major difficulty a compromise solution that
evades the substance of the problem, offers no sense
of vision or leadership and merely delays the day of
reckoning."

Presidential leadership—or the lack of it—certainly will
affect the market conditions of the future, even as it
affects them now. In my view the politics of postponement,
practiced at this particular time in history, can only
exacerbate an ugly situation. Referring to the violent
changes in our society, and the violent reactions to them,
Anthony Lewis wrote recently: "In the end the answer
must be political leadership. Unless politicians, especially
conservative politicans, can offer an alternative persuasive
to the frightened majority, we may have a society run by
policemen."

* Maurice Mann, Assistant Director of the Bureau of the Budget,
recently voiced sharp criticism of the tardiness and inaccuracy of
government figures on inventories and retail sales: "In my opinion, we
are playing Russian Roulette with our economy." And Paul W.
McCracken, chairman of the President's Council of Economic Advisers,
has complained of recent revisions in official estimates of the U.S.
money supply that the "figures are falling apart on us."

Investors, therefore, must consider the quality of political leadership as well as the reliability of government reports in any evaluation of their effect upon the market in the future. Also to be noted is the ironic fact that in the last quarter-century the stock market has fared better under so-called inflationist Democratic administrations than under so-called pro-business Republican administrations. This may be explained by the theory that the Republicans, a minority party, historically have not had the confidence of the people the Democrats, the majority party, have had. If this is so, it illustrates dramatically how confidence in political leadership affects stock prices, and it confirms Nixon, with his credibility albatross, as a poor prospective tonic for the market.

In all probability, nothing short of peace in Vietnam will give Nixon credibility—and only if it is not too costly or delayed too long. Peace, being historically bullish, may send stock market prices climbing, at least over the short-term. President Johnson's March 31, 1968, speech halting the bombing of North Vietnam was sufficient to trigger a major market reversal upward the day after it was delivered. A look at previous postwar periods reveals that after the Spanish-American War, stock prices rose 38 percent within twelve months; after the First World War, 36 percent; after the Second World War, 29 percent; and after the Korean War, 27 percent. The last three increases, in fact, were achieved despite declines in both business activity and corporate earnings. With peace in Vietnam, the massive poverty problem, for example, both at home and abroad, could be a profit-oriented opportunity for American business. Modern business, increasingly market-oriented, is well aware that the poor are a huge untapped market which can be tapped once they have been raised above the poverty level and have discretionary income to spend.

So the government's effect upon the economy goes beyond the level of the confidence it inspires; it also sets

65

economic directions by its pursuit of war or peace. And it does more. As the largest single purchaser of goods and services, it is a major participant in the economy, with all the economic leverage which size confers. In 1929 the federal budget was only 2 percent of the GNP. Now it is more than 20 percent—"much too big a cannon," presidential advisor Herbert Stein has noted, "to be allowed to run loose on the deck of the economy."

But even more potent than the above factors are the subjects of the next chapter, the government's fiscal and monetary policies. Their impact upon the economy—and the stock market—makes them the third of the major fundamental factors that investors should understand.

1991 ADDENDUM

21 years ago I noted that when stocks of large companies *double* prior major lows they often run into *trouble* [page 50]. It has also become important to know that stocks which are very low in price, or where the fundamentals are especially dynamic, sometimes *triple, quadruple, quintuple,* or even more. Indeed, one *yardstick* I have found especially valuable is that the outer limits of a very dynamic advance are often the *square of the low.* Contrarily, on the way down, yardsticks such as a *cut-in-half* [50 percent off a major top], or a *double cut-in-half* [75 percent off the top], indeed, even a *triple cut* [less 87-1/2 percent], are valuable tools. Later, we'll see how these yardsticks and concepts worked out for the stock market as a whole, for the U.S. dollar and for a variety of individual stocks.

4 / Money, the Root of All...

Who shall decide when doctors disagree?

—ALEXANDER POPE

No fundamental factor more purely correlates to stock prices than money. A subject of great complexity, it also is one of bitter controversy among the experts, each of whom can support his theories with a raft of impressive economic esoterica. Here, however, we shall not attempt to fathom the deep mysteries of economics; rather, we shall try to achieve a basic understanding of how money affects investor attitudes and equity prices.

In neo-Keynesian economics, *fiscal* policy—manipulative changes in the federal budget through taxation and federal spending—is the government's strongest tool for "fine tuning" the economy, that is, keeping it on an optimum noninflationary upward path. For better or for worse, this was the theory, first espoused in the New Deal and later elaborated upon by John F. Kennedy's advisers, which underlay the government's economic policies of the 1960's. The 10-percent surtax of 1968, designed to curb inflation, was one example of its application.

Present policymakers, however, take a different view of the government's economic role. They do not believe in excessive fiscal manipulation. "The role of fiscal policy is to maintain a moderate, predictable and stable budget surplus," Herbert Stein said recently. This surplus, he ex-

67

plained, would permit *monetary* policy—the regulation of the supply of money—"to do its thing."

The reliance upon monetary policy is characteristic of the so-called Chicago school of economics, which is personified by presidential adviser Milton Friedman, a long-time critic of the neo-Keynesians. Friedman believes that regulation of the money supply is the most important economic tool at the government's disposal; that over the short-term it controls the rate of growth of the economy, and over the long-term it governs the rise or fall of prices.

Certainly, the heavy impact of the money supply upon the market is clearly demonstrable. To repeat, peace historically has been bullish. But closer examination of the market's peace rallies reveals that the availability of money —or the lack of it—had much to do with their timing and staying power. "It is quite easy," said John W. Schulz, a partner in the NYSE firm of Wolfe & Company, "to relate each of the stock market's peace demonstrations and each of its subsequent hangovers since at least the Spanish-American War to the ebb and flow of the money supply."

A look at the record confirms this. With the fall of Manila in August 1898, stock prices and the money supply increased until April 1899, when money became scarcer and more difficult to borrow, and the market declined, wiping out the entire post-Manila gain by September. The same pattern was repeated after the First and Second World Wars. For two years following peace, money expanded rapidly and stock prices rose; then, when the money supply expanded less rapidly or shrank, stock prices declined sharply. The post-Second World War decline did not abate until the early 1950's, during the Korean War, when money again became more available. During the protracted Korean peace negotiations the market fluctuated within a narrow range, after an initial 10-percent rise at the start of negotiations in July 1951. The money supply increased at a rising rate during 1951, but the *rate* of increase declined in 1952; in 1953 it came to a standstill, and stocks declined, wiping out almost all the gain since July 1951.

This is similar to what happened in 1966, when the DJIA declined from 1001.11 in February to 735.74 in October. Even though the money supply expanded at a rate of 5 percent, the rate was down from 9.5 percent, and lowering the rate produced what the United States Commerce Department called the "greatest credit stringency in many decades," or what is widely known as the "credit crunch" of 1966. The market's recovery in 1967 was fueled by a return to a 9.5-percent increase in the money supply.

Most investors underestimate the effect of the availability and cost of money upon the economy and upon the stock market. As money becomes more available and easier to obtain it becomes cheaper in terms of interest (at least over the short-term*), and there is nothing like available money to stimulate stock prices. "Money shall make my mare to go," concludes an old nursery rhyme.

Conversely, of course, as money becomes scarcer, it becomes hard to get and its cost increases. Like any commodity, money is subject to the stresses of demand; and when everyone wants to borrow it at the same time, its "price"— the interest rate—rises, and credit restrictions widen, dampening both the economy and market investment.

---

* Milton Friedman, in his book, *A Monetary History of the United States 1867–1960* (written with Anna Schwartz), contends that, as available money filters through the economy, incomes rise, increasing consumer spending and demands, which business meets by plant expansion financed by loans—the increased demands for which raise interest rates over the long-term. "The delayed effect of monetary expansion is to raise interest rates," says Friedman, "and this is reinforced when you have inflation." Recent experience appears to confirm this. Noting the long upward trend in interest rates during the 1960's, the Federal Reserve Bank of St. Louis explained that this trend was "the result of the increase in demand for funds relative to the supply over the whole period. The rapidly growing demand is related to the excessive growth in total spending and the resulting inflation and, in turn, the excessive growth of total spending may be attributed to the government deficit and monetary expansion in these years."

What, in fact, *is* money, and how is it created and extinguished? "Money is as money does," explains the *Monthly Economic Letter* of the First National City Bank of New York. "Money is anything which is generally accepted in payment for goods and services. It also serves as a store of value and performs other functions, but it is the medium of exchange function which sets money apart from other financial assets. (You can't buy a cup of coffee with a Treasury bill.)"

Since money is the only means apart from barter by which transactions can be made, individuals and businesses need cash balances in order to buy; every interchange of goods and services requires a corresponding flow of money. "The internally held money supply is thus closely linked to the level of domestic economic activity," explains Citibank. "If more money is available, individuals and businesses (economic units) have excess cash balances to spend." This increases demand for goods and services, and if the economy is already at a high level, prices are pushed up. But, a reduction in the money supply leaves persons with an inadequate amount of cash to complete planned purchases; they are forced to cut back and rebuild their cash positions. This decreases demand and takes the pressure off prices. It is this power to influence the nation's economic activity that makes changes in the money supply so important.

In the United States, coin and currency make up only a fraction of the money supply. Most of the nation's money consists of bank deposits—rows of figures on bank ledgers, sums which are transferable, in the case of demand deposits, from one holder to another by means of checks. The ebb and flow of money is determined by credit. Money is *created* when a bank makes a loan to (or buys securities from) any person or entity which is not a bank. It is *extinguished* when a bank receives loan repayments from nonbanks (or sells securities to them).

Monetary policy—and ultimately, of course, the cost and

availability of money—is the responsibility of the Federal Reserve System, which regulates the money supply through its power to control credit and bank reserves.

Operating through twelve regional banks, the Federal Reserve is not required to follow the Administration's monetary policy, but it usually works in concert with it. Indeed, as the nation's central bankers, the Federal Reserve Board may be obliged to follow policies that *accommodate* federal financing which, as an independent body, it might not otherwise pursue—a situation brought sharply into focus during the massive $25-billion deficit of Lyndon Johnson's last year in office.

According to Albert E. Burger of the Federal Reserve Bank of St. Louis, the two most widely used indicators of the effect of monetary policy upon the economy are "money, defined as currency plus demand deposits held by the non-banking public" and "bank credit, defined as the loans and investments of commercial banks." It is the *monetary base*, however, which is the chief determinant of the money supply. The monetary base is an asset supplied to the private sectors of the economy by the monetary authorities. It consists principally of Federal Reserve holdings of U.S. Government securities (the largest component), the U.S. gold stock and Treasury currency outstanding.

Burger explains that "changes in the amount of base money supplied to the public and banks have been, on the average, the major cause of changes in the stocks of money and bank credit; and from the sources side, the amount of base money supplied is under the complete control of the Federal Reserve."

This control is exercised through *open-market operations,** which involve the buying and selling of U.S. Government securities by the Fed. Buying creates additional re-

* The Reserve's policy-making body is the Federal Open Market Committee which usually meets every third Tuesday. It consists of the seven governors of the Reserve Board plus five of the twelve presidents of the regional Reserve banks. The Federal Reserve Bank of New York carries out the Committee's policy directives.

serves, selling depletes them. The Fed conducts these transactions at its own specific initiative, and they are used by it to offset other changes in the monetary base over which it has less direct control.

The policies of the Fed itself affect the legal *reserve requirements* of member-bank deposits, the *discount rate,* and *Regulation* Q *interest-rate ceilings.* Together with open-market operations, these are the instruments—casually alluded to but seldom explained in the financial press —by which the Fed regulates the money supply.

We saw above how open-market operations work. As for the other instruments, the law requires member banks to carry reserves which the Fed can determine within statutory limits. The banks have been ingenious in getting around reserve requirements during periods of tight money. Some formed one-bank holding companies enabling them to sell nonregulated "commercial paper"—unsecured corporate notes. They also resorted to enormous borrowings of "Eurodollars"—U.S. dollars on deposit in banks outside the country. Eurodollar borrowings by U.S. banks surged up $9 billion in 1969 until the Fed imposed a 10 percent reserve requirement on borrowings late in the year.

The discount rate is what the Fed charges member banks for loans. When the Fed wants to discourage loans, it raises this rate.

Regulation Q gives the Fed the power to determine the maximum interest that banks may pay to their depositors. Beginning in the early 1960's, faced with the loss of deposits to higher-yielding investments, commercial banks began actively seeking such funds by issuing large-denomination "certificates of deposits." These rose from less than $3 billion to almost $20 billion in the next several years. But since the banks may not raise their yields above the rates set by the Fed, during periods of tight money CD's spill out as quickly as they originally flowed in. This severely depresses stock market credit, as we saw in 1969, when the rate ceiling shook out about $12 billion.

When the Fed adopts a policy of monetary restraint, interest rates rise, particularly in the short-term categories. The rise in interest rates, however, is not the primary means by which restraint becomes effective; rather, it becomes effective by reducing the availability of money. "A bank which is borrowing from the Federal Reserve," explains one banker, "will be much more disposed to refuse some loan applications and tighten up on loan terms than it would be if it were not having to borrow. And nothing can be more emphatic in making restraint effective than for some applicants to have their requests for loans refused or reduced or granted only on the basis of a more rapid payback of principal. Not only are such applicants forced to cut back on their planned expenditures but the knowledge that loans are hard to obtain will influence others toward a course involving less borrowing."

Surprisingly enough, widespread interest in the relationship of money to stock prices is a comparatively recent development. Previously, only a few of the more sophisticated economists and security analysts bothered to study the phenomenon. Now, with more interest in the subject, there is more exploration of how to relate money flow to equity prices. We have seen how the money supply affects the stock market. David Jenkins, writing in the *Daily Bond Buyer,* mentions two other significant monetary factors that relate to market action, the ratios of bank debits to bank loans and the ratio of bank loans to total deposits:

The ratio of debits to bank loans is significant because it illustrates how rapidly the economy is turning over its resources. If debits are rising faster than loans, then spending activity is high, but it is not being financed by an extravagant use of credit. If loans are rising faster than spending, on the other hand, the economy is overextending itself, inventories are being overbuilt, and trouble is ahead.

The ratio of loans to total deposits is a simple measure of liquidity. "When this figure is low," Jenkins explains, "liquidity is high, and banks have plenty of room to extend additional loans. When liquidity is low, the banks are getting close to being 'loaned up,' and further expansion in the economy must await further money-easing moves by the Federal Reserve." In short, this index of liquidity measures the extent to which the credit base of the country can support additional expansion.

Barron's recently suggested looking at *how* money is being used by analyzing the data on bank clearings. An upward trend of bank clearings, for example, indicates that effective money circulation is increasing, thus offsetting the effects of tight money.

Working with economists at the Massachusetts Institute of Technology, the Federal Reserve Board's staff has been conducting a special study assessing the role of monetary policy in our economic affairs. The study shows that open-market purchases which boosted bank reserves enough to cause an eventual 4-percent increase in the money supply would, in a year's time, result in a 1-percent rise in the GNP. By the end of two years, this same policy would increase GNP by about 2.5 percent, and at the end of three years by 3 percent. So, the Fed's power to raise the GNP by almost $30 billion is impressive; at the same time the lag between the Fed's decision-making and its effect upon the economy is uncomfortably long.

The MIT–FRB study also showed that monetary policy has a large dollar impact on consumer expenditures, even though the effect is small in terms of percentage (because consumer expenditures are such a huge item). "The way monetary policy affects consumption," board governor J. Dewey Daane explained in a recent speech, "is, in considerable part, through its impact on the value of equities. I suppose it will come as a surprise to no one that monetary policy is revealed to have a potent effect on the stock market. And it turns out, according to this research, that fluctuations in equity prices seem to have a measurable direct effect on consumption." The study indicates that an important segment of discretionary income over the past decade has come from capital gains in the stock market, *i.e.*, consumers count on these gains as part of their regular income, which, to that extent, determines their spending and saving patterns. This implies, of course, that a major stock market break can do much to curb inflation, a thought which is not unknown to policymakers.

Monetary policy also has a direct effect on equity prices. A slowdown in the growth of the money supply curtails the amount of money available for purchases of stocks and bonds, and interest rates consequently rise to levels at which the public is willing to accept lower cash ratios. Higher interest rates, however, mean lower bond prices and capital losses.

Money supply also can be related directly to price-earnings ratios. When the money supply expands at a high rate, investors apparently are willing to pay more for earnings, and price-earnings ratios are bid up; in contrast, when money and credit are less available, investors often insist on paying less for earning power. For example, the cost of buying earning power of a representative group of growth companies over the past five years has varied between forty times earnings and fifteen times; the correlation with rates of change in the money supply is reasonably close. So, as important as it is to follow earnings trends of individual companies and industries, it is perhaps even more important to gauge the price that investors are willing to pay for such earnings; and in this particular, the trend of money supply change may provide an excellent early warning clue. Indeed, though the emphasis of investors invariably is on corporate earnings, the rate of change of money supply may be as good or even a better indicator of stock prices.

Market tops usually have been indicated in advance or coincidentally by declines in the rate of change for the money supply, and since the determinant of it is principally the monetary base, it follows that the principal component of that base, *the Fed's holdings of Treasury securities, could be the single most important general market indicator of a fundamental nature.* Just as the Fed's persistent

75

selling of government bonds in its open-market operations may signal initiation of a period of restraint, its aggressive purchases of Treasury securities may signal the reversal of this policy and the advent of easier money.

It is important to remember, however, that while monetary restraint can choke off most stock markets, it does not necessarily follow that an ample money supply assures higher stock prices. In the long run it is investor psychology that determines whether and to what extent money is injected into or withdrawn from the stock market.

Since 1960 the money supply has expanded and contracted at annual rates ranging from plus 13.5 percent to minus 2.8 percent. The current Administration, hoping to curb inflation, has said it would like to eliminate this fluctuation and stabilize the expansion rate at a level of about 4 percent annually, which is in line with the real growth of the nation's production of goods and services. In apparent agreement with this policy, the Fed in 1969 reduced the expansion rate. Following average growth for the years 1967–68 of a 7.3 percent rate, money grew by 4 percent during the first five months of 1969, then fell off to essentially no growth at all for the rest of the year and into early 1970.* "Monetary analysis," reported the Federal Reserve Bank of St. Louis, which sometimes is described as the unofficial statistical arm of the Chicago school, "suggests that this slowing in the growth of money . . . will have a significant restraining impact on total spending in the economy."

Reducing the rate of monetary expansion, however, risks backing the economy into a recession. Chief monetary theoretician Milton Friedman himself points out that every

* The *Monthly Economic Letter* of the First National City Bank of New York explains that "the actual impact of the slowdown has been even more severe than is apparent from the figures. As the demand for money is determined by the dollar value of transactions, price changes are as important as changes in real output in fixing the level of desired cash balances. When changes in the money supply are adjusted for inflation, the zero growth since June becomes a 5 percent annualized rate of decline."

recession in the United States but one (1869–70) has been preceded by a decline in the expansion of the money supply. To exacerbate the problem, even when real growth declines, inflation doesn't ease until six months or a year later, making the economic situation politically untenable. Indeed, as the Fed applied the monetary screws in 1969, Friedman accused it of overdoing it and predicted disastrous consequences for the county if the screws were not loosened. "We cannot go quickly from nearly 8 percent a year—the recent rate of growth in total dollar income— to zero percent without a severe economic contraction. Inflation has an inertia of its own," he said. "Some retardation in growth and some increase in unemployment is an inevitable, if unwelcome, by-product of stopping inflation. But there is no need for—and every reason to avoid —a retardation of the severity that will be produced by a continuation of the Fed's present monetary overkill."

In the recessions of 1957–58, 1960–61 and 1966–1967, the Fed, responding to political pressures, sharply expanded the money supply, compounding its original error of overexpanding, then contracting it. Whether or not this pattern will repeat itself in the early 1970's will become evident only when, in the words of economist Henry Kaufman, a partner of Salomon Brothers & Hutzler, "the economic indicators begin to slide and business expectations turn somewhat hazy." But whether or not the pattern repeats itself, for the investor the important point is that historically the effect of deflationary forces upon the market is bearish. This is what he must remember if he is to be more right than wrong in such a period.

The stock market is affected not only by the *availability* of money but by its *cost* as well. As we shall see, when money can be invested at sufficiently high rates in bonds or other debt securities with virtually no risk, substantial funds are drawn out of the stock market, where equities are always a risk. Indeed, at times, as we shall see in a later chapter, highest-grade bonds can prove an excellent speculative vehicle. Yet the typical bond-buyer has courted disaster during the past thirty-years. A representative bond price index reflecting AAA (highest quality) bonds, adjusted for the inflation rate, shows a drop in excess of 70 percent between 1940 and 1970. Even when bond yields and living costs both increased during the earlier period of 1902–1920, there was a loss of purchasing power of 69 percent. But bond-buyers have not always lost; for example, between 1920 and 1940 (after making adjustments for the inflation rate) bond-buyers profited more than 120 percent as bond prices rose more than 50 percent while living costs declined 30 percent.

The cost of money rose in 1969 to the highest level in more than a century. In June the nation's banks raised their prime rate 1 percent to 8½ percent, the biggest one-step boost in history. (The prime rate nominally is the rate that banks charge customers of the best credit standing. In fact, it is more like the list price of an automobile. It is in effect a base price from which negotiations start, but each loan is negotiated separately.) In February 1970, the U.S. Treasury offered 8¼ percent interest on an 18-month note, the highest interest since 1859, to holders of maturing notes. "They've decided to hang as many carrots out in front of the horses as they can," one banker observed. But the 1969 squeeze was so extreme that public holders of almost a quarter of $7.6 billion in government securities maturing in September refused 8 percent offered on new notes and demanded cash instead.

Actually, such high interest costs tend to be self-defeating because few substantial long-term capital investments can prove economic with an interest cost near 10 percent. Public utilities, which absorb about one-half of all the new capital raised by U.S. corporations each year, are especially vulnerable. It is no accident that the utility stocks have an excellent record as a leading indicator of the stock market as a whole.

That investors are quite sensitive to interest rates is shown by the spread between long- and short-term interest rates and by the flows between bonds and stocks as their respective yields reach extreme highs and lows. Lenders like to put their funds out at long-term, which keeps long-term rates relatively low. But when borrowers believe rates may fall later, they tend to borrow more at short-term, which drives up short-term rates.

When money is both expensive and scarce many sophisticated investors invariably shift their capital out of stocks and into bonds at a certain critical point because when the yield on bonds, as on all loans, is so much higher it makes riskier stock investments less attractive. Indeed, the yield spread between stocks and bonds is a useful indicator of probable market trends. I calculate it by taking the yield on the 30 Dow Jones Industrials, deducting it from the yield on the 40 Dow Jones Bonds, then dividing the difference by the yield on the Industrials only. The resulting spread reveals how much more a dollar invested in bonds will earn compared with the same dollar invested in stocks. For example, for the week ending December 13, 1968, bonds yielded 6.84 percent, stocks 3.23 percent. The spread was 3.61, which is 112 percent of the stock yield. This means that a dollar invested in bonds earned more than twice as much as a dollar invested in stocks. Not surprisingly, the stock market declined precipitously immediately thereafter.

My experience indicates that, while there is no absolute ratio at which the spread portends a market decline, a topping spread over a prolonged period is ominous. In the period from late December 1965 to early February 1966, for example, the yield-spread ratio rose to exceed 70 percent for six successive weeks; in the seventh week, the market topped out and started the major 1966 collapse. The prolonged high yield-spread ratio was, of course, an excellent sell signal.

Another useful monetary indicator is *Barron's* weekly

Confidence Index, which is the ratio of the average yield of 10 high-grade corporate bonds to the average yield on 40 lower quality corporate bonds. In essence this Index measures the confidence of large-quantity bond-buyers, who presumably are one of the most sophisticated groups of investors. When they move toward the high-grade bonds, into the direction of safety because they are concerned about the future, the CI declines. When they are more optimistic about the future they move toward the higher yields of the lower-grade bonds; then the CI rises.

While there is much disagreement over how to use this indicator as a forecasting tool, I have had excellent results with a ten-week moving average of it. When this average turns sufficiently to break the existing trend, stock prices frequently also break their trend 90 to 120 days later.

Studies show that long-term returns in the stock market, including both dividends and price appreciation, approximate 10 percent. With bond yields approaching 10 percent in 1969, bonds obviously should have appeared more attractive to institutional money managers, particularly those who manage pension funds. These men are concerned with the longer term, and bonds assured an almost risk-free return well in excess of the 5 to 6 percent inflation rate, in contrast to the considerable risk stocks presented in the yo-yo market of 1969. Ironically, many pension fund managers in late 1969 and early 1970 were switching large sums into quality growth stocks just as they were topping out—a classic example of pathetic market timing. Some lost 10 percent of their purchase cost in several days.

In a later chapter I discuss one kind of outstanding speculative opportunity in high-grade bonds; here it is sufficient to say that sophisticated investors always seek the highest return commensurate with the risks assumed —and when bond yields are extraordinarily high, bonds may fit this bill better than stocks do. What is important to remember is that during such periods the stock market always will be vulnerable.

One further thought about the availability and cost of money may be useful in putting into perspective *why* a favorable stock market environment requires an orderly money market: In the past twenty years 95 percent of the credit needs of our economy have been financed through debt instruments, not through stocks. So the ability to borrow money at economic rates has virtually made possible financing of federal, state and local governments, of business and of consumers. The inability to borrow, then, means the inability to purchase at high levels, and without the ability to purchase, how will public programs be implemented, and to whom will business sell its goods and services? The economy as we know it today simply cannot survive in its present form without adequate supplies of credit.

While the cost and availability of money are the most important fundamental determinants of stock prices as a whole, no assessment of the role fundamentals play in the stock market would be complete without considering *fiscal* policy also, and the relation between the fiscal and monetary roles. Indeed, in recent years a substantial controversy has erupted in the ranks of economists over the relative importance of fiscal vs. monetary actions. This widely discussed argument is of more than academic interest to investors, since national policymakers belong to one school or the other, and the policies they choose as well as the means by which they apply them affect the stock market. It isn't necessary to have an expert knowledge of all the details, many of which are irrelevant or unimportant with respect to stock prices; but one must have some basic knowledge of and insights into the framework of fiscal and monetary policies so that regularly reported news items can be interpreted (or disregarded) with respect to their effects on stock prices.

Despite the present administration's emphasis upon the importance of monetary policy, the Depression and the huge federal budgets of the last thirty years have made it clear that every administration, regardless of party, is committed—and will continue to be committed—to the Keynesian principle of "compensatory finance": the principle that the government must compensate through its taxing and spending policies for either shortfalls or excesses in the private-enterprise economy. Indeed, in recent years this principle has been evoked (if not always implemented) to meet the needs of the millions of Americans still living in conditions of poverty and near-poverty.

In the interplay among fiscal and monetary policies and the inflation rate, however, the experience of the last few years indicates that the very *size* of the federal budget and the way this money is spent have a pervasive influence on the economy.

As the Vietnam War expanded in 1966, the budget deficit rose to almost $9 billion in fiscal 1967 (year ending June 30, 1967). In fiscal 1968 the deficit increased to more than $25 billion, as Lyndon Johnson tried to finance both the war and domestic programs. Since then the federal budget has been less expansive. The nation's leadership, under the pressure of a majority of Americans who insist that the national priorities lay elsewhere than in Southeast Asia, has begun to face economic reality. Fiscal 1969 ended with a budget surplus of $3.2 billion, and the Nixon Administration first predicted a still larger one for the fiscal year ending June 30, 1970, then later forecast a deficit unless Congress acted favorably upon the President's proposals to extend the income-tax surcharge at 5 percent through June 1970 and to repeal the 7-percent investment tax-credit. This political arm-twisting illustrates why— since Congress holds the federal funding and taxing powers—fiscal policy is in the final analysis a political question.

In the long run, monetary policy also is subject to political considerations; but the political pressures are not so immediate. Perhaps that accounts for the fact that monetary-policy decisions usually are immediate and clear-cut and fiscal-policy decisions usually are delayed political compromises.

The initial findings of the FRB–MIT study indicate that both monetary and fiscal policies have powerful effects upon the nation's economy. Monetary policy can be changed quickly; but its effects are delayed from one to three years because it takes time for the Fed's open-market operations to be reflected in changes in long-term interest rates, and even more time for these rate changes to be reflected in investment decisions. In contrast, fiscal policy takes more time to change, but its effects are felt more quickly. "As to their relative merits," economist Stephen B. Packer said recently, "it seems fairly evident that fiscal policy is superior for stimulating the economy and money policy for curbing growth. Fiscal policy was ascendant during the 1930's and the early 1960's, when we were trying to overcome prolonged, excessive unemployment. Monetary policy was ascendant in the mid-1950's, when we were trying to halt seemingly inexorable price inflation. It is ascendant again today. Debates over which technique is unconditionally superior to the other are not likely to be fruitful."

In fact, concluded Packer, the stemming of the current inflationary spiral may depend more upon the ending of the Vietnam War than upon the application of either fiscal or monetary policies. Not only would the end of the war divert billions of dollars back to the domestic economy, it also would have a profound psychological impact upon the people, "and provide a politically acceptable justification for the increase in unemployment that may be necessary before price inflation is reduced to more acceptable levels."

Indeed, it is the psychology of inflation that is the chief problem. "The expectation of continuing inflation," says Dr. Peter B. Kenen, head of Columbia University's Economics Department, "has sort of been worked into people's thinking, which means that people will demand wage increases that correspond to past cost-of-living increases, which will mean in turn that prices are going to go up some more." Sidney Homer, an economist and partner of Salomon Brothers & Hutzler, calls this inflationary psychology "even more dangerous than the present inflation."

Inflationary psychology is an almost universal belief that excessive inflation is here to stay, that the government either cannot or will not halt it, that prices will continue to rise 5 percent or more every year. For example, although manufacturers were operating at less than 85 percent capacity in 1969, investment in new plant and equipment boomed, despite record interest rates on loans. Businessmen, noting that the cost of construction and equipment was rising rapidly, apparently felt that it was better to build immediately, even if the facilities were not yet needed, than to wait and pay more later.

That people expect inflation to continue is not surprising. Since mid-1965, when American involvement in Vietnam significantly expanded, consumer prices have risen from an average of 3.5 percent annually to 6 percent in 1969.

It wasn't always so. During the seven years prior to 1965, consumer prices rose an average of only 1.3 percent a year, which these days is not considered very inflationary. In fact, for those years American price stability was unmatched anywhere in the industrial world, and the economy (except for the 1960–61 recession) was generally prosperous. Wage increases averaged about 3.5 percent, which was nearly in line with the growth in productivity. Today, however, a dangerous wage-price spiral has replaced restraint and stability. Wage increases are running as high as 6 percent—to compensate for higher prices; and price increases are averaging the same—to pay for higher labor costs. A Harris Poll study in 1969 revealed that a family of four with an annual income of $10,000 in 1959 whose income had risen 50 percent since then, to

$15,000, had gained only $575 in real income. Inflation and taxes had taken the rest.

Everyone agrees that the recent rate of inflation is intolerable and that it must be reduced to a manageable level. Many economists feel we can live with a price increase of as much as 1.5 to 2 percent a year (as measured by the gross national product price deflator). At a rate of increase much above 2 percent, however, problems start to appear in the capital markets, in our international monetary relations and in the psychological reactions of business and consumers. An excessive inflationary rate also threatens to increase the already sizable deficit in the United States balance of payments. Excessively high prices make it difficult to export American goods—they cannot compete in foreign markets. Highly priced American products also make lower-priced foreign imports more attractive to American buyers.

Looking over the horizon, however, an official of Connecticut General Life Insurance Company predicted not long ago that a 10-percent interest rate on mortgages will be common in ten years; that by the year 2,000 bread will cost $1 and gasoline $1.25 a gallon. I don't think so; I think this is more a manifestation of inflationary psychology than valid economic prognostication. But the immediate future promises no real respite, not even in a possible recession. A look at the record reveals that the cost of living rose in four of the last five recessions. The increase has been especially steep during recessions that followed big expansion periods—and this last expansion period has been the longest on record. It appears that, after a long party, a severe hangover is in sight.

Nixon has instituted deflationary fiscal and monetary policies, but whether he will make a serious effort to reduce defense spending, which is the prime pumper up of the inflationary balloon, remains to be seen. Money that is spent for consumer goods theoretically creates as much supply as demand; but money spent for "defense"—that is, war and arms—creates no marketable consumer goods to offset demands, which results in a bidding up of prices in consumer goods. "So long as $80 billion a year is being pumped into our $900-billion economy with no equivalent creation of supply," insists one observer, "the inflationary pressure is almost irresistible."

The problem is not so much inflation but the *rate* of inflation. There is a bigger difference than is apparent between an inflation of 1 or 2 percent and an inflation of 4 or 5 percent. "In the latter case," economic writer Edwin L. Dale, Jr., explains, "the value of the dollar is cut in half in ten years or so, savers get almost no 'real' return, pensioners suffer a visible, yearly loss of real spending power. In the former case, the small rise in prices . . . is almost offset by gradual improvements in the quality of things we buy."

It is popularly assumed that inflation does not adversely affect the stock market, that equities in fact are a hedge against inflation. Not so. In recent times—the past twenty years—common stocks have performed favorably as a group in preserving the purchasing power of the dollar. Inflation rate-adjusted stock prices rose almost 350 percent during the last two decades, with serious declines in only a few of the years. But we would be making the habitual mistake of experts if we simply projected this record for the next three decades. The last twenty years is not the final model of human experience. From 1909 to 1921, for example, when living costs approximately doubled, stock prices declined and, when adjusted for the inflation rate, equities actually lost almost two-thirds of their value. Equities also dropped in value more than 40 percent between 1936 and 1949.

A modest inflation does tend to foster a favorable atmosphere for a rising market, as people seek to convert depreciating dollars into equities. But as the rate of inflation accelerates, stock prices are severely affected. A study by the International Monetary Fund, Organization for

Economic Cooperation and Development, correlated stock
prices to rates of inflation in various countries from 1955
to 1966. The table below, prepared by the IMF, shows the
relationships:

COUNTRY	1955–60 ANNUAL RATE OF INFLATION	1955–60 CHANGE IN STOCK PRICES	1960–66 ANNUAL RATE OF INFLATION	1960–66 CHANGE IN STOCK PRICES
France	5.8%	+ 78.5%	3.5%	− 18.8%
Germany	1.8%	+231.7%	2.9%	− 32.2%
England	2.6%	+ 61.1%	3.6%	+ 10.2%
Italy	1.9%	+152.7%	4.5%	− 24.8%
Netherlands	2.6%	+ 89.6%	3.9%	− 4.5%
Japan	1.5%	+200.0%	6.1%	+ 32.3%
Switzerland	1.3%	+ 76.0%	3.7%	− 28.4%
Average	2.5%	+127.1%	4.0%	− 9.5%

Further analysis of the data, including evaluation of
shorter periods, reveals that there is no automatic correlation between stock prices and inflation rates over the
short-term; but that over the long-term, as the table
indicates, an inflation rate in excess of about 3 percent
annually tends to become unmanageable and depress stock
prices. For investors, then, the rule of the game is: Enjoy
the ride while you can, but keep your parachute handy.
As one observer has noted: "There is no faster cure for
runaway expectations than a declining market."

In periods of runaway inflation, investors often buy
traditional natural-resources stocks, real estate or equities
of companies dealing in real estate. They also look for
high-grade glamour stocks, what one analyst describes as
"companies which have demonstrated competitive ability,
superior management and the capacity to overcome the
cost-push element of inflation." If the balloon bursts, however, these so-called "inflation hedges" also get pricked.
Indeed, I doubt that there are any really reliable inflation
hedges *per se* in the stock market. As we shall see later,
the best of all hedges against the vagaries of the economy

and of the stock market, as well as against the occasional stupidities of politicians, monetary and fiscal authorities, is the successful timing of purchases and sales of common stocks.

In 1969 the issue was joined when the Fed firmly announced its intention to break the back of inflationary expectations. It is more important than ever that it succeed, however painful the remedy may be; failure would entail the breakdown of certain of our institutional arrangements. If the Fed succeeds, it will be bearish at first for stock prices but bullish over the longer term as price stability returns to the scene. But if the Fed fails, all bets are off, for who will know what anything is worth?

The Fed's perserverance—or the lack of it—poses a key question for investors: When will the System make credit more available to avoid a recession?

"They have talked themselves into a corner," said one distinguished banker. "They not only have to think about the direct effect of what they do but of the effect on expectations. And once you begin determining policy on the basis of expectations, the task becomes impossible."

But perhaps the question should be: Is not a recession the very price which must be paid to kill inflationary expectations? We have seen how inflation feeds on itself. In the same way, deflationary forces, once set in motion vigorously enough, are like a truck rolling downhill— difficult to stop and reverse before reaching the bottom.

In considering the impact of monetary and fiscal policies upon the stock market, we also must look across the sea to the European money markets. The world is small, and the fate of the dollar is inextricably bound to the fate of the pound, the franc, the mark and the lira. The frequent correlation between the action of the London and New York stock markets, for example, is no accident. Indeed, the price index of British Industrials, taken in conjunction with other measurements, is a useful indicator for predicting probable action of the New York market.

The financial relationships—and the machinery that regulates them—between nations is worthy of a book in itself, but here we will focus only on those aspects of international finance which are particularly germane to stock prices. These considerations rest upon a common economic interest: world trade.

For most companies the effect of world trade is indirect; but for the shipping and airline industries, and for firms with foreign subsidiaries, mining properties or overseas markets, the effect is direct—sometimes too much so. In 1969, for example, the stocks of Occidental Petroleum and of the Anaconda Corporation plunged under threats of expropriation of rich foreign properties. Indeed, to the extent that corporate earnings are contingent on foreign events they are more vulnerable than those derived almost completely from domestic sources and markets, and the stocks of such companies sell at lower PE ratios and higher yields. This does not make them bargains, as unsophisticated investors usually assume; it simply reflects the inherent risk.

World trade itself (expressed in imports) has grown at a steady rate since 1961, from $124.6 billion to $224.5 billion in 1968. But this very growth carries within it the seeds of international monetary disaster. The problem is the inadequacy of international reserves, gold and such key currencies as the U.S. dollar, to settle debts created by an imbalance of trade between nations. As trade grows, so do the imbalances; but as the imbalances grow, the reserves shrink. Since 1961, the world's reserves of gold and key currencies have declined steadily from 50 percent of imports to only 34 percent in 1968.

The present system of international monetary exchange, the *gold exchange standard,* was adopted in 1944 by forty-four nations at Bretton Woods, New Hampshire. At that time there was a severe dollar shortage—every country owed money to Uncle Sam. To stabilize the values of the currencies among its member countries, and to insure a dependable cooperative international payments system, the International Monetary Fund (IMF) was created.

The fund is actually a pool of gold and currencies, currently amounting to some $25 billion and contributed by the member countries, now numbering 111. A member country that finds itself strapped for foreign exchange can borrow funds from the IMF to tide itself over while it uses the time to take any necessary action to improve its own economy.

The currencies of the IMF member countries are interrelated through a "fixed parity" system, parity being based upon the U.S. dollar, which itself is fixed in terms of gold (1/35th of an ounce). In daily trading a nation's currency may fluctuate no more than 1 percent above or below its fixed exchange rate. This proviso, however, does not apply to the United States. America's role in essence is to be the world's banker and stand ready to sell gold at $35 an ounce. So the various national currencies relate to the dollar and all relate to the price of gold. If a nation's currency threatens to fluctuate beyond its 1-percent limit, its central bank must intervene in the market with sales or purchases of its currency—purchases being paid for in dollars or gold.

The demand for one currency against another arises because the economies of different nations move at different paces under different political, social and economic conditions. The real problem, says Darryl Francis, president of the Federal Reserve Bank of St. Louis, "stems from the fact that the domestic value of a currency, which depends on the domestic price level, may not be equal to the international value of that currency, which depends upon the exchange rate between that currency and other currencies. . . ." Some mechanism, Francis adds, is needed to correlate these two values. Some nations spend more money abroad than they take in, and vice versa, leading to a deficit or a surplus in their so-called *balance-of-payments*. In 1969 the United States suffered another year of a net deficit in its balance of payments, the eleventh deficit in the last twelve years. This deficit of $7 billion, the worst ever, by jeopardizing the dollar, threatens to shatter the entire international monetary mechanism, the financial consequences of which would be felt by every individual in the Western world.

Even without this problem, the international monetary system is constantly in a state of crisis as currency exchange rates rise or fall. When an IMF member nation (except the U.S.) has a persistent and growing imbalance of payments, it must do one of two things: *de*value, if the imbalance is a deficit; or *re*value, if it is a surplus. Britain, under pressure of a chronic trade deficit, devalued the pound from $2.80 to $2.40 in 1967. Two years later France, faced with heavy inflation and rapidly dwindling gold and dollar reserves, was forced to devalue the franc 12.5 percent. That same year Germany, with a persistent and substantial surplus, was obliged to revalue its currency upward.

A government will do almost anything to avoid devaluing or revaluing its currency. Even when faced with the inevitable, politicians will refuse to acknowledge it. Sports buffs are familiar with the symptoms. When the owner of a professional team gives his manager or coach a "vote of confidence," it is only a matter of time, perhaps days, before the owner fires him. Currency devaluation works the same way. When the British pound was in trouble in 1967, the Chancellor of the Exchequer insisted that there was "no possibility" of devaluation. His statement was made on a Friday. That weekend the pound was devalued. The next week the Chancellor resigned.

During the West German currency crisis of the spring of 1969, an official government spokesman assured newsmen that the government's decision against revaluation of the mark was "final, unequivocal and for eternity." Asked to define "eternity," he replied: "That is a metaphysical question I am not qualified to answer."

The money speculators, however, bet that "eternity" would be short-lived, and indeed it proved to be so. On September 29, 1969, in violation of IMF rules, the West German Government ordered the nation's central bank to allow the mark to "float freely," that is, to rise (or fall) in value in accordance with the demands of the free market. It immediately soared, of course, to a premium of more than 5 percent, and speculators who had poured some $4 billion into West Germany in anticipation of the upward revaluation began taking profits. Less than a month later, the new West German Government, with the approval of the IMF, formally revalued the mark upward by almost 10 percent.

This action brought immediate relief to the international money markets, relieving pressure on the recently devalued franc and the ever-troubled pound. "I think we have our sore thumbs bandaged now," said one international banker. But that is all the West German revaluation was: a first-aid measure. Recurring international money crises of one kind or another have become routine in the last few years, and few economists believe that the IMF will survive much longer without drastic reforms. "The monetary system is like an elastic that has been stretched and stretched," another central banker said recently. "Perhaps there is a little more stretch left, perhaps not."

The system itself always has been based upon gold because, as the great Danish economist Per Jacobsson once noted, gold "cannot be arbitrarily created as credit can." The dollar is the world's premier currency today partly because it is presumed to be redeemable for gold—and because it is backed by America's vast economic power. In 1969 the dollar accounted for payment of some 70 percent of commercial transactions, up from 60 percent the year before. Some commentators have gone so far as to suggest that the gold standard is dead and that the new standard of common value in the world is the dollar. With gold no longer contributing to reserve expansion, economist Ernest W. Luther has noted that "the system has developed a lopsided and wholly unhealthy dependence on continued deficit financing by the United States." This financing is in the form of U.S. dollar holdings by foreign countries. Yet the acceptance of this dependent relationship is diminishing steadily because those nations with dollar surpluses realize that the acceptance of dollar accumulation could lead to the loss of their economic sovereignty. The United States, after all, can print an unlimited supply of dollars.

What the world really needs is a system independent of U.S. policies and under which the U.S. also can enjoy the option for growing reserves. The IMF recently took a step in this direction by the creation of Special Drawing Rights, known as "paper gold," a new form of international payment.

Meanwhile, despite the pressure on it, the dollar continues to command a high degree of world confidence. As one foreign economist explained to an American correspondent: "No one doubts the power behind your dollar. All we doubt is how you will use that power." Discussing America's use of its power, economist Eliot Janeway wrote in *The Economics of Crisis*: "For America to aspire to the role of world policeman or of self-appointed surrogate for a world peace-keeping authority, is to fall into the old Greek sin of hubris—of overweening pride which challenges the gods and tempts fate to strike it down."

Corporate success; confidence in government; fiscal and monetary policies; inflation; international finance—these are the major fundamental factors that act upon the stock market. They are all, of course, interrelated. Like the colored spirals in op-art constructions, they form economic patterns that are at once complex, subtle, diverse and often unpredictable.

Hundreds of economic indicators have been devised to predict the effect upon the market of fundamental factors. I have discussed a few of those which I consider the most useful—the money-supply measurements, the yield-spread ratio, the Confidence Index, and so on. Most of the others, in my opinion, are of little value to the average investor because they don't correlate to stock price-action. For those who are interested, however, a virtually complete listing of fundamental indicators can be found in the Commerce Department's monthly publication, *Business Conditions Digest*. Actually, one never knows where a new indicator will pop up. Harvey Brenner, writing in a recent issue of the scholarly *Journal of Social Psychiatry*, reported that business fluctuations, "no matter how slight," are reflected in the ratio of admissions to psychiatric hospitals: when the economy goes up, admissions go down, and vice versa. Brenner claimed that a high ratio of admissions of high-level business executives—especially manic-depressive cases—indicated future economic decline because these people are the first to sense trouble and react to it. "The people at the top get wind of the coming economic changes early and lead the general curve of mental hospital admissions," he said. "Indeed, a standing joke among psychiatrists is the advice to doctors who hold stocks to keep their eyes on the number of manic-depressives being admitted to mental hospitals."

Manic-depressive executives aside, however, it seldom is possible to fathom all the patterns created by the major fundamental factors, which is why it is difficult to predict their effect upon the market. Just how difficult it is can be seen by a study of the Chrysler Corporation's fortunes since 1968.

Throughout June, July and August of 1968, any number of favorable fundamental reports were published on Chrysler in particular and on the automotive industry in general. In *Forbes*, for example, it was reported that for Chrysler 1968 would be "the sixth consecutive year that the company's share of the automobile market has increased—a period during which the company more than doubled in size." The report concluded that "Chrysler's earnings this year could be in the $5.50-per-share area" (up from $4.35 in 1967). The *Wall Street Journal* quoted Chrysler's chairman Lynn Townsend as raising his forecast of auto-industry sales in 1968 from 9 million to a record 9.3 million and predicting that 1969 sales would be "at least equal and possibly higher." In further interviews with Townsend and with Chrysler's president Virgil Boyd, the *Journal* recorded the officers' view that company earnings might even exceed $6 a share. Meanwhile, *The New York Times* reported a rise in automobile sales and headlined a story based upon a projection by the Census Bureau "New Car Demands Seen Continuing."

On the basis of these and other reports that appeared almost daily, and encouraged by Chrysler's record of aggressive marketing, many brokerage houses and advisory services recommended purchase of Chrysler stock, which then was selling in the 60 to 70 area. My own divergence analysis, however, indicated the probability that sophisticated investors were distributing their holdings of Chrysler and that unsophisticated investors, barraged by the stream of favorable present fundamentals, were buying at the top. This was the exact reverse of the situation of the previous fifteen months, when divergence analysis had indicated sophisticated buying of Chrysler, raising it from the 30 area in early 1967 to its then current level. The fundamentals were encouraging, all right, but they appeared to be only part of the story. On August 19, 1968, I reported: "C magnificently managed company. In recent years has aggressively achieved ever-greater market penetration at expense of world's toughest competitor, GM. Earnings expected up sharply this year and those who view automobile market optimistically for next year estimate *C*'s 1969 earnings at $7. Nonetheless, if as we forecast, the market is about to undergo major decline, and if our measurement of investor psychology in *C* is sound, it may be about to suffer a major decline."

Actually, the fundamental data on the automobile industry, *when closely examined*, was not nearly as bullish as it appeared. Much had been made of phenomenal automobile sales in recent months: new car sales had jumped from an annual rate of 9 million to 10 million. But surveys by the University of Michigan and others indicated that one-third of the buyers were buying principally because of the low prices then available due to heavy clean-up discounts prior to receipt of the 1969 models, which would sell at sharply higher prices. Dealers had about 1 million 1968 models on hand, and heavy clean-up sales would continue for some time. So the current buying surge was essentially a *borrowing* from 1969 sales, and as the deflationary aspects of the surtax-spending reduction took hold, the current consumer enthusiasm for the lower-priced 1968 models could be expected to swing to resistance to the higher-priced 1969 models.

On the basis of my divergence analysis and the above reading of the fundamental data, I recommended selling Chrysler short between 64 and 68. Within several weeks Chrysler's stock started down (followed a few months later by the market itself), despite the fact that the company's per-share earnings did climb, as predicted, to $6.23 for the year. Hit hard by institutional selling of its stock (the funds sold 1,151,400 more shares of Chrysler than they bought, and fifteen funds completely eliminated their holdings of the company from their portfolios), Chrysler dipped to 50 by January 1969. The company then lost about 15 percent of its share of the 1969 auto market, and its stock dropped to the 35 to 40 area, where it hovered during the last half of the year. By early 1970 the stock dropped further to the low 20's.

This pattern often recurs. When favorable fundamental

news emerges about a company, sophisticated investors who had purchased the company's stock many months before in anticipation of the upturn may use the opportunity to unload the stock at a profit as unsophisticated investors, impressed by the widely publicized fundamentals, buy in at the top.

The moral is clear: Fundamental information often is enlightening in explaining past price-action of the market but its direct predictive value is limited except as part of an integrated approach. The market usually deals with the unknown, in effect registering sophisticated opinion about the future. By the time most fundamental data has been published, the stock price-action already has taken place.

To assess sophisticated opinion, we must employ an integrated approach that incorporates not only fundamental data but technical analysis and psychological measurements as well. Technical analysis is our next consideration.

1991 ADDENDUM

In recent years I developed a method to measure the *growth rate** of money and to *correlate* it with stock market *breadth* [as measured by the Daily Advance/Decline Line, pp. 120-1]. In the chart on page 97B I use the *weekly Adjusted St. Louis Monetary Base*, data for which is available every Thursday afternoon by telephone from the Federal Reserve Bank of St. Louis [not the biweekly data which is published every Friday, usually with a two week lag]. In this way, I feel I'm able to track money on a week-to-week basis but in a long term context. Moreover, these data are real and completely unrelated to what the Federal Reserve may say to the media [pp. 91-2], i.e., the data measures what the Fed is *doing,* not what it is *saying.* This method doesn't always work and the timing isn't precise; however a rapid growth rate of money *after* it's been in an historically low area almost always is a big plus for the stock market. Contrarily, note how peaks in stock market breadth are often identified by peak growth rates of this measure of money.

At year end 1990, even amidst signs of Fed easing by cutting banks' reserve requirements and the discount rate, the growth rate of the Base was falling sharply. Indeed the Base itself was virtually unchanged during the 16 weeks ended December 26, 1990 [in $billions]:

September	12	318.5	November	7	318.3
	19	318.9		14	319.1
	26	319.0		21	320.2
October	3	316.2		28	319.5
	10	320.1	December	5	318.7
	17	317.4		12	317.7
	24	319.0		19	320.3
	31	316.5		26	321.5

* The growth rate which I originated is a rate of change of the difference between the Base's 10-week and 40-week moving averages. Since many popular computer programs provide Welles Wilder's RSI, which provides a similar configuration to my own method, I have used his method in this and other new charts.

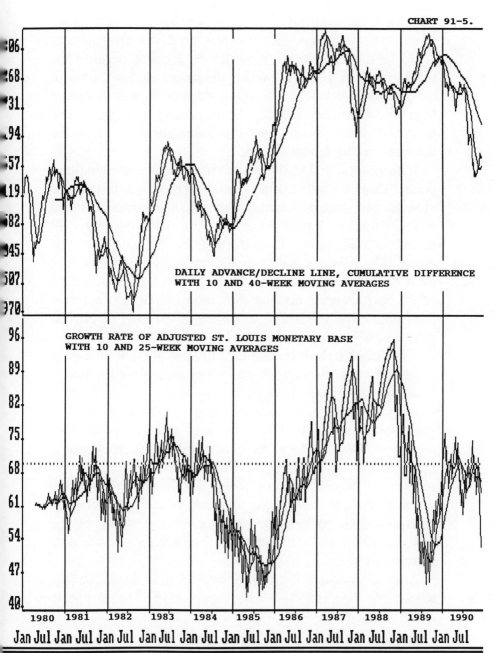

CHART 91-5.

DAILY ADVANCE/DECLINE LINE, CUMULATIVE DIFFERENCE
WITH 10 AND 40-WEEK MOVING AVERAGES

GROWTH RATE OF ADJUSTED ST. LOUIS MONETARY BASE
WITH 10 AND 25-WEEK MOVING AVERAGES

ROWTH RATE ADJUSTED ST.LOUIS MONETARY BASE & DAILY STOCK MARKET BREADTH

What these data may well mean is that despite Fed easing it was not easing enough and that both business and consumers were unwilling to spend until they first reliquefied themselves. If the Base continued not to grow or if the growth rates failed to rise sufficiently, it would be a major negative for stock prices in 1991. However, the unusually low levels of the growth rate would also allow the Fed to ease far more than was expected. Indeed, the beginning of a major rise may have been signalled by the Base's surge to 325.9 for the week ended January 2, 1991.

With Federal budget deficits in recent years some ten times greater than they were twenty years ago [pp.81-2], the popular view has become that deficits are the villain in 1990s' financial crises. However, I tend to agree with economist Peter L. Bernstein who argued in 1983 that the "villain is *not* the deficit. The villain is government spending. Any expenditure must be financed. In the case of the government, that means either borrowing or taxation." A more important factor in determining the level of stock prices is the level of interest rates, in my opinion.

It is difficult to determine exactly how the absolute level of interest rates affects stock prices. For example, even though bank rates in Britain have been very high in recent years— near 15 percent during most of 1990—stocks there haven't gone down much. The best all around indicator of whether money is "too" tight or very easy, insofar as stock prices are concerned is, I believe, the *Ratio of Treasury Bill Futures to Treasury Bond Futures* on page 97D. Note how the surging squeeze of 1987 finally got to stock prices. By mid-1990 emerging *tightness* was also clearly evident as shown by the upward spiking ratio. By this same yardstick, policy was *easy* at year end 1990.

Another indicator I've created does seem to reveal whether stocks are "too" expensive or cheap relative to corporate bond prices.

CHART 91-6.

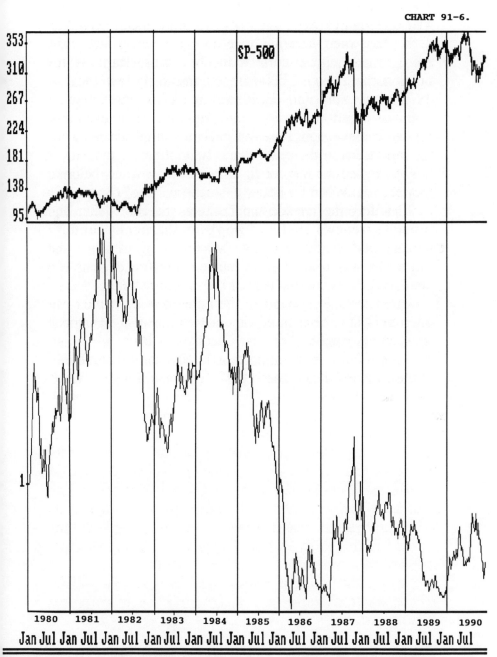

SP-500

353
310.
267.
224.
181.
138.
95.

1

1980 1981 1982 1983 1984 1985 1986 1987 1988 1989 1990

Jan Jul Jan Jul Jan Jul Jan Jul Jan Jul Jan Jul Jan Jul Jan Jul Jan Jul Jan Jul Jan Jul

SQUEEZE OR EASE ? RATIO TREASURY BILL FUTURES TO TREASURY BOND FUTURES

Money, the Root of All...

The chart on page 97F shows the *Weekly Advance/Decline Line* with a Ratio of it to the Dow Jones 20 Bonds Index. The least squares trend* of this *ratio* shows a linear correlation of + 0.97 whereas *perfect* is + 1.00 or - 1.00. This fairly precise mathematical correlation does show clearly, in my opinion, that there is a definite relationship between the *level of long term corporate bond rates* and stock prices. Indeed, I am surprised that some economist has never examined this close connection. I use this indicator simplistically: when the ratio is *above* the least squares trend it means that stocks are *too expensive relative to bond yields*, whereas below it they are not. When far below it, stocks are "too" cheap.

Regarding the relationship between the U.S. dollar and other currencies [pages 88-93], in the next chapter I demonstrate what I believe to be convincing evidence that the dollar was near a major buying juncture at year end 1990, despite its enormous weakness in recent years.

And whereas 21 years ago the London stock market was often thought to be an important factor influencing American stock prices [pp.88-9], it subsequently has become obvious that one of the more important foreign indicators, today, is the Japanese stock market. We examine Tokyo's Nikkei index next, also.

* *Least squares* shows the mathematical relationship between two different data series. This tool is available on most popular computer programs.

CHART 91-7.

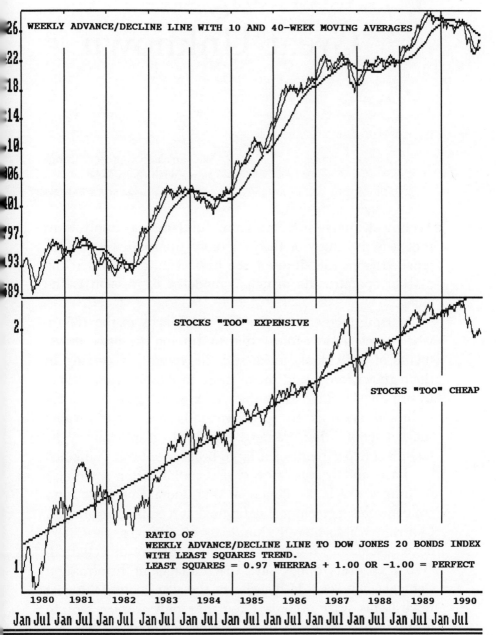

WEEKLY ADVANCE/DECLINE LINE WITH 10 AND 40-WEEK MOVING AVERAGES

STOCKS "TOO" EXPENSIVE

STOCKS "TOO" CHEAP

RATIO OF
WEEKLY ADVANCE/DECLINE LINE TO DOW JONES 20 BONDS INDEX
WITH LEAST SQUARES TREND.
LEAST SQUARES = 0.97 WHEREAS + 1.00 OR −1.00 = PERFECT

1980   1981   1982   1983   1984   1985   1986   1987   1988   1989   1990

Jan Jul Jan Jul Jan Jul Jan Jul Jan Jul Jan Jul Jan Jul Jan Jul Jan Jul Jan Jul Jan Jul

CORRELATION OF WEEKLY STOCK MARKET BREADTH TO DOW JONES 20 BONDS INDEX

97F

5 / Charting the
Great Unknown

We can easily represent things
as we wish them to be.
—AESOP'S FABLES

Technical analysis differs from fundamental analysis in that it is the study of the actions of the market as distinguished from the study of the basic values on which the market operates. Its principal mode of expression is the chart.

Charting of the market-action dates back to the 1880's, when some traders found that by tracing the price movements of individual stocks and the volume of trading in them they often could make more profitable transactions by improved timing. Since then, technicians have expanded technical analysis to cover virtually every conceivable market-action that can be depicted graphically. The technical department of a large brokerage firm, blanketed by charts and graphs of every description, often resembles nothing so much as a Pentagon War Room. One go-go fund concentrates its technical data in what it calls "Information Central," where literally hundreds of averages, ratios, indexes, oscillators and other indicators are carefully charted. "We keep everything," says the manager of Information Central, who regards his charts the way a horticulturist regards his prize orchids. "You may only want a certain graph once a year, but when you do, it's here."

Charts, say the chartists, reflect what the market knows

—or thinks it knows. What they mean is that charts depict actual market price-action, and market prices take into account every possible bit of fundamental information. In fact, the purists among chartists insist that they prefer not to know *anything* about the companies whose price-action they study; such knowledge only prejudices their interpretation of the charts. These technicians forecast future stock price-action solely on the basis of their evaluation of the past price-action represented by the neat pinpoints, lines and curves on their charts.

Charts themselves, of course, predict nothing; they only indicate what a stock—or group of stocks, or the market—has done, is doing and, theoretically, should do. Stock prices tend to move in *trends*, continuing moves in a given direction. These trends usually are classified by direction—that is, bull, neutral or bear—and by durability and amplitude. A *long-term*, or *major*, trend may last from one year to several years; an *intermediate*, or *secondary*, trend may last from a few months to a year or more; and a *short-term*, or *minor*, trend may last as little as a few days or continue for some weeks. All of these trends may in turn operate within the framework of longer-term patterns extending over decades; such historic tendencies are called *grand* trends.

The technician assumes that trends tend to persist over a substantial period of time and that price patterns tend to recur. He bases his forecast of price movement upon these patterns. "They are not infallible, it must be noted," write Robert D. Edwards and John Magee in their book, *Technical Analysis of Stock Trends,* the technician's Bible, "but the odds are definitely in their favor."

The "random-walk" theorists, however, challenge this assumption. Using higher mathematics to support their theory, the random-walk people insist that stock prices have no memory, that each day on the market starts anew and that there is only a 50-50 chance that a stock price will continue to follow a trend. The principle of random-walk is like that behind the theory that says each time a coin is flipped it has a 50-50 probability of coming up heads or tails, no matter what has happened on the previous flips. The past history of a series of stock price-changes "cannot be used to predict the future in any meaningful way," says Professor Eugene Fama, a leading random-walk theorist. "The future path of the price level of a security is no more predictable than the path of a series of cumulated random numbers."

"If the random-walk model is a valid description of reality," concludes Professor Fama, "the work of the chartist, like that of the astrologer, is of no real value." But chartists are very touchy on the subject of their relevance. Indeed, so are the money managers, who are reluctant to admit to their clients that many of their investment decisions are based upon squiggles on lined paper. "How would people react," a veteran Wall Street observer asked recently, "if they thought that they were being charged for all the risk, and some jerk in the closet was spinning a roulette wheel and when the bell rang fund managers were taking it as a buy signal—according to the temperature and humidity?"

Actually, the fault in most conventional technical analysis, I believe, lies not in charts but in chartists. Some of them become so involved in their patterns and trendlines they invest them with anthropomorphic qualities. Their charts, like the painting in Oscar Wilde's *The Picture of Dorian Gray*, take on a life of their own; after a while they become the *sine qua non* of any investment decision.

The danger here is of falling into a self-defeating cycle; that is, chartists as a group, by slavishly relying on their charts, may cause the very price breakout they are trying to predict. "Charting is somewhat like a cult," says a successful technician. "If someone interprets a chart and then buys heavily, the others will follow." But such a move, which essentially is a false breakout, contains within it dangerous backlash potential. And what happens if, on the basis of the charts, everyone decides to sell at the same time?

Ralph Rotnem, a former president of the New York Society of Security Analysts, put charting in perspective when he said: "In self-defense one must know about charting and what it says—in the 1930's you had to know the Dow Theory because people acted solely on it."

I use charts in my own work, for I believe it is no coincidence that certain market advances and declines reverse themselves at certain technically defined points. But I don't regard technical trendlines and patterns as sacred, nor do I think they should dictate investment decisions. Charts are a vital tool in such decisions, but only when integrated with fundamental data and psychological measurements.

In the long run, says one highly respected technician, technical analysis boils down to the "analysis of change—those things that tell us when the abnormality is happening." This, of course, implies the consideration of many other factors besides squiggles on graph paper. Some of these already have been discussed, others will be explored following our examination of technical analysis.

Our study of technical references necessarily must be brief. Technicians often consult a staggering array of charts, indexes and indicators; to treat them all would require a book in itself. In any case, I don't believe investors should so immerse themselves in technical references because this creates the same confusion that inundating oneself with fundamental information does; furthermore, many indicators repeat one another's conclusions. Therefore, I shall discuss only the basic charts, patterns, indicators and concepts that I have found to be most useful as aids to forecasting stock price movements.

Some of these concepts are not commonly known, except to the most sophisticated Wall Street investors. I would be less than candid if I did not admit that the increased exposure which this book will give them probably will dilute their effectiveness somewhat. But this should not concern us unduly because technical analysis is only one consideration of the approach to the market outlined in this book, an approach that is premised upon psychological insight, not technical formulas.

As for charts themselves, I have found that many investors are confused by them. It is not surprising. Many otherwise excellent charts try to show too much or are inadequately keyed; and frequently their highlights are not correlated with the then current situation in the market. A picture may be worth a thousand words, but not if it is blurred. In my own charts I try to present a picture that accents those features that distinguish the stock market's action or that of an individual stock for a particular period. This gives me a better grasp of what is happening on the market in both particular and general situations. I use plain, arithmetic-scale graph paper in which each box is assigned an equal value. Some technicians argue that logarithmic-scale paper is preferable, but I believe this is one of those technical refinements not worth pursuing because it creates as many operational problems as advantages. These advantages, say chartists Edwards and Magee, "are not so great as to require one to change who because of long familiarity and practice prefers an arithmetic sheet."

We will consider three kinds of charts: *historic long-term,* which shows the weekly or monthly price range of a stock for a long period ranging from a few years to as many as thirty or more; *daily basis,* a similarly drawn chart that depicts a stock's trading range each day for a period of about six months; and *point-and-figure,* which reflects significant price changes of a stock without regard to time.

Both the historic long-term and the daily-basis charts are line, or bar, charts, in which a vertical bar extends from the lowest to the highest price of the stock for the month, week, or day being recorded. A short horizontal "tick" across the bar, or extending from it to the right, indicates the closing price for that period. Most chartists record volume, also with bars, at the bottom of the graph.

Chart No. 2 is a historic long-term record of the price action of the common stock of the Polaroid Corporation (PRD) since 1955. Each bar represents the high and low price of PRD for one month. A chart like this gives an investor perspective, provides what economist Pierre A. Rinfret calls "an economic history that bare numbers cannot duplicate."

The PRD historic chart is interesting both for what it does and does not indicate. Note that PRD traded between a high of about 33 and a low of about 11 for a period of more than six *years* beginning in 1959; and that, beginning in July 1965, the stock rose dramatically, almost tripling within a year to about 90. As noted in Chapter Two, Edwin H. Land and James P. Warburg sold their 600,000 shares of PRD just several days before the stock began its dramatic climb. It is obvious now what poor timing that was. But PRD's historic chart *at that time* did not indicate any such imminent dramatic upside breakout. On the contrary, it indicated that the price at which the stock was sold, 30, was close to the high which PRD had reached over the last ten years. The moral of this is: Never make investment decisions solely on the basis of a chart. (That is not to imply that Messrs. Warburg and Land did, but to emphasize that it shouldn't be done.)

The PRD chart, however, does tell us something. Observe that from 1965 through 1968, the stock advanced within the framework of an "advance channel," an area bounded by two parallel lines connecting the upper and lower limits of price-action. Every time the stock approached the overhead channel line it topped out, then declined precipitously, indicating that an investor should think twice before buying in near the top—as in June 1968, when the fundamental data on PRD was highly favorable and many brokers were recommending its pur-

CHART 2. HISTORIC LONG-TERM RECORD OF THE MONTHLY PRICE RANGES OF THE COMMON STOCK
OF THE POLAROID CORPORATION (PRD)

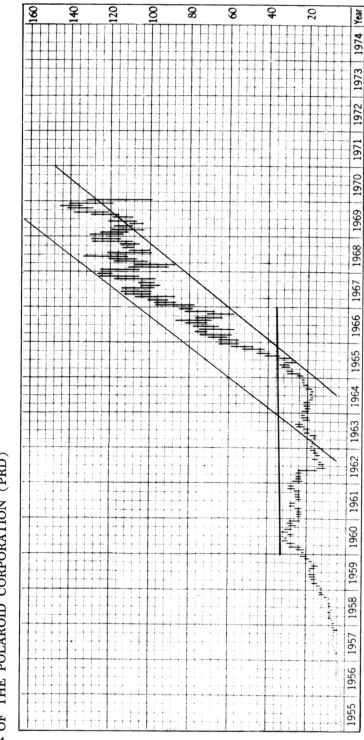

Chart courtesy of M. C. Horsey & Co.; trendlines and text by the author

CHART 3. DAILY-BASIS RECORD OF THE PRICE
RANGES OF POLAROID FROM APRIL 15, 1968, TO
NOVEMBER 8, 1968

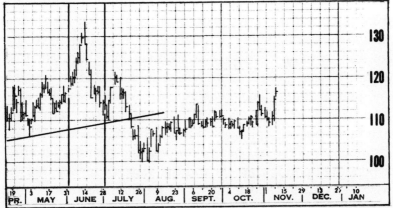

Chart courtesy of Trendline; trendlines and text by the author

The thin rising line is the neckline of a classic head-and-shoulders
formation.

chase yet PRD declined from over 130 to 100 in a month.

The stock also reversed itself each time it approached
the bottom channel line. But in March 1969 it broke through
the bottom channel line for the first time in five years,
indicating that the steady advance of the past five years
might no longer continue as smoothly.

Chart No. 3 is a daily-basis record of the trading in PRD
over a more than six-month period. I have marked off
June 1968, the same month represented by a single bar
on the historic chart. We can see that in the beginning of
June PRD was trading near 118, that it rose to near 134
by June 13 and declined again to near 110 by the end of
the month. A daily-basis chart like this helps the investor
assess a stock's current situation, but obviously it becomes
more useful when correlated with an historic chart. In
fact, both daily-basis and historic charts should be correlated with the third kind of chart, point-and-figure.

Where bar charts are two-dimensional, measuring both
price-change and time, a point-and-figure chart is one-
dimensional; it measures only price-change itself. It has
the advantage of compacting into a small space a stock's
major price-changes, and may be especially helpful in pro-

105

viding confirmation of estimated price tops and bottoms. Most important, however, it gives the investor a different perspective on the price pattern of a security. As sophisticated investors know, and amateur chartists have discovered to their dismay, a stock may look very good on a daily-basis chart yet seem less than desirable on a point-and-figure graph. The question is: What does the total picture look like? A woman may appear very attractive in a facial photograph, less so in a full-length one and even disappointingly so in a back view—or the other way around, depending upon her assets and the viewer's tastes. But the wise man always looks for the three-dimensional picture. The investor must do no less when judging a stock.

Many chartists rely primarily upon point-and-figure charts, because says one, they produce "much purer, more accurate and dependable trendlines." The same chartist, illustrating the value of point-and-figure versus bar charts, points out that a chart showing 5-point moves of the DJIA back to 1914 "might take up only ten inches of paper, and the long-term trends would stand out with a blinding and revealing clarity. A bar chart, however, including time, would take yards of charts and be too large to be interpreted quickly." Quite true, but it is time that determines the rate of gain in any investment transaction, and it is time that is an important element of investment behavior—points overlooked by most investors.

Chart No. 4 is a point-and-figure record of the price changes of PRD in the same period, from April 15 through November 8, 1968, shown on the daily-basis chart of PRD (Chart No. 3). Each box under 100 represents 1 point; over 100, 2 points. This is standard practice. The columns of X's represent price gains, the O's price losses; the two columns always alternate. If numbers appear in some boxes, this refers to the months of the year, a marginal reference that is sometimes added to point-and-figure charts. A price-change equal to at least three boxes is required before a reversal is recorded—that is, a move is made to the next column. This eliminates minor fluctua-

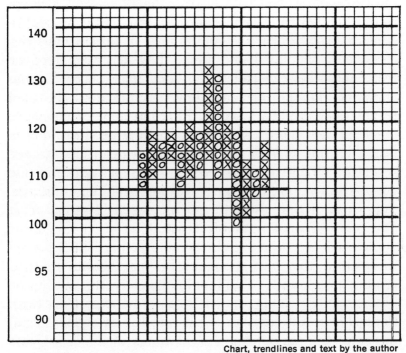

Chart, trendlines and text by the author

The horizontal line at 108 is the neckline of the head-and-shoulders
formation also shown in Chart No. 3.

tions. So, if a stock trades between 50⅛ and 52⅞ for a
period of six months, a daily-basis bar chart will show the
fluctuations, but a point-and-figure chart will indicate no
price-change at all. Of course, when PRD trades in the
above-100 range, its price must change at least 6 points
(2 points per box) to be recorded on the chart.

The PRD point-and-figure chart illustrates a "head-and-
shoulders" formation, a classic chart pattern, one which
chartists Edwards and Magee call "by all odds the most
reliable of the major reversal patterns." The head-and-
shoulders formation also is clearly visible on the daily-
basis chart of PRD. The left shoulder of the formation
represents a strong rally and extensive advance, then a
decline. This is followed by the head, which represents a
greater advance, then a decline to a point below the top

107

of the left shoulder and usually near the bottom level of the previous recession. The right shoulder represents a third rally, which falls short of equaling the head and declines to a point near the bottom level of the previous two recessions. The line drawn across the bottom points of the three recessions is called the "neckline." According to chartists, violation of a neckline portends a major trend reversal. As the chart shows, PRD did make a downside breakout past the neckline at 108, but it declined only to 100, then rose to 116; so the basic upward trend was not reversed. Which reminds us that chart patterns indicate possibilities—and in some cases probabilities—not certainties, and that they are no more reliable than most other conventional market-forecasting tools.

Although the head-and-shoulders pattern of PRD proved misleading, this formation can be very helpful in forecasting price trends when it is integrated with other measurements. This is illustrated by my own experience with Control Data Corporation (CDA) in August 1968. On August 19 CDA announced that earnings in the fiscal year ending June 30 had been $2.12 per share, more than double the previous year's figure of $0.95. Good fundamental news. The stock also was selling at 155, near its recent top of 170. But the glamour group (of which CDA is one), which I watch closely, gave evidence of topping, and CDA itself just had completed etching a massive head-and-shoulders formation, as shown on Chart No. 5. Furthermore— and this was crucial—divergence analysis showed that sophisticated buying of CDA, and unsophisticated selling of it, which had been heavy as the stock rose, had reversed itself by late July; sophisticated investors now appeared to be distributing their holdings, and unsophisticated investors were increasing theirs, a portent of decline in the price of the stock. From the available evidence I concluded that CDA was not likely to exceed its overhead shoulder line and that in fact it looked ready to make a downside breakout below the right neckline of its head-and-shoulders, in

CHART 5. HEAD-AND-SHOULDERS FORMATION OF CONTROL DATA CORPORATION (CDA)

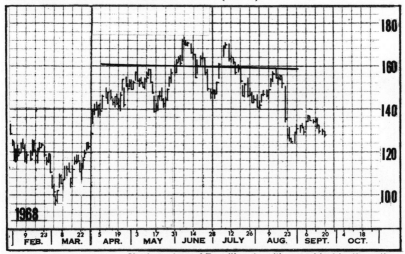

The horizontal line is the shoulder line of the head-and-shoulders formation.

the 140 area. The publication of favorable fundamental data could be ignored as being grist for unsophisticated investors, sophisticated investors having anticipated the high earnings and acted upon the knowledge months ago.

On August 19, 1968, when CDA closed at 155⅞, I recommended short-selling it at 154 to 168. Two days later CDA plunged to about 135 and the next day it dropped to below 125.

Charts Nos. 6 and 7 show head-and-shoulder formations etched by two blue chips, General Foods and Johns-Manville Corporation. Along with divergence analysis, they prompted me to recommend short sales of both stocks, and both subsequently made downside breakouts from the lower right necklines of the head-and-shoulders. I have often found blue-chip head-and-shoulder formations to be reliable technical references. Because the blue chips are less volatile in their action than glamour stocks, their patterns reflect the action as though it were being taped, so to speak, in slow motion for instant replay.

The head-and-shoulders formation is only one of many chart patterns. Our principal interest, however, is in basic

CHART 6. HEAD-AND-SHOULDERS FORMATION OF GENERAL FOODS CORPORATION (GF)

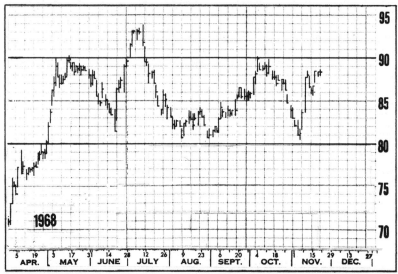

Chart courtesy of Trendline; trendlines and text by the author

Note the shoulder line at the 90 area and the neckline at the 80 area.

CHART 7. HEAD-AND-SHOULDERS FORMATION OF JOHNS-MANVILLE CORPORATION (JM)

Chart courtesy of Trendline; trendline and text by the author

Note how the stock persistently weakened after declining below its neckline.

CHART 8. TREND ILLUSTRATIONS

formations that indicate *tops*, *bottoms*, *uptrends* (as illustrated on the Polaroid historic chart), *downtrends* and *consolidation* areas (also known as "boxes"). Almost all the other patterns are essentially variations of these.

Chart No. 8 illustrates a "box", a congestion area representing a narrow, relatively flat trading range from which an upside or downside breakout subsequently occurs. This is a so-called consolidation pattern, which means supply and demand are about balanced, and "support" and "resistance" levels are fairly strong. A support level is the price level of a stock at which sufficient demand (buying) appears to halt a downside breakout, at least tem-

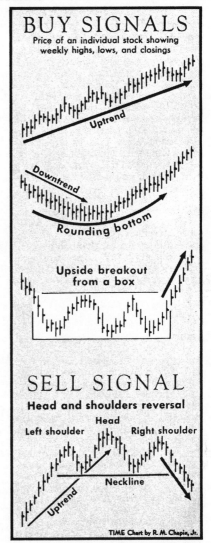

Chart courtesy of Time Magazine

porarily; a resistance zone is the price level at which sufficient supply (selling) appears to halt an upside breakout. The strength of these levels depends somewhat upon the extent of the stock's lateral (sideways) movement; the longer the movement, the stronger the support and resistance levels. Of course, when the stock finally does break out, there is no way of knowing beforehand from the chart alone which way it will go; this is where divergence analysis is useful.

Chartists refer to many more patterns—*triangles, wedges, flags, pennants, scallops, diamonds, rounding tops, rounding bottoms*, etc.—but some of these border on the esoteric and need not concern us. There also are more complex, longer-term patterns, such as the "whipsaw" in the form of an "expanding triangle" and the "fan" formation; these graphically depict the psychological and material struggle between sophisticated and unsophisticated investors. Later we shall see how to avoid being a victim of such patterns, which usually defy conventional technical analysis.

Trendlines, which indicate up and down trends, are straight lines connecting the highs or lows of a stock's pattern. Chartist James Dines likes to "anchor" his trendlines at the bottom from which a new high has progressed, claiming that no major market crash can occur until such a trendline has been penetrated. But this is essentially an exercise in semantics.

Many charts are drawn with simple curves against the background of bar charts of prices covering the same period. Chart No. 1 in Chapter Two, showing the ratio of bearish-to-bullish opinion of the leading investment-advisory services, was plotted by connecting each mathematically determined point from one time interval to the next. When the curve rises to a peak a majority of these experts are relatively bearish; a minority are relatively bullish. When the curve dips, the reverse is true.

Most charts of indicators are drawn with such simple curves. As with chart patterns, there are hundreds of indicators, ranging from an Index of Speculative Confidence to the Gold Mining Disparity Index; but only a few are consistently really significant. I already have mentioned some, like Price-Earnings ratios in Chapter Three; and the ten-week moving average of *Barron's* Confidence Index and the yield-spread curve in Chapter Four; and I discuss other indicators throughout the book. Some technicians attach more importance to one indicator than another, and many interpret the same indicator differently. Indeed, if all indicators used by all technicians were listed, each with their respective interpretations and weightings, we would have a bouillabaisse, with something for everyone—and a net value of zero. As with fundamental data, many indicators are at times repetitive, at times conflicting. Therefore, anyone who uses any indicator—fundamental, technical or even psychological—as an absolute measure becomes a prisoner of it, no longer able to think for himself.

The entire purpose of indicators is to provide *clues,* however tiny, to the direction stock prices will take. Those using the clues as an exercise in mathematics, as most technicians do (when more than 50 percent lean in one direction they act on those mathematical probabilities), show little awareness of human nature. They assume that the crowd is always and absolutely wrong. This is far from the case. As we show later, the crowd is rarely *absolutely* wrong, almost always *relatively* wrong, and for brief periods even right. Indeed, it is this occasional sweet taste of success that encourages their almost perpetual relative wrongness. The important technical clues we receive, then, almost always are ephemeral in nature—often changing within relatively brief periods of time. Yet they are of real value provided we don't expect more of them than they are capable of yielding.

Some of the other indexes that I use are market *averages* —the average price movements of various combinations of stocks. These averages are useful in forecasting stock prices, but investors tend to forget that the trend of any individual stock may be—and often is—opposite to the trends of the market averages. "You do not buy and sell the averages," says analyst George Chestnutt. "You buy and sell individual stocks. It is more important to know the trend of your individual stock than it is to know the trends of the market averages." Nonetheless, group averages and general market averages are vital tools in determining whether the climate is right for a particular stock to move.

The most widely used averages are those computed by Dow Jones: 30 Industrials (the DJIA), 20 Rails (revised in 1970 to include airline stocks and now known as *Transportation* average), 15 Utilities and a 65-Stock Composite of all of these groups. Reported hourly, the Dow Jones Averages are computed by adding the prices of the stocks in each average and dividing these totals by the number of stocks in each group. The DJIA divisor, however, has been adjusted downward over the years to compensate for stock dividends and splits. As of February 6, 1970, it was 1.894. Revisions are promptly reported in the financial press.

Both the DJIA and the Rails Average figure in the Dow Theory, the granddaddy of all stock market technical studies. According to Dow theorists, major bull or bear trends are indicated when the Rails Average and the DJIA, one after the other, set new highs or lows. (One average acting without the other indicates nothing.) I am not a Dow theorist, but I believe these indexes are useful indicators. I also use the Utilities Average, which has an excellent record as a portent of the major direction of the DJIA, a better record in this respect than the Rails, which tend to coincide with the DJIA rather than lead it.

Chart No. 9 shows the record of the three DJ Averages and the British Industrials during the market swings from 1966 to 1969. In the 1966 decline, the Utilities bottomed in August and the Rails and the DJIA in October. In 1967 the Utilities, again leading the way, topped out in April, a move followed by the Rails in August and by the DJIA in September. Note also that when in February 1969 the Utilities failed in a fourth "now or never" attempt to penetrate the overhead trendline projected through the important tops of 1966, 1967 and 1968, this average plummeted, and was followed by a precipitous decline of the DJIA a few months later.

The British Industrials Average, as noted in Chapter Four, also has proven to be a fair leading indicator of our stock market. The double-top etched by this average in

CHART 9. COMPARATIVE CHARTS OF WEEKLY PRICES OF DOW JONES INDUSTRIALS, RAILS (TRANSPORTATION), UTILITIES AND BRITISH INDUSTRIALS

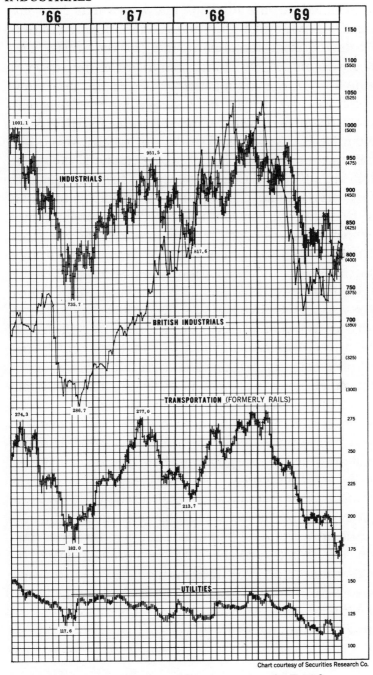

Chart courtesy of Securities Research Co.

The three Dow averages are weekly price ranges; the British Industrials are weekly closing prices.

September 1968 and January 1969 after a two-year advance provided a clue that the major direction of the DJIA was likely to be downward in 1969.

The DJIA sometimes is criticized as not being representative of the stock market in general. This is true, obviously, with only thirty stocks comprising it, but so many investors use it that I am convinced it is a reliable barometer of mass psychology and, therefore, a useful tool for forecasting price trends. A more broadly based index is Standard & Poor's 500 Stocks Average, which I also utilize. The broadest-based average, of course, is the NYSE Index, which includes all the common stocks on that exchange and is weighted by capitalization. Statistically, it is the most accurate market average that can be constructed. Chart No. 10 shows the DJIA, Standard & Poor's 500 Stocks and the NYSE Index for the period from 1965 to 1969. Note the similarities and differences at crucial market turning points.

The Amex Price Index shows the average price changes of all the common stocks on that exchange. Unlike the NYSE Index, it is not weighted by capitalization. Because the Amex lists less-seasoned and, in most cases, lower-quality stocks than the NYSE, its Index is a useful indicator of speculative activity in the market. In fact, the Amex is the only national exchange that provides the data necessary to measure the activity in inferior issues. The issues traded over-the-counter and elsewhere are less stable even than those on the Amex, but these sources do not provide the data necessary to measure their activity.

Even more useful as a psychological measurement is the ratio of Amex to NYSE *volume* against the background of stock price-action of the DJIA, as shown on Chart No. 11. Some fine companies trade on the Amex—for example, seasoned growth issues like Syntex, the drug company, and solid, old-line, high-yield issues like Alan Wood, the steel company. But many Amex issues are "cats and dogs" that sell for just a few dollars a share. An abnormal increase in

CHART 10. COMPARATIVE CHARTS OF DJIA, S & P 500 AND NYSE COMPOSITE INDEX

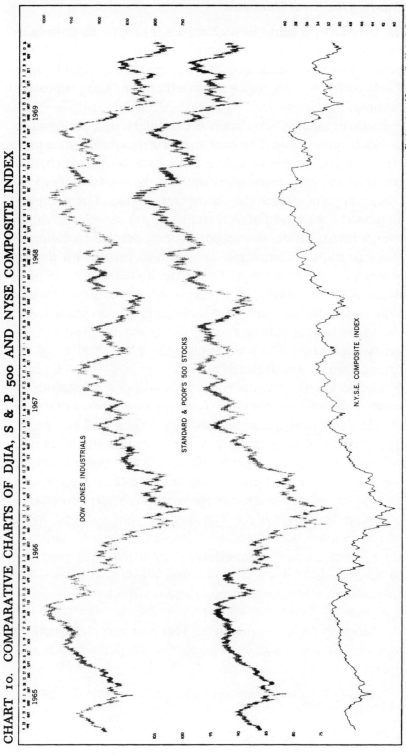

Chart courtesy of Comparative Market Indicators

The DJIA and S & P 500 indexes are daily-basis line charts and the NYSE index is constructed from daily closing prices.

the volume of trading in such issues is often a clear indication of uninformed, unsophisticated investor activity—people buying shares (on a mathematically disadvantageous basis) in companies about which they know virtually nothing.

Mathematically, the disadvantage of buying penny-ante stocks is quite clear. The brokerage commission* on a purchase of 100 shares of a $50 stock is $46.55, less than 1 percent; the commission on the sale is the same, so less than 2 percent covers the entire transaction. The commission on the purchase of 100 shares of a $3 stock is $10, or 3.33 percent; selling costs another 3.33 percent in commissions, so the stock must rise at least 6.66 percent for the investor just to break even. And a stock selling for under a dollar must rise more than 10 percent just to pay commission costs. So anyone who habitually buys penny-ante stocks without a substantial reason is paying an unnecessarily high entry fee just to play the game and must be categorized as uninformed.

The action of such investors as a group is a measure of unsophisticated enthusiasm. Note on Chart No. 11 that in October 1967, for example, this enthusiasm was at a peak. The Amex volume soared to 67 percent that of the NYSE volume. October 26, 1967, in fact, was the busiest day in the Amex's 118-year history up to that point—8,290,000 shares traded, 1.2 million more than the 7,090,000 shares that were traded on Black Tuesday, October 29, 1929. Most of this volume was in the very low-priced issues. The volume "leader" was Burma Mines, a company with assets of about 8¢ a share. Its stock rose from below $1 to almost $2, then within a few days dropped again to below $1. Observe also that the DJIA topped out at or shortly after peaks of the Amex/NYSE volume curve. This was especially noticeable in 1966 and 1967, but also useful throughout 1968 and 1969.

* The NYSE proposed new commission rates in February 1970—higher for small investors and lower for large investors.

CHART 11. RATIO OF AMERICAN STOCK EXCHANGE VOLUME TO NEW YORK STOCK EXCHANGE VOLUME

DOW JONES INDUSTRIALS

% AMERICAN STOCK EXCHANGE VOLUME
% NEW YORK STOCK EXCHANGE VOLUME

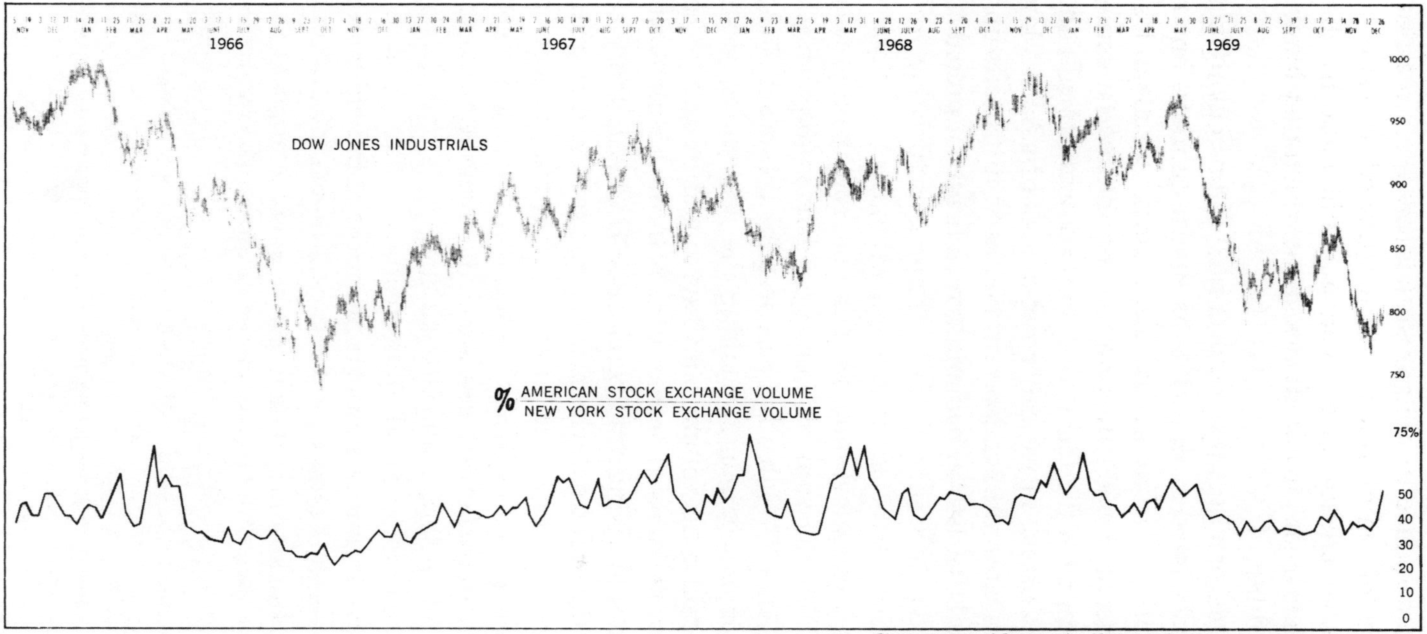

Chart courtesy of Comparative Market Indicators; curve and text by the author

Independent of the various market averages are the "breadth of market" indicators, measurements of the total market climate. The most commonly used is the Advance-Decline (A-D) line. It consists of a cumulative total of the number of NYSE stocks that advance over those that decline, or vice versa, and is plotted on a chart against the background of the DJIA, as shown on Chart No. 12*.

The A-D line should slant up in an advance, down in a decline; but it has no real significance unless it moves counter to the DJIA. If it starts downhill while the DJIA is still rising, as we can observe it did in April–May 1969, it indicates market deterioration; and if it heads uphill while the DJIA is still declining, it indicates a probable reversal in the near future. The A-D line is a fairly accurate indicator of major tops and general-market declines but, like most technical references, it is vague about precise timing.

I go one step further and relate *trading volume* to the A-D line to evaluate the underlying condition of the market. This can be done by taking the *percentage* of advancing-to-declining volume and dividing it by the percentage of advancing-to-declining stocks. If the result is above 100, the underlying volume is more favorable than is reflected in the A-D line, which suggests that the A-D line (and the general market) will turn up. A result of below 100, however, indicates that the underlying volume is deteriorating and that the A-D line (and the general market) is likely to turn down. As with all indicators, trend is more important than an absolute reading.

For example, if weekly advances of individual stocks total 700 and declines total 500, the percentage of advances to declines is 140, which on the surface appears to be favorable. But if the underlying volume for the week is 33 million

* To plot an A-D line, begin the chart at an arbitrary point, say 1,000, then total the number of NYSE issues that advance and decline at the close of a day, or a week, and add or subtract the net difference to the 1,000. For example, if 750 stocks advance, 350 decline and 200 remain unchanged, add the net advance of 400 to the original 1,000. The second point on the graph is then 1,400. If the next closing shows 500 stocks advancing, 550 declining, and 250 remaining unchanged, subtract the net decline, 50, from 1,400. The third point is then 1,350, and so on.

CHART 12. ADVANCE-DECLINE LINE AND THE DJIA

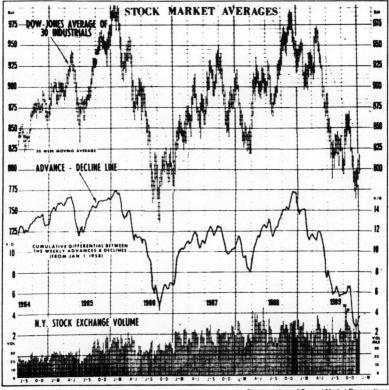

Chart courtesy of Current Market Perspectives

advancing and 30 million declining, for a percentage of advancing-to-declining volume of 110, then dividing 110 by 140 would yield a ratio of 78.5, indicating that, despite the apparently favorable A-D line, the market's advance was outrunning volume advances and showing underlying deterioration.

This indicator is useful in evaluating short-term trends, even those of a day or an hour, but I usually use it on a weekly basis to give me added perspective on the general condition of the market. The data for its construction is regularly available in *Barron's* and from other public sources.

I also use an overbought-oversold indicator constructed from the same two components as above. But, *instead of dividing* the advancing volume/declining volume percentage by the advance/decline percentage, I *multiply* both percentages. For example, the two cited above if multiplied —140 x 110—gives the answer 15,400. When the trend is rising, the market is approaching an overbought status and is vulnerable to correction; when the trend is in a low area, the market is oversold and therefore technically ripe for a rise. This tool is particularly useful in indicating when prices have been carried by emotions—hope in the former instance, fear in the latter—beyond the point at which they might have been expected to stop.

The significance of volume itself often is misinterpreted. Some experts consider an increase in volume during a rally and a decrease during a decline bullish, and a decrease during a rally and an increase during a decline bearish. Often this is so, but the fact is that many declines start on low volume, and frequently a decline ends only after a sharp increase in volume—that is, a "selling climax." But even a selling climax can be misleading; some declines end merely by petering out on low volume. Most investors, however, react in accordance with the experts' formulae. For example, when a record 21 million shares were traded on the NYSE on Thursday, June 13, 1968, many brokers reported that the huge volume created panic among investors. One broker, quoted in the *Wall Street Journal,* said: "I don't know when I've had so many customers call me and say they were scared." The reason behind the record volume was simple enough: the market had been closed on Wednesday but the brokerage houses had remained open, so the Thursday volume essentially reflected two days' trading. But, as we have seen, the market is not rational. That is why it is so important to understand the psychology that prompts investors' actions.

Historically, volume and price trends have moved in tandem over the long term, with volume peaks preceding price peaks. But with the recent tremendous increase in volume this relationship has been changing; volume peaks now often coincide with or even trail price peaks—another illustration of the need for keeping a sharp perspective on technical references.

Another important indicator is the action of stocks grouped by industry—automotive, chemical, airline, etc. Chart No. 13 shows each major industry's performance for 1969. With this data an investor can match the performance of an individual stock—say, Chrysler Corporation—against that of the industry. Note, too, the substantial difference in performance among the different industry groups, ranging from Real Estate's gain of 14.7 percent to Sulphur's loss of 54.8 percent. Obviously, no matter how brilliant a stock selection may be, the odds against its performance are heavy unless its group is "alive."

One of the most sensitive indicators of sophisticated investor action is a group index of my own devising, the Glamour Price Index. The GPI is composed of eleven blue-chip glamour/growth stocks which, because they are highly volatile—ordinarily 2½ times more so than those in the DJIA—are favorite vehicles of sophisticated investors. Their PE multiples are, of course, always very high, which makes them among the highest-risk stocks. These equities are:

Beckman Instruments	Minnesota Mining &
Burroughs	Manufacturing
Comsat	Polaroid
Fairchild Camera	Teledyne
IBM	Texas Instruments
Litton Industries	Xerox

The index is constructed by adding up all the highs and lows of these stocks and multiplying by a figure that adjusts the sums for stock splits that have occurred since the Index first was formulated. The multiplier for the GPI was 1.78 at the beginning of 1970.

I plot the GPI against the background of the DJIA, as shown on Chart No. 14, because any divergence between the price-action of the GPI and the DJIA is significant. For

CHART 13. INDUSTRY GROUPS PERCENTAGE PERFORMANCE—1969

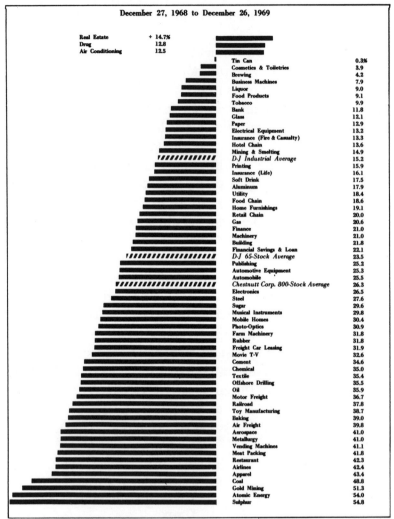

December 27, 1968 to December 26, 1969

Industry	%
Real Estate	+ 14.7%
Drug	12.8
Air Conditioning	12.5
Tin Can	0.3%
Cosmetics & Toiletries	3.9
Brewing	4.2
Business Machines	7.9
Liquor	9.0
Food Products	9.1
Tobacco	9.9
Bank	11.8
Glass	12.1
Paper	12.9
Electrical Equipment	13.2
Insurance (Fire & Casualty)	13.3
Hotel Chain	13.6
Mining & Smelting	14.9
D-J Industrial Average	15.2
Printing	15.9
Insurance (Life)	16.1
Soft Drink	17.5
Aluminum	17.9
Utility	18.4
Food Chain	18.6
Home Furnishings	19.1
Retail Chain	20.0
Gas	20.6
Finance	21.0
Machinery	21.0
Building	21.8
Financial Savings & Loan	22.1
D-J 65-Stock Average	23.5
Publishing	25.2
Automotive Equipment	25.3
Automobile	25.5
Chestnutt Corp. 800-Stock Average	26.3
Electronics	26.5
Steel	27.6
Sugar	29.6
Musical Instruments	29.8
Mobile Homes	30.4
Photo-Optics	30.9
Farm Machinery	31.8
Rubber	31.8
Freight Car Leasing	31.9
Movie T-V	32.6
Cement	34.6
Chemical	35.0
Textile	35.4
Offshore Drilling	35.5
Oil	35.9
Motor Freight	36.7
Railroad	37.8
Toy Manufacturing	38.7
Baking	39.0
Air Freight	39.8
Aerospace	41.0
Metallurgy	41.0
Vending Machines	41.1
Meat Packing	41.8
Restaurant	42.3
Airlines	42.4
Apparel	43.4
Coal	48.8
Gold Mining	51.3
Atomic Energy	54.0
Sulphur	54.8

example, the 38-percent up-move of the GPI in the spring of 1968 anticipated the DJIA rally from 863 to 994 in the fall; and the topping of the GPI in June 1968 was an important clue that the fall DJIA rise was a tail-ending rather than an initial bull move. And in 1969, during the May to July decline, the GPI declined only 14 percent compared with the DJIA's decline of almost 20 percent. This alerted

124

me to the possibility of the glamour stocks outperforming the basic-industry stocks during any market rally. Note that from July to late September, while the Dow remained in a tight 5-percent trading range from 800 to 840, the GPI rose almost 25 percent from its low of 1856 to the high of 2301. This dynamic action demonstrated clearly that the general market was likely to follow the GPI up and break out of its trading range, which is precisely what happened. But by late October the GPI topped out and began declining even while the DJIA moved higher into mid-November. This was an ominous sign, suggesting that the Dow's move would abort. It did. This kind of drastic price divergence, when viewed in the light of other indicators noted elsewhere, has a clear meaning—that sophisticated money frequently deserts (distributes) glamour and vogue stocks under cover of DJIA strength and usually invests in (accumulates) the volatile market leaders under cover of DJIA weakness.

Some experts have suggested that a general-market advance can occur with the glamours going in the opposite direction; but this confuses the typical tail-end strength of basic-industry stocks with a basic advance for them. The market can no more advance without glamour participation than the New York Jets could have won the 1969 Super Bowl without Joe Namath.

Generally speaking, glamour stocks lead market rallies and follow declines in an overall up-move. In major market decline movements, glamours are the last to break down. This happened both in 1962 and 1966 as well as in late 1969 and early 1970. The reason for this may be that glamour stocks are intrinsically the creatures of confidence, and until confidence is broken, the glamour issues will stay alive. When confidence is broken, however, the glamours break the worst of all.

We now come to some concepts I use regularly that will be unfamiliar to most investors. The first is the "rule of three," which is useful in estimating terminal

CHART 14. THE SCHEINMAN GLAMOUR PRICE INDEX AND THE DJIA—WEEKLY PRICE RANGES OF BOTH

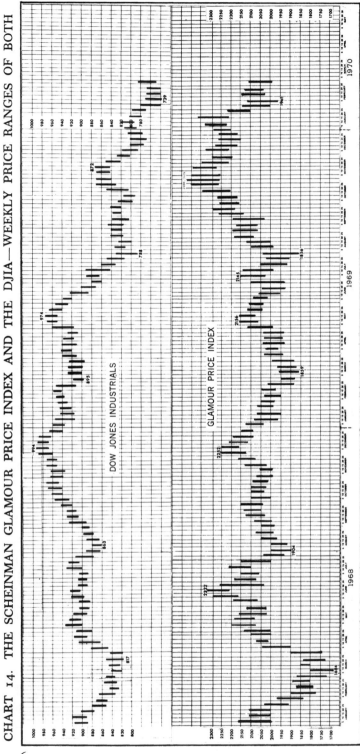

Chart by the author.

phases of both short-term moves and long-term trends. For reasons about which one can only speculate, individuals tend to do things in sets of three. Studies show that most of us, when knocking on a door, knock three times, sometimes four, but rarely two or five times. This tendency may be deeply rooted in the natural family unit of father, mother and child, which is given religious expression in the concept of the Holy Trinity. The stock market, which, after all, is a reflection of human emotions, also frequently acts in the same way. Sometimes it adds a fourth movement, which usually is characterized as a "now-or-never" action, climactic in nature. That the market—and individual stocks, too—typically (but not always) moves in a series of three steps is apparent in both very short-term moves as well as those encompassing several years.

The 1966 market decline, shown on Chart No. 15, is a perfect illustration of this phenomenon. This long decline, from DJIA 1001.11 to 735.74, took place in four well-defined steps—three major slides followed by a climactic fourth. The first-step slide of 96 points terminated at the March low of 905.40. This was followed by a recovery rally to the April high of 961.91, a gain of 56 points. The second-step slide from the April high ended at the May low of 859.13, a drop of 103 points; the recovery rally topped out in June at 910.35. The third-step slide from the June high bottomed at 759.92 in August, then the market rebounded to 822.93 in September. And the fourth-step slide from the September high ran 87 points to a low of 735.74, from which point began the full recovery, ending at the December 1968 high of 994.65.

Note that each of the first three declines was progressively more severe and that each recovery was substantially weaker. The second-step decline of 103 points was greater than the first step's 96 points, and the third step's 151 points was far greater than the second step's. And while the first rally retraced approximately 60 percent of the first decline, the second rally recovered only 50 percent of

CHART 15. FOUR-STEP 1966 MARKET DECLINE OF THE DJIA

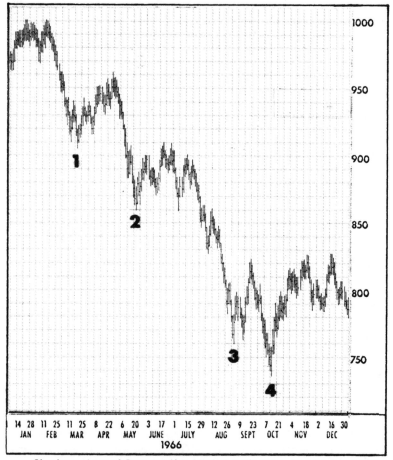

Chart courtesy of Comparative Market Indicators; text by the author

its loss and the third one regained only 40 percent of its loss. These three declines exhausted the emotions of the unsophisticated investors, and the climactic fourth one broke their backs. This overall pattern, as we shall see, may provide some useful lessons for projecting future DJIA action.

The second concept, resistance-line measurement, is even less well known. Pioneered by theoretician Edson Gould, it is based upon what are perhaps the two principal determinants of crowd psychology in the marketplace—price-change itself and elapsed time to achieve it. The resistance-line concept attempts to measure these two ele-

128

ments of mass psychology mathematically, weighing both the *vertical* price-change and the *horizontal* elapse of time. Resistance lines can be based upon any set of important tops and bottoms. The theory is that a trendline *rising* at one-third (or two-thirds) the rate of an advance movement is likely to provide resistance to a subsequent decline, but if violated, the decline will accelerate at the point of penetration. Similarly, a trendline *declining* at one-third (or two-thirds) the rate of a decline movement may provide resistance to a subsequent advance movement, but if penetrated, the advance will accelerate at that point.

Sometimes it works, sometimes it does not; it is not foolproof. But I use resistance lines because I find them more accurate than ordinary trendlines and—most importantly —because they are drawn *before* the price-action takes place. And when they are integrated with divergence analysis, I have found them valuable in deciding on the timing of the market as a whole as well as of individual transactions. For example, the market decline from December 1968 through July 1969 terminated almost precisely at the ascending one-third speed resistance line that rises at one-third the rate of the actual advance from the 1966 crash low to the December 1968 high of Standard & Poor's 500 Composite Stocks Index.

By using this tool (in conjunction with others) it sometimes is possible to buy and sell individual stocks off the tape almost exactly when the stock is finding support or making a breakout. Chart No. 16 shows how this was possible with Libbey-Owens-Ford in 1968, and also illustrates the construction of resistance lines. Note that the declines of August and September stopped almost precisely at the resistance line, thus suggesting these as buy points; and that when the line was penetrated in November, the stock dropped precipitously, making this a point for either short sales or, if one owned the stock, for protective sales to limit losses.

The situational element—that is, the price-action pattern within well-defined technical trendlines—sometimes reinforces prospects indicated by divergence analysis and the resistance line concept. When this happens the result is what may be the fastest and most reliable action in the market based on technical measurements and concepts. For example, on Chart No. 17, which records the action of Procter & Gamble for the ten-month period from July 1967 to May 1968, the convergence of the double-bottom baseline with the resistance line indicates that a breakout is—by very definition—certainly imminent, making the stock a good buy. If the base is violated, the stock can be sold with very little loss. And if the resistance line is penetrated, the upside action should accelerate and provide a substantial gain. In this case, the divergence analysis for PG was very favorable, indicating a likely upside breakout, which is what indeed did occur. The stock rose from the low 80's to 100 before reaction set in.

A third concept, unit measurement, is also based upon the evaluation of crowd behavior. Also pioneered by Gould, unit measurement is especially helpful in estimating the terminal points of both advances and declines, particularly in individual stocks, including volatile high fliers. Its measurements are expressed in terms of bull and bear "units." A bull unit consists of the number of points of an initial advance by a stock or price index following the bottom of a prior important decline, succeeded by a subsequent reaction which, however, remains above that bottom and then is followed by a second advance that goes beyond the first one. A bear unit is formed in the same manner but in the opposite direction. These measurements often portend the length of the overall advance or decline and indicate levels at which a trend may meet resistance or—as we shall see— a violent reversal. Price-action *with* the primary trend frequently "works off" units three times (sometimes four times) in accordance with the "rule of three." Contra-trend movements often work off the unit 2⅓ times. Chart No. 18, a daily-basis computer-drawn line chart from January 1966 through October 1969, illustrates both a bull and bear unit—how they "worked out" in actual practice—in one

CHART 16. LIBBEY-OWENS-FORD DAILY-BASIS PRICE-ACTION SHOWING RESISTANCE LINE CONSTRUCTION AND APPLICATION

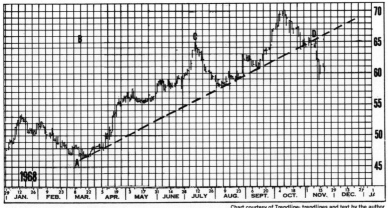

Chart courtesy of Trendline; trendlines and text by the author

The dashed two-thirds speed resistance line rises at two-thirds the rate of the actual rise from the March low (A) near 46 to the July high at 65 (C). Point (B) is directly above (A) and on a horizontal plane with (C). The distance between (B) and (C) is the basis of measurement, with (C)–(D) equaling (B)–(C) and constituting (A)–(D) as a two-thirds speed resistance line. (Twice the distance of (C)–(D) would constitute a *one*-third speed resistance line.)

CHART 17. SITUATIONAL BREAKOUT PAST THE RESISTANCE LINE, PROCTER & GAMBLE (PG)

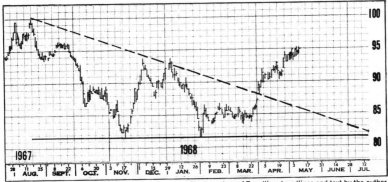

Chart courtesy of Trendline; trendlines and text by the author

The descending resistance line (dashes) declines at two-thirds the rate of the actual decline from the August high of 100 to the February low of 81½.

CHART 18. ANTICIPATING TOPS AND BOTTOMS OF HIGH FLIERS: UNIT MEASUREMENT OF THE XEROX CORPORATION (XRX)

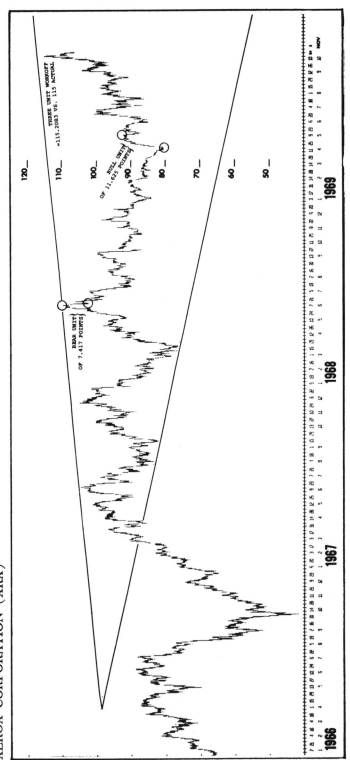

Chart by the author.

of the most volatile glamour stocks of modern times, the Xerox Corporation (XRX).

Despite the volatility of XRX, it is a "regular" stock, regular in the sense that its price-action reflects mass psychology with a reasonable degree of faithfulness. From its April 17, 1969, low point of 80.33 (adjusted for 3-for-1 split) XRX formed a bull unit, as illustrated on the chart, by its initial advance to a May 16 high of 91.9583 (also split adjusted). Assuming that the move by XRX would be *with* the primary trend, normal expectation would be that the bull unit should work off three times. This yields an upside target of 115.2083. The actual high on October 21 was 115.

To illustrate the precision with which XRX worked off units in a previous instance, refer to the bear unit formed following the June 13, 1968, high of 109.5 (split adjusted) by its initial decline to 102.083 by June 18, 1968. The bear unit of 7.417 points called for a downside target, if worked off four times, of 79.832. It actually reached 80.333 on April 17, 1969, within half a point of the projection. It is also useful to observe that the decline itself took place in four well-defined down steps.

If we look at the DJIA from 1959 to 1964, as shown in Chart No. 19, we can see the classic "whipsaw" formation, the unequal battle between sophisticated and unsophisticated investors. The trendline M-E is the upper limit of the major expanding triangle T-M-E and defines the outer limits of the market's price-action for that period. At the 1959, 1960 and 1961 tops, sophisticated investors sold and unsophisticated investors bought—positions that were reversed at the 1959, 1960 and 1962 bottoms. Each time the unsophisticated investor was burned. The fourth attempt to penetrate the M-E trendline, however, in 1964, was successful. This was no accident and is deeply rooted in principles of crowd psychology. Having bought at the top for *three* successive years, and each time having been decisively wrong, unsophisticated investors sold in 1964 when the market again hit the M-E trendline. Again they were decisively wrong.

The whipsaw is essentially a psychological game, like Musical Chairs. The rule is that it often takes three times to fool the crowd. That is why the fourth attempt to breech a trendline is known as the "now-or-never" attempt.

Chart No. 19 also illustrates the Elliott Wave Theory, which is related to the rule of three. Originally described by Robert Rhea and R. N. Elliott, this pattern consists of a series of "waves," up and down, each succeeding one of which is "corrected" by the pattern created by the first set. Elliott's theory is based upon the Fibonacci series of numbers, in which each number equals the sum of the two preceding numbers—for example: 1-1-2-3-5-8-13-21-34 and so on. These ratios often are found in nature—for example, in the whorls of sunflowers and pineapples. Elliott believed that prices in the market fluctuate in natural ways, that trend moves tend to appear in five waves, counter-trend moves in three.

As we can see on the chart, when advances proceed in three steps—the normal expectation of a move *with* the trend—the three up-moves interrupted by two reactions make up a five-wave pattern. Wave theory as such, however, is of interest more as a concept to be taken into account rather than an active working tool for timing purposes because of the ambiguities of waves-within-waves and the elaborate efforts required of wave-theory adherents to constantly re-explain the theory to conform to market action.

A word here about the newest tool in security analysis, the computer. Certainly data processing equipment serves a real purpose in cutting down the time between the availability of information in raw form and its processing to the stage where the money manager can use this information to make timely portfolio decisions. I myself use the computer to process data and draw charts because the results are both available more quickly and far more precise for my needs than could possibly be achieved by hand. But many well-known money managers have taken the computer one step further and attempted to program it to time

CHART 19. THE WHIPSAW—MAJOR EXPANDING
TRIANGLE OF THE DJIA

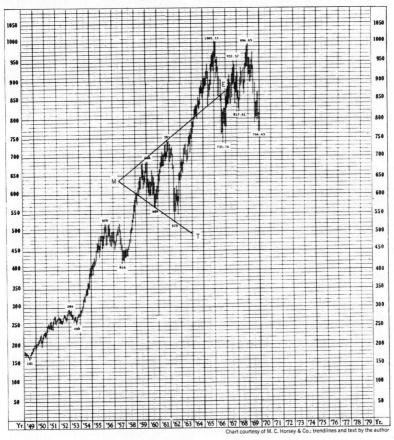

Following the 1964 breakout above the triangle, note how the 1965
decline terminated precisely at the same trendline.

the purchases and sales of securities. Some managers even
claim that the computer is the magic answer to timing stock
selection.

I do not know the programming details of all such computers in operation today (most of them are cloaked with
elaborate security arrangements to assure secrecy), but all
those which I know anything about I have found to be programmed essentially on the basis of the "relative-strength"
concept. This is no more nor less than the conventional
technician's basic premise that a trend in motion is likely
to continue until it is broken. The computers are put to

135

work to find out as early as possible when a trend has become established, and when an established trend has broken, the aim being to jump on and off the bandwagon before the next guy. But since the next guy also is starting to use a computer, or plans to use one in the future, it is obvious that the entire exercise eventually must become self-defeating. Furthermore, this approach suggests that human nature as it operates in the stock market is simple enough to be programmed. This simply is not so. Indeed, in my limited exposure to computer-based decisions, I have found the machines increasingly vulnerable to whip-saw action. An example of this occurred in early October 1969, when a technical downside breakout of the DJIA took place, causing most technicians and relative-strength programmed computers—including a multimillion-dollar computer operation at one of the most prestigious firms on the Street—to turn decisively bearish. I myself did not turn bearish, at that time, despite the technical evidence, because not only were my divergence-analysis measurements still favorable but the GPI still was in a well-defined uptrend; indeed, the DJIA showed support precisely at its relevant resistance line. The market rallied sharply immediately thereafter, the glamour stocks rising to all-time highs by the end of the month, and the computer-directed institutional investors were left out of the game, some of them having made short sales at precisely the wrong time.

These then, are some of the technical tools I use. Some of them are common, some are not. None of them works all the time or in all situations. As one of the most respected technicians has said: "Stocks are like women; what stimulates one will leave another cold." That is why I never act upon fundamentals or technical references alone; indeed, even integrating these two approaches with divergence analysis is no guarantee of success. But, as we shall see, it does increase the odds in one's favor.

1991 ADDENDUM

This will be not only the most challenging new material in this book, but also I hope the most rewarding because I believe it provides practical tools for gauging investment psychology on a day-to-day basis, in specific investment situations. Perhaps these tools are even more important now than 21 years ago because since then there has been a proliferation of investment information, due to the information explosion. This means that even though a plethora of fact and opinion are available, most of it does not seem to have a meaningful relationship in helping decide whether to buy or sell a specific investment at a given time and given price. Moreover, today's instant communications technology means that information which formerly took months and even years to disseminate, now takes place in weeks, days or even hours. Indeed, rapidly growing technology stocks whose earnings have stumbled were off as much as 50 percent or more in a single day—or less—in 1990.

Consequently, *short term* now means *today*, *intermediate term* means somewhere between *weeks* and months, whereas the *long term* is for very discerning investors. In brief, in order to excel as an investor one needs to demonstrate sufficient situational awareness to anticipate, as well as respond to, a fast-paced, dynamic, tactical investment environment. But even though I feel *future shock* is in place in 1991, I also continue to think that *long term cycles* such as *decennial patterns* and the 4-year presidential cycle are relevant. I discuss these in chapters 6 and 10. With this background in mind, let's examine the tools and yardsticks, the judicious use of which can help determine when to get on and off, as well as some specialized bellwether indices.

Technology Stocks

More than 20 years ago I constructed a Glamour Price Index [pp.123-6,149-151,164] as a measure of *sophisticated* investor confidence. Today I use the *Hambrecht and Quist Technology Stock Index* and particularly its *sub-index of rapidly growing, smaller technology companies,* the *H & Q Growth Stocks Index.* The Technology index is dominated by household names such as IBM, Digital Equipment and Texas Instruments. The chart on page 136C shows the six-fold advance from 1974 to 1987, as well as 1990's break of an 11-year uptrend. Though many investors and particularly large institutional investors continue to focus on what I describe as the "Techs", I believe their day in the sun is over. This is not only because the Techs became "too" big but—more importantly—because of the inherent tendencies of popular technologies to be cannibalized. Thorstein Veblen wrote about this phenomenon earlier in this century in his essay, *On The Merits of Borrowing and the Penalty of Taking the Lead.* Veblen said it is the newcomer who is best able to leapfrog existing technology not only because he "borrows" from it but also because he has no vested interest in maintaining it when it becomes obsolete.

Therefore, it is the smaller, more rapidly growing [sales and earnings] technology companies which are more deserving of our investment focus, though more difficult to invest in because their PE multiples are typically very high. Whereas companies which have flowered from their earlier stages of relatively undiscovered super-rapid growth but still have far more potential are core growth stock investments for the Nineties, in my opinion. These include such names as Amgen, Intel and Microsoft.

My chart of what I call the "Growths" is on page 136D. From the 1988 low this index rose more than 50 percent to its 1990 peak. That was a virtual *double top* with the 1987 peak and an important clue that the stock market,

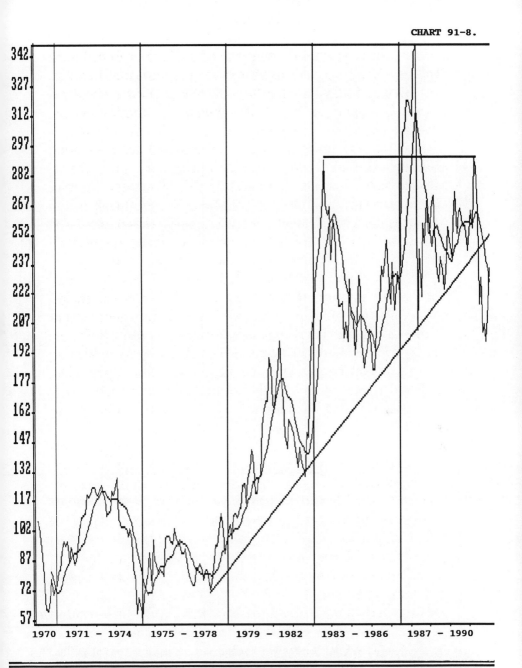

CHART 91-8.

HAMBRECHT & QUIST TECHNOLOGY STOCK INDEX, MONTH END: JANUARY 1970-DECEMBER 1990

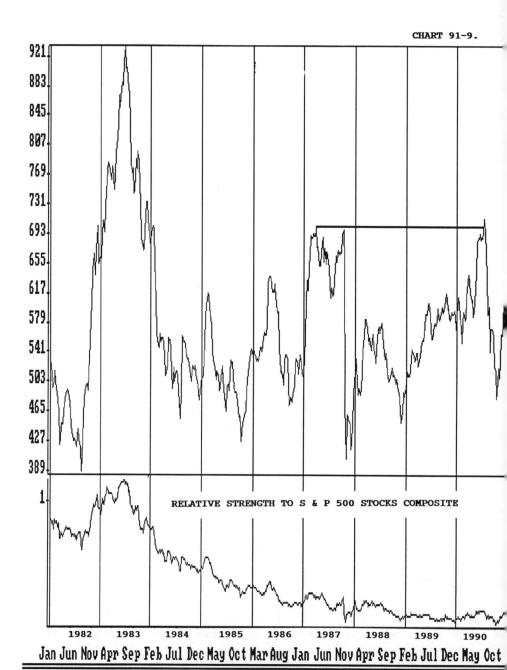

CHART 91-9.

RELATIVE STRENGTH TO S & P 500 STOCKS COMPOSITE

1982 1983 1984 1985 1986 1987 1988 1989 1990

Jan Jun Nov Apr Sep Feb Jul Dec May Oct Mar Aug Jan Jun Nov Apr Sep Feb Jul Dec May Oct

HAMBRECHT & QUIST GROWTH STOCK INDEX + RELATIVE STRENGTH: JAN.1982-DEC.1990

136D

itself, might fall in third quarter 1990. The Growths then lost about one-third of their value in two months! With the index at 625.16 on December 31, 1990, a further rise of about 15 percent would bring it back to the 1987 and 1990 peaks. However, since I believe 1990 witnessed an *every other* 4-year stock market cycle low, I think the Growths' longer term potential is to match the much higher 1983 peak. One potential sign of this may be the rising *Relative Strength* during the last quarter of 1990. I agree with my friend Joseph McNay of Essex Management in Boston who is perhaps the most discerning technology-oriented investor I know. In a recent *Barron's* interview he said that areas of investment which would be particularly fruitful include "companies that deal in cost reduction for U.S. companies, such as the computer-aided engineering, computer-aided design companies. Companies that help increase productivity…help reduce costs, offer new services or offer new products." He added, "Biotechnology has been a mainstay for us, and we continue to be there."

Despite recent years' interest in and hype about the Elliot Wave Theory [pp.134-5], I still prefer to keep it simple with the *Rule of Three*, as illustrated later: expect *three* attempts, be prepared for the fourth.

How to Use Resistance Line Measurement to Define Buy & Sell Zones

I continue to believe that *resistance lines* [pp.128-30] remain valuable tools, as illustrated, for example, in the chart on page 136F of the Value Line Industrials. Just as the break below the 2/3 speed resistance line in 1987 meant that there would be a further drop to the 1/3 speed line, the 1987-1989 rally terminated just below the higher parameter. Now, the 1990 break below the 1/3 speed line suggests to me that a logical upside target for 1991 is back to it. That would be a gain of about 20 percent from the year end 1990 close

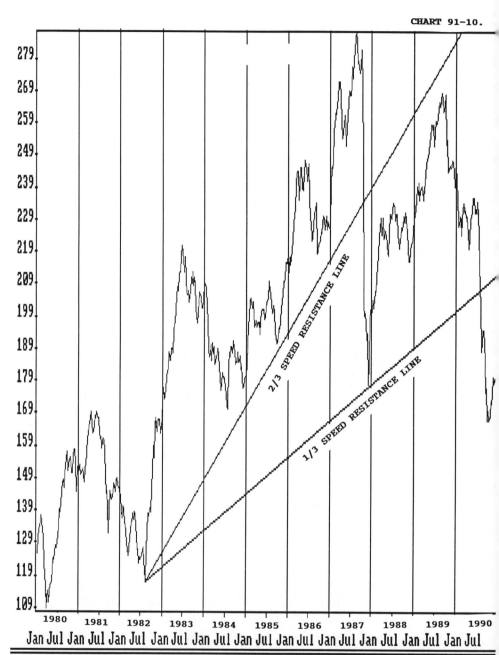

CHART 91-10.

2/3 SPEED RESISTANCE LINE

1/3 SPEED RESISTANCE LINE

VALUE LINE INDUSTRIALS WITH RISING 1/3 AND 2/3 SPEED RESISTANCE LINES

136F

near 180. This conclusion, however, doesn't rule out longer term upside potential because the overall 1987-1990 decline was almost 50 percent off the top. The importance of a low which is a cut-in-half is discussed later. Indeed, 1991-1992 might well become an *outside* year as in 1982-1983 during which the Value Line Industrials doubled. I discuss this in the next chapter.

The chart on page 136H of the *Nasdaq Composite*, the home to most of the rapidly growing technology stocks, illustrates how accurate the 1/3 speed resistance line from the 1984 low was in helping determine that 1990's late-year low was a major one.

The *Tokyo Nikkei Index* chart on page 136I also shows how after the break of each of the two rising resistance lines the declines accelerated. Off almost 50 percent from the year end 1989 peak, at the 1990 low below the 20000 level, I feel Tokyo is overdue to extend its rally, perhaps back to the now overhead 1/3 speed line, as much as 5000 points higher than Nikkei's 1990 close. After that, I don't rule out at least a test of the 1990 low, or worse—a *double cut-in-half* to the 10000 level.

Declining resistance lines are equally valuable as shown by the behavior of the *Commodity Research Bureau's Futures Price Index* in the chart on page 136J. After upside penetrating the declining 2/3 speed line in late-1987, the CRB index accelerated its advance back almost to the overhead 1/3 speed line. That line stopped it in 1988. Subsequently, the declining 1/3 speed line seems to be providing the simple message that so long as the index remains below it, inflation will not be a great problem.

*How to Use Unit Measurement to Estimate
the Length of Advances & Declines*

Unit measurement [pp. 130-3] continues to be enormously valuable, I feel. Here are some recent examples. Unit measure-

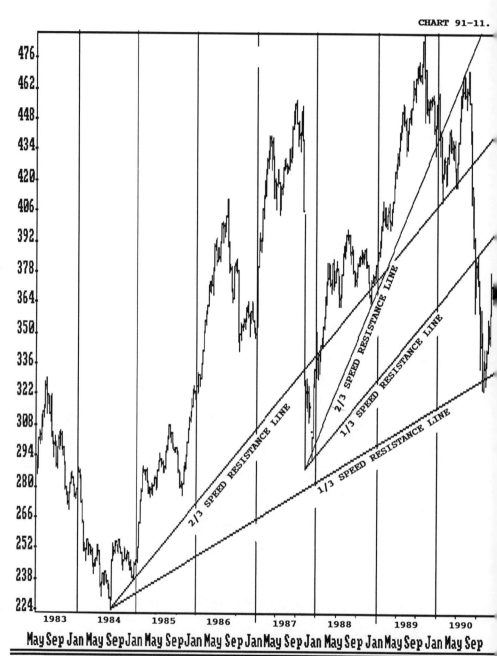

CHART 91–11.

2/3 SPEED RESISTANCE LINE

2/3 SPEED RESISTANCE LINE

1/3 SPEED RESISTANCE LINE

2/3 SPEED RESISTANCE LINE

1/3 SPEED RESISTANCE LINE

NASDAQ COMPOSITE WITH 1984-BASIS & 1987-BASIS RISING RESISTANCE LINES

136H

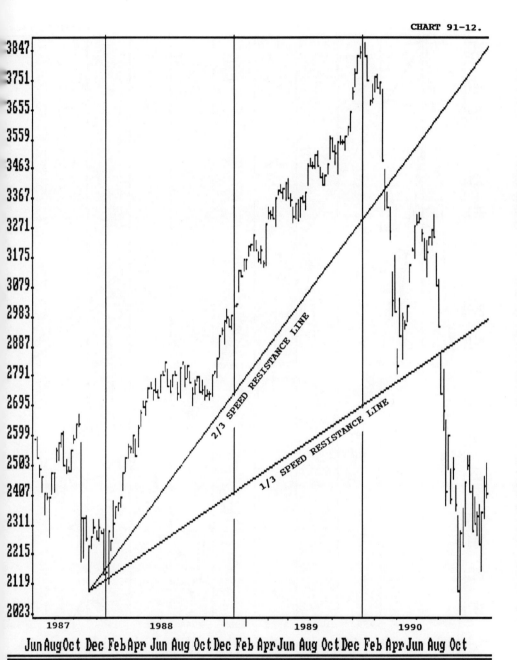

CHART 91-12.

JAPAN NIKKEI INDEX WITH RISING 1/3 AND 2/3 SPEED RESISTANCE LINES

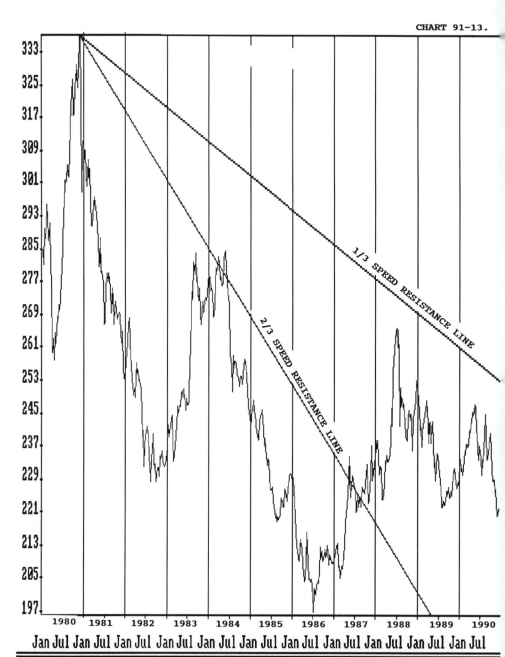

CHART 91-13.

CRB FUTURES PRICE INDEX WITH DECLINING 1/3 AND 2/3 SPEED RESISTANCE LINES

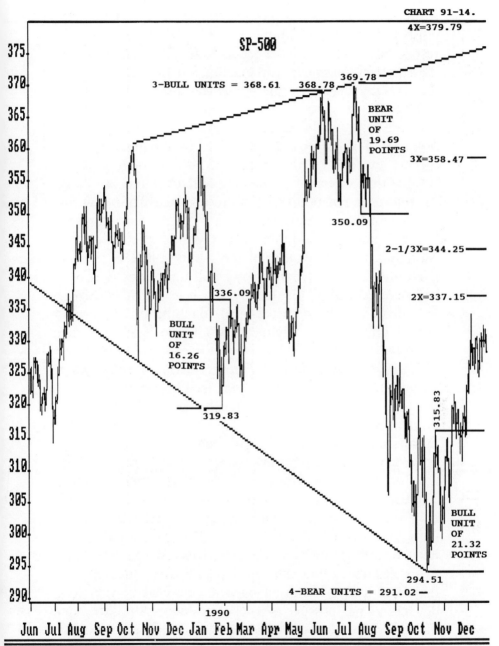

CHART 91-14.

SP-500

S & P 500 STOCKS COMPOSITE, DAILY WITH BULL AND BEAR UNIT COUNTS

ment accurately helped to define the July 1990 peak of *Standard & Poors* 500 Stocks Composite, chart on page 136K. The theoretical 3-bull unit target of 368.61 was very close to the actual double top of 368.78 and 369.78, respectively. The October 1990 low, also, reflected unit measurement inasmuch as the actual low of 294.51 was less than 1.2 percent above the theoretical 4-bear unit count of 291.02.

Subsequent to the October 1990 low, I believe a new *bull unit* of 21.32 points was etched by the initial advance off that low. The December 6, 1990 intraday high of 333.98 was less than 1 percent below the 2-bull unit target of 337.15. Therefore, a reaction, such as took place from near the 2-bull unit level, means that theory suggests an ultimate 3 or 4 bull unit workoff [after the intervening reaction is over]. Moreover, this *recognition* of the 2-bull unit level tends to mean that the *contratrend* 2-1/3 bull unit target of 344.25 will be exceeded. Consequently, I believe the stock market will head higher in 1991 until reaching either 358.47 [3-bull units] or a marginal new all-time high to 379.79 [4-bull units].

Treasury Bonds Nearest Futures, chart on page 136M, likewise faithfully recognized unit measurement, as well as the *Rule of Three*. The summer 1989 decline from the peak of 101.281 was the first large step down in the overall bear move which ended at the third step September 1990 low of 86.875. Moreover, that low recognized with great precision the theoretical contratrend 2-1/3 bear unit level of 86.854. Thereafter, a bull unit was etched with upside targets of 3 or 4 bull units [99.544 and 103.767, respectively]. 4 bull units would match the 1986 peak. However, my feeling is it will be difficult for Treasuries, which closed 1990 at 95.719, to exceed the 3-bull unit level on the first attempt since that level is also identified by a weekly chart's 1986-1989 downtrend, i.e., possible overhead resistance. A positive sign, though, is that Zero Coupon Treasury Bonds of 2015 have already decisively exceeded their own 4-Bull unit level. This

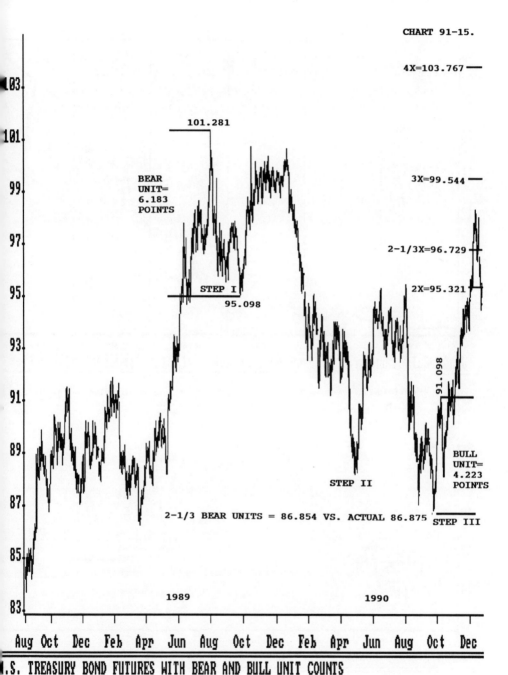

CHART 91-15.

4X=103.767 —

101.281

BEAR
UNIT=
6.183
POINTS

3X=99.544 —

2-1/3X=96.729 —

2X=95.321 —

STEP I
95.098

91.098

BULL
UNIT=
4.223
POINTS

STEP II

2-1/3 BEAR UNITS = 86.854 VS. ACTUAL 86.875 STEP III

1989   1990

Aug Oct Dec Feb Apr Jun Aug Oct Dec Feb Apr Jun Aug Oct Dec

.S. TREASURY BOND FUTURES WITH BEAR AND BULL UNIT COUNTS

136M

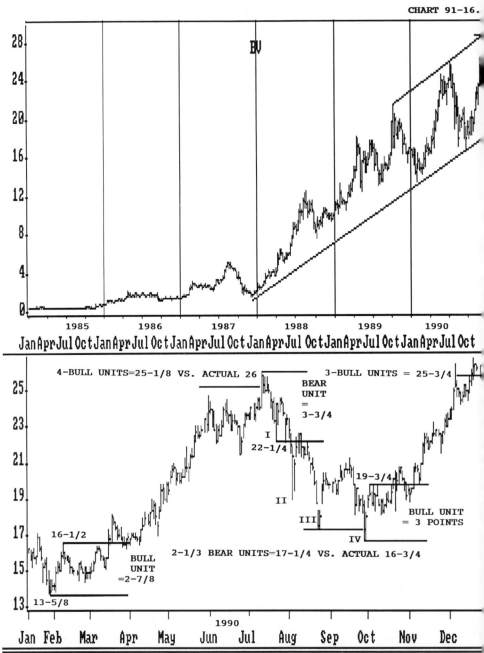

CHART 91-16.

BLOCKBUSTER ENTERTAINMENT, DAILY WITH UNIT COUNTS & WEEKLY + LONG-TERM TRENDS

implies their ultimate workout to 6 or 8 bull units. This more positive outcome for the bond market may also be warranted by the bearish action of the CRB Futures Price Index, as shown earlier, i.e., a low inflation environment.

Finally, let's look at the 1990 action of one of the most volatile stocks, *Blockbuster Entertainment*, chart on page 136N. The January-July advance exceeded the 4-bull unit level by 7/8 of a point whereas the actual July high was 1-1/8 points below the doubling level. Close enough. The July-October decline, which took place in *four* steps, ended at 16-3/4, only a 1/2 point below the contratrend 2-1/3 bear unit level of 17-1/4. Also close. The new bull unit etched by the October advance suggested 3 or 4 bull units working off, i.e., a target area between 25-3/4 and 28-3/4. I doubt that the 4-bull unit level will be exceeded, or if so by much, because the long-term chart [on the same page] shows the higher level also being targeted by the top of the rising trend which is projected through Blockbuster's major highs of the past several years. As this longer term picture illustrates, owning Blockbuster has been like riding a roller-coaster, with excellent opportunities to buy and to sell. It also shows the importance of using short-term tools only within the context of long-term parameters. Moreover, I caution that in some cases units are not easily discernible and sometimes they simply aren't there. This is one reason for using other yardsticks, some of which we examine next, including a case where unit measurement doesn't seem to be working.

The Cut-in-Half Rules and Their Opposites:
Double Trouble

When a broadly based price index doubles a prior important low or declines by half from a prior important high, this is almost always an excellent place at which to act—sell or buy. The best recent example seems to be that

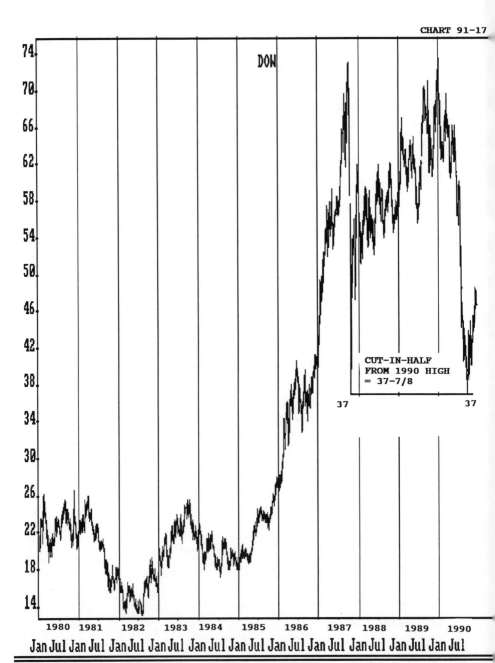

CHART 91–17

DOW

CUT–IN–HALF
FROM 1990 HIGH
= 37–7/8

DOW CHEMICAL WITH CUT-IN-HALF LEVEL FROM 1990 PEAK

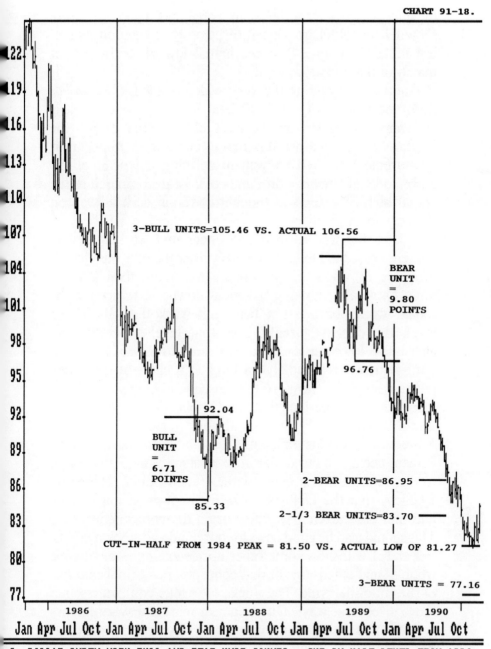

CHART 91-18.

3-BULL UNITS=105.46 VS. ACTUAL 106.56

BEAR
UNIT
=
9.80
POINTS

96.76

92.04

BULL
UNIT
=
6.71
POINTS

85.33

2-BEAR UNITS=86.95

2-1/3 BEAR UNITS=83.70

CUT-IN-HALF FROM 1984 PEAK = 81.50 VS. ACTUAL LOW OF 81.27

3-BEAR UNITS = 77.16

.S. DOLLAR INDEX WITH BULL AND BEAR UNIT COUNTS + CUT-IN-HALF LEVEL FROM 1984

136Q

Charting the Great Unknown

provided by the Value Line Industrials [page 136F] which
doubled between mid-1982 and mid-1983, then collapsed
by almost 50 percent between 1987 and 1990. In 1990,
Dow Chemical [chart page 136P] closely recognized its cut-
in-half level of 37-7/8 at the actual low of 37 [a perfect
match of the 1987 low, also].

Another example is the very widely traded *U.S. Dollar
Index* on page 136Q. This Federal Reserve Board index is
an average weighted on the basis of trade that tracks the
Dollar's value against ten major currencies. Since unit
measurement worked so well in defining the peak of the
1987-1989 advance—3-bull units of 105.46 compared to the
actual high of 106.56—I thought it would work as well on
the way down.

Indeed, the well-defined 1989 bear unit worked well in
the sense that the Dollar fell sharply after the unit was etched,
dropping by about 20 percent in little more than a year's
time. Originally thinking a logical downside target for the
Dollar would be a 2-1/3 bear unit workoff to the 83.70
level, the decisive breaking of that level suggested the
alternative lower target of 3-bear units to 77.16. However,
I subsequently realized that a long-term chart of this index
peaked in 1984, near 163. Consequently, I was able to
recognize after the fact that the October low of 81.27 was
undoubtedly "the" low, an almost perfect cut-in-half.
Moreover, it sounds eminently reasonable to me that a 50
percent decline in our dollar in six years is more than enough
to discount the worst case for the United States. Therefore,
I believe that the Dollar's 1990 low is of great importance
and that our currency will now begin to appreciate in value.
This should also be good news for our bond and stock markets.

Later, I will show some other upside examples of "double
trouble" and extensions of that concept, after a final example
of the cut-in-half rule. The stocks of smaller companies often
move in extreme ways. During a bear market they sometimes
get cut-in-half more than once, i.e., a double cut-in-half [off
75 percent], or even a triple cut [off 87-1/2 percent].

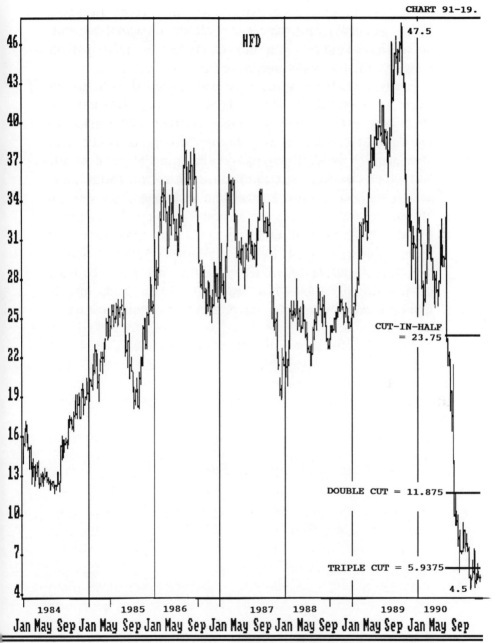

CHART 91-19.

HFD

47.5

CUT-IN-HALF
= 23.75

DOUBLE CUT = 11.875

TRIPLE CUT = 5.9375

4.5

1984 1985 1986 1987 1988 1989 1990

Jan May Sep Jan May Sep Jan May Sep Jan May Sep Jan May Sep Jan May Sep Jan May Sep

OME FEDERAL : THE TRIPLE CUT-IN-HALF. OFF 90.5 PERCENT FROM 47.5 TO 4.5

Indeed, between 1929 and 1932 the Dow Jones Industrials was off 89 percent. Such was the recent case of Home Federal, the California savings and loan, whose chart is on page 136S. From the 1989 peak of 47-1/2, HFD appeared to have recognized its cut-in-half level in early 1990 by rallying about 50 percent from moderately above that level. After that rally was over, however, it was all the way down. The double cut level of 11-7/8 didn't stem the decline, nor did even the triple cut, near 6. By year end 1990 the stock sank to a low of 4-1/2, which is 90.5 percent off the top. The very equivalent of the DJIA 1929-1932 collapse! This shows why it is wise to use such tools judiciously. Looking ahead, however, the most important decision an investor considering Home Federal needs to make now is whether or not it is likely to go into bankruptcy. If not—and I think not—the upside potential for HFD may be huge. I believe a longer term target *squaring the low* is possible. That would be back up to near 20, a level also suggested by the 1987 low, in my opinion. I illustrate the concept of squaring lows in chapter 8.

6 / Divergence Analysis: Timing Stock Selections

The greatest of all gifts is the power to estimate things at their true worth.

—LA ROCHEFOUCAULD

The unexplored element of the marketplace, says one of the most successful money managers on the Street, "is the emotional area. All the charts and breadth indicators and technical palaver are the statistician's attempts to describe an emotional state."

This is the area within which divergence analysis operates. As I explained in Chapter One, divergence analysis attempts to measure the behavior of groups of investors. Group behavior invariably is motivated by emotional factors; as Gustave Le Bon said in his famous treatise on crowds, the fundamental fact of group psychology lies in the "intensification of the emotions" and in the "inhibition of the intellect." In the stock market these emotions usually are hope and fear—hope of profit, fear of loss.

Of the two, fear probably is the more potent. Indeed, it is fear, the fear of isolation, that drives men into crowds in the first place. Most investors are psychologically incapable of playing the "loner" in the market, as the most sophisticated investors do. For the average investor, the crowd provides emotional comfort, especially during periods of market stress. In the words of that old pre-Freudian adage, "misery loves company."

The influence of fear is more pervasive than we realize. Most investors insist they are in the market "for the money." Of course they are, but there also is that unspoken need to get into the game, to join the party, to belong.

Group psychology is dramatically illustrated during bull markets. Each new advance in prices attracts a new group of less sophisticated buyers—who drive prices up still higher. When the market finally reaches an unrealistically high level and reacts, the same buyers become depressed to the point of affecting the most intimate aspects of their lives.

As I noted earlier, insight—that is, an understanding of behavior—is what enables sophisticated investors to win consistently in the market's version of Musical Chairs. There is no magic formula; certainly divergence analysis is not one. In recent years, mutual funds have been thought to be the magic formula: the average investor, who knew little about the market and didn't have the time to study it, would have his money managed by experts, professional money managers. But, as we have seen, the performance of mutual funds as a group leaves much to be desired, and with the increasing proliferation of funds, it now is as difficult to pick the few that will perform well this year as it is to choose individual stocks. And, in any case—and as stated earlier—individual investors can outperform funds because individuals have greater mobility getting in and out of issues.

The fact is, the investor cannot abnegate his responsibility. Whether he manages his own portfolio, buys mutual funds, takes investment advisory services, retains investment-management counsel or gives his broker full discretion, in the final analysis *he* must bear the responsibility for his decisions. He pays the bills. At the very least, as noted earlier, in view of the mixed quality of professional opinion, he must be able to assess intelligently the performance of any professional services he engages.

The name of the game is to buy low and sell high (or, in short selling, to sell high and buy low). Success in this lies in the timing of stock purchases and sales. It is not enough to know that a particular company is financially sound and has excellent growth prospects; one also must know *when* to buy its stock—and when to sell it. "To know values," said Charles H. Dow around the turn of the century, "is to know the meaning of the market." But Dow also said that wise investors, knowing values above all else, buy them when there is no competition from the crowd. Indeed, they buy them from the crowd during periods of mass pessimism, and sell them to the crowd in return for cash during late stages of advancing markets. An investor must know the fundamental worth of a company, the growth prospects for it and its industry group, as well as how monetary and fiscal conditions affect these values. But a knowledge of fundamental values is not the same as an understanding of how the market capitalizes them.

Fundamental factors and technical references, as we have seen, deal with what is known. With these approaches as background, we are now ready to examine a less-known element—the human behavior that produces the technical patterns. To *anticipate* its effect upon the market and thereby improve the timing of investors' purchases and sales is the goal of divergence analysis.

The market as a whole, said Dow, "represents a serious, well-considered effort on the part of far-sighted and well-informed men to adjust prices to such values as exist or which are expected to exist in the not too remote future." Actually, the market cannot always be judged as a whole because it is composed of three distinct groups—the blue chips, the main body of stocks and the performers. These groups change only insofar as they vary in size. The blue chips are the least variable, being by definition relatively stable issues. But the other two groups constantly vary vis-à-vis. When the number of stocks in one group increases, the number in the other group diminishes. In a bull market, for example, performers may account for 20 to 25 percent of all stocks; in a bear market, only 1 to 2 percent. The difference is absorbed into the main body of stocks.

Dow's comment raises the interesting question of whether or not stock prices can be forecast with any degree of reliability. Certainly, investors have not hesitated to try. More than thirty years ago Richard Dana Skinner pointed out that "more zeal and energy, more fanatical hope, and more intense anguish have been expended over the past century in efforts to 'forecast' the stock market than in almost any other single line of human action." The harvest, needless to say, has not matched the sowing.

But that doesn't preclude the possibility of forecasting stock prices with a reasonable degree of accuracy. We now know, for example, that the laws of probability apply to human actions as well as to physical phenomena. Edward R. Dewey and Edwin F. Dakin of the Foundation for the Study of Cycles have written that "certain activities of people, viewed en masse, fall into definite patterns, some of which repeat themselves with periodic rhythm. . . . These patterns will not tell us what any given *individual* will do— any more than laws in physics will tell what a particular atom will do. . . . But the patterns do reveal how masses are likely to act at given times. And to that extent they are a formulation of law."

There is a rhythm to the market, a pulse of alternating waves of investor optimism and pessimism, just as surely as there is to the ebb and flow of the tides. Successful investment timing comes of matching one's major decisions to this basic rhythm—no easy task, of course, since individual stocks often play counterpoint to the basic melody of the market.

One's ear, then, must be sharp, and always tuned in, but some tactical precepts are useful. Long-term investors, for example, should look to assume investment positions at or near major market bottoms and take long-term profits at or near major market tops. Short-term investors should trade each leg of the advance and decline. To a trader, it should make no difference whether the market goes up or down. Even a major decline movement consists of both advance and decline legs. So does a major advance movement. The only material difference is that in a decline movement the down legs are longer and more intense than the up legs, and in an advance movement the reverse is true.

The tendency of prices to rise or fall during specific time cycles is well established. For example, the market traditionally rallies every summer. Since 1897 the DJIA has made an important advance about 75 percent of the time from a May–July low to a June–September high. In most years the advance from low to high runs 10 to 20 percent; but in those years when the market is topping or part of an overall decline movement, the advance is usually between 5 to 10 percent. And what could be more consistent than a year-end rally? Every year since 1897 has had one. Indeed, the extent of its magnitude and duration usually has been a clue to the price action for the year following it.

A look at the record over the last seventy years reveals other cyclical trends: About two-thirds of the time January, July, August and December are the strongest months; February and September are the weakest. The market is stronger on the first three days of the month than on all other days about 60 percent of the time. Since 1952, Monday generally has been the weakest day and Friday the strongest.

Decade patterns reveal that years ending in 7 often are characterized by precipitous spilloffs during the third quarter, years ending in 8 often show a major market advance before the end of the year. For the past seven decades, the beginning of significant market weakness usually has shown up within the last two months of the 8 year. And typical early-to-mid-year weakness in 9 years generally has been followed by a strong late-year advance. But late-9-year strength usually has peaked by early in the next year and often has been succeeded by a major decline into late in the new year of the new decade. Even in 1929, when the market declined almost in half from September to November, there was nonetheless a sharp recovery rally of more than 50 percent from the November low to an April 1930 high. Following that recovery rally the market made a deep, precipitous decline that didn't terminate until more than two years later.

There also has been remarkable constancy in the intervals between market high points and market low points throughout the entire bull market that commenced in 1949. The five bear-market lows of 1949, 1953, 1957, 1962 and 1966 have been separated by intervals averaging four years and four months. Taking June 1949 as a starting point, anyone buying precisely at fifty-two-month intervals would have been within one month of the exact low point in every case with the exception of 1958. Even then the bottom was only four months away, and the circumstances of that year were such that buying opportunities near the low point prevailed for six months after it, so it really wouldn't have made any difference.

The market peaks, beginning with the 1948 high, and adding highs of 1953, 1957, 1961 and 1966, all were separated by intervals ranging between fifty-one to fifty-five months. Each interval was approximately one month shorter than the prior one. If this cycle repeats itself, the next important market high would appear early-to-mid-1970 and the next important low would materialize by the end of 1970. As we can see, this cyclical pattern is not inconsistent with the decade pattern for 1970.

From time to time astrologers, climatologists, oceanographers and other specialists attempt to explain these periodic biases in terms of their fields. But we really don't know why these patterns recur, only that they do. While they are seldom so precise as to set a transaction by, they are useful guides when correlated with fundamental, technical and psychological measurements. As Gerald Loeb says: "It will pay to give some thought to this subject. We do have warm days in winter and cool ones in summer. They are always the exceptions."

To deal with these patterns, one must focus one's attention on probabilities, not on cause and effect. "The quantum physicist," said the great English physicist A. S. Eddington, "does not fill the atom with gadgets for directing its future behavior, as the classical physicist would have done; he fills it with gadgets determining the odds on its future behavior. He studies the art of the bookmaker, not of the trainer."

This is what I have tried to do with divergence analysis. Of course, divergence analysis is only the beginning; much research remains to be done in the study of human behavior in the stock market. Statistics have been kept for only a few generations, and even this limited data is inadequate for the task of refining the work here begun. We are, Dewey and Dakin have said, "like doctors following Pasteur, who had incontrovertible evidence that germs exist, but in only a few instances had isolated the germs involved in particular human states."

Nevertheless, we have plowed ahead, and tried to put to practical use what insights we have acquired. In this chapter we shall see how divergence analysis can be used in making more reliable forecasts of stock prices. These are not predictions in the ordinary sense of the word but probabilities posed by the data itself. I do not believe that anyone can foresee the future, and certainly no one can predict with consistent accuracy what a stock or the stock market will do in a year or even in several months. Divergence analysis, as I explained in Chapter One, attempts to record and measure what sophisticated and unsophisticated investors as groups are actually doing—whether buying, selling or short selling—at key market turning points *before* important price changes take place. The actions of investors in the stock market produce the data on which divergence analysis is based. Investors also react to fundamental news and technical measurements. The production of data and the reaction to it results in a short-term synthesis, which is the measure of investor psychology at any given time.

The only other definitive attempt to measure human behavior in the stock market is represented by the odd-lot theory, which seeks to interpret the psychology of the small, unsophisticated investor from a record of his activity. The theory expressed in its crudest form is that when odd-lotters sell it is a good time to buy, and when they buy it is a good time to sell. Actually, the odd-lot investor acts no differently than the investor who deals in round lots (100-share lots), but only the odd-lot data is segregated statistically for public distribution.

Years ago the odd-lot theory was highly useful; today it is much less so because it is so widely known and followed. Also, it is essentially a simplistic, one-dimensional approach to a complex and many-faceted activity. It fails to take into account the relationship of the odd-lotter's behavior to that of other groups. The competitive element of the game, the invidious emotional reactions of one group to the actions of another—these factors make it imperative to evaluate group behavior within the context of all the groups that comprise the stock market.

Contrary to conventional belief, these days the typical unsophisticated investor often, if not usually, buys at the bottom and sells at the top—apparently sophisticated actions that appear to belie the "unsophisticated" label. What happens is that the typical investor buys *after* a major top and continues to buy all the way down to the bottom. His buying at the bottom is the climax of a continuous buying binge that begins whenever he thinks a stock looks "cheap"—and to him "cheap" is lower than yesterday's price. If a stock was $60 last month and is $50 this month, it appears cheap even though it may be on its way down to a $20 bottom. In the same way, the typical investor who sells at the top has been selling all the way up since the breakout from the bottom.

So the crowd is not always absolutely wrong; it merely is invariably *relatively* wrong when compared with the loner group of sophisticates. Odd-lotters, for example, were clearly right when they sold at the tops in 1965, 1967, 1968 and 1969, judging by the absolute ratio of their selling to their buying. Compared with the activity of specialists and floor traders, and other statistical aggregates, however, their performance was relatively less right—that is, relatively wrong.

The unsophisticated investor is riven by those "antagonistic impulses" described by Freud. He may be ready to shoot craps at the drop of a hot tip, yet his usual posture is extremely conservative and may be characterized as a search for value. Stanley Kaish, assistant professor of economics at Rutgers University, concluded from a statistical study of odd-lot buying vs. selling that "the odd-lotter is basically a conservative participant in the stock market. If . . . he is unsuccessful in the market, it is because the issues he sells are not really *over*priced but rather have risen deservedly and will continue to rise after he sells them. The stocks he buys are not really bargains, but instead have fallen deservedly, and will continue to fall. If the odd-lotter does the wrong thing at the wrong time, as the odd-lot theory suggests, it is certainly not because he is reckless. Instead it appears that his interpretation of the 'proper' action in light of price changes of securities is too conservative."

This is in contrast to the sohisticated investor, whose favorite investment and trading vehicles are the volatile glamour stocks. The sophisticated investor values performance more than intrinsic worth. The average investor is far less venturesome. He needs repeated advice, comfort and assurance before committing himself to act, and by the time he does act, he is often too late. He confuses the underlying intrinsic values of stocks with the constantly changing value at which the market prices them. These are two different concepts.

The present decline in odd-lot transactions in the market, which began some years ago, is considered bullish by odd-lot theorists. That would be consistent with the theory but inconsistent with other factors. For example, increased ownership of common stock by institutions and these institutions' sharply increased percentage of portfolio turnover have paralleled the decline in odd-lot transactions. It seems clear that the decline is largely a mechanical result of increased institutional participation in the market. Indeed, since mutual-fund shares are owned principally by relatively unsophisticated investors, I don't see how the decline of odd-lot transactions can be considered bullish; the unsophisticated action has merely found other channels.

The fact is that the *absolute* action of odd-lotters no longer is as useful an investment indicator as it once was. The classic odd-lot pattern of buying at the top and selling at the bottom is still of value to us as an indicator when it occurs; the problem, however, is that it doesn't occur very often anymore. It is the *relative* action of the odd-lot investor that is particularly relevant today. This is measured in divergence analysis within the context of the behavior of more sophisticated investors and against the background of stock price-action. The crucial questions are not how many shares or percentage of shares the odd-lotters are buying, selling or short selling but rather whether—and to what extent—odd-lot actions run parallel to or *diverge* from the actions of more sophisticated investors against a particular background of price-change.

As I noted earlier, sophistication in investment behavior is relative and ascends a scale. A precondition to becoming a more sophisticated investor is to acquire some psychological insights into human behavior at work in the stock market—beginning, if possible, with one's own behavior. I have already discussed some of the psychological mechanisms that affect individual behavior. Here we shall measure the investment behavior of statistical groups, dividing them into sophisticated and unsophisticated actions.

It may be suggested by some that measuring certain stock market transactions from the incomplete data that is made available from public sources is an inadequate basis on which to construct theories of investor behavior and of investment psychology. But as Freud said in dealing with similar criticisms: "Suppose you are a detective engaged in the investigation of a murder, do you actually expect to find that the murderer will leave his photograph with name and address on the scene of the crime? . . . Let us not undervalue small signs: perhaps from them it may be possible to come upon the tracks of greater things."

How do we find these "small signs"? By analyzing the data covering differently categorized daily market transactions—for example, those of odd-lots, of 100-share lots, of 1,000-share lots, of floor traders, of specialists, et al., each category segregated where possible into buying, selling and short selling. Certain of these segregated categories can be further broken down into industry groups—for example, steels, chemicals, airlines, the DJIA, the glamours. From this empirical data—most of which in raw form is available from the ticker tape, the stock exchanges, the SEC and the financial press—it is possible to draw some conclusions with respect to the behavior of each category and the probable resultant stock price-action.

During several years of research, I measured and recorded hundreds of categorized investment actions, examining the behavior of each against differing price-action backgrounds. First I tested the concept on a historical basis for several years to see which statistical curves correlated most directly with subsequent price-action. Then I juxtaposed into sets those categories in which the actions consistently tended to diverge at major market turning points. Finally I posted the divergence-analysis curves against the price-action background covering the same period to determine which curves seemed to have predictive value.

Needless to say, scores of tests proved worthless, and these I discarded. In the end I was left with several dozen sets that appeared to be reasonably consistent. They followed a pattern in which the curves ran relatively parallel, or randomly fluctuated, over a period of time while the price of the stock (or the group index) continued in whatever direction it had been going, but in which the curves diverged before market turning points—tops, bottoms and breakouts from base areas.

Having satisfied myself that the concept worked on a historical basis, I then made trial runs by selections in the actual market of eighty-one stocks. The experiment began with a letter to a professional adviser of mine who had asked that I put my forecasts on record. In the letter, dated October 5, 1966, I wrote that "based on the data I follow there is extremely clear evidence that was available this morning that the market [which then was in a major bear phase] is about to turn around with a sharp rally on the upside. I repeat this notwithstanding that the Dow Jones Averages were off −7.80 today. When I say 'about to turn around,' I mean within the next day or two but in any event at the latest by early next week."

Three trading days later, on October 10, the 1966 bear market did bottom at DJIA 735.74.

I had selected thirteen stocks, all long, to test. In my letter I listed them and said that "the following stocks, which closed at the prices indicated today, will all go up with a profit of between 15 percent to 50 percent on cash invested (70 percent margin) within the next two to four weeks."

The results of this (in retrospect) brash forecast are given below. Before I review them, however, and the results of the later trial run of sixty-eight stocks I selected,

I want to make clear that all gains and losses are based upon the high (or low) price that followed the selection (unless the selection was prematurely closed out because of a divergence-analysis reversal, in which case the price then prevailing was used). In other words the net gains and losses were not based on sell recommendations because in most cases I did not make any then. Sell decisions are an aspect of investment management, which is related to but distinctly different from stock selection, as we shall see in Chapter Eight. In my first trial run I did not concern myself with management, only with selection and timing,* since even the best manager needs a valid selection to begin with. So I merely compared the price-action of my selections against the price-action of various representative market indexes—the DJIA, Standard & Poor's 500 Index and my own GPI. Of course, I used the same criteria for gains and losses for these indexes as I did for my selections.

My purpose here, then, is to demonstrate market timing and stock selection, not management performance, which is reviewed later. The following data should in no way be interpreted as a claim on my part to be able to match in practice the theoretical selling or buying of a valid selection at its peak or valley. No one can sell and buy consistently at peaks or valleys; in the stock market this is the impossible dream.

A record of the thirteen stocks selected on October 5,

---

* Market timing and stock selection in themselves represent two distinct investment approaches. In stock selection one looks for strong stocks. The idea in market timing is to decide the direction of the market trend and invest in stocks that move with the averages, getting in (or out) as close to the bottom (or top) as possible. This approach was long favored by old-guard investors. The difficulty with it, however—aside from the problem of pinpointing tops and bottoms—is that the trend may be too short to generate a profit and the investor may get caught in a whipsaw. Shortened intermediate-term general-market swings, together with higher capital-gains taxes (especially on short-term gains) have made the stock-selection approach more popular in recent years. The concentration on growth has also been a factor. Actually, both approaches have their virtues, but the most profitable course obviously is a combination of the two. It also is the most difficult, of course.

1966, using August 9, 1967, as a peak date, shows that all the stocks rose. As a group they gained 80 percent. Their annual *rate of gain*—a concept that we will examine in detail in the next chapter—was 158.5 percent. The gain and rate-of-gain figures were 24 and 29 percent for the DJIA, 30 and 37 percent for Standard & Poor's 500 Index and 80 and 122 percent for the GPI. Of the thirteen selections themselves, eight may be categorized as glamour-growth stocks and five as more conventional issues. Dividends and commissions were omitted from these calculations.

The results were too uniformly good. My adviser, thinking that I had perhaps been lucky in timing the market bottom and that this luck had carried over to my selections, suggested that I test on a broader basis, selecting both longs and shorts. So, beginning on March 28, 1967, I selected 68 stocks over a fourteen-week period. The record of these selections, using August 23, 1967, as a cut off date, shows that of the fifty-five longs fifty-one rose and four declined, and of the thirteen shorts ten declined and three rose. The longs rose an average of 12.6 percent in an average of sixty-one days, the shorts declined 5.4 percent in twenty-four days. As a group, the sixty-eight stocks gained (declined where short) 10.5 percent in fifty-four days, an annual rate of gain of 71 percent. During this period the DJIA rose 7 percent in 136 days, an annual rate of gain of 16 percent; Standard & Poor's 500 Index rose 6 percent in 136 days for an annual rate of gain of 17 percent; the GPI rose 12 percent in 105 days, a 42-percent annual rate of gain. Again, dividends and commissions were omitted from the calculations.

The experience was educational. For example, the timing of the first short sale clearly was wrong; it did not meet the requirement of short selling—particularly of glamours—only on strength. But this mistake led to the formulation of the present GPI, which has proved to be a useful timing confirmation tool. One of the most significant conclusions, however, was that divergence analysis enabled me to avoid serious losses. For example, when the divergence-analysis curves subsequently indicated a reversal in a short position I had selected at 107, I was able to close it out at a small profit and, more important, avoid a substantial loss as the stock rose to 153.

Also interesting was the excellent performance of the selections compared with the performance of the GPI, for despite a few glamour-growth issues, the selections were mostly "safe and solid" stocks, some of them the bluest of blue chips. Of these presumably "dull" issues only a few showed minor losses; most of the rest showed absolute gains of from 3 to 40 percent. This indicated that it may be possible to time the swings of blue chips for substantial gains at low risk—a profitable way to play the game.

That was the end of my experimentation. From February 1968 to June 1969, I selected and closed out 166 transactions, 125 long and 41 short, as an investment adviser. Measuring from selection price to subsequent peak before the transaction was closed out shows that the annual rate of gain for the longs as a group exceeded 100 percent; for the shorts it was almost 118 percent. While my management of these selections—long and short—as groups proved profitable, it did, of course, fall far short of these theoretical potentials.

Over the years I have abstracted a number of usually reliable divergence-analysis sets from hundreds of possibilities, about fifty for the market as a whole and about a dozen for individual stocks. Difficult? Not at all. Different categories are organized into sets, each set consisting of two juxtaposed indicators representing sophisticated and unsophisticated action. For example, the simple ratio curve on Chart No. 20 represents weekly market transactions in two categories: odd-lot short selling and short selling by NYSE specialists. They form a *set* indicating a relationship between a *like* sophisticated and unsophisticated action (NYSE specialists obviously are more sophisticated than odd-lotters). When the curve rises, specialists sell short relatively less, odd-lotters sell short relatively more; in other words, the former are relatively optimistic and the latter are relatively pessimistic. A dip in the curve indicates the reverse. Note that the curve is posted against the background of the DJIA price-action.

I find this ratio curve a highly reliable indicator. Its usefulness is limited by the fact that the NYSE Statistical Department does not make the necessary data available until two weeks after the actual transactions; but it gives me some perspective on major market movements. As the chart shows, the curve peaked in March 1968, the specialists' optimism portending the subsequent rally to the May high of 935.68. The curve peaked again prior to the August 1968 low of 863.33, suggesting the likelihood of the 131-point rally that followed. And by the end of February 1969, the curve's peak coincided with the market's bottom of 895.39, following which a sustained rally developed. Note how the curve "valleyed" at the May top, after which the market plunged 187 points to the July low; by then the curve had moved up in three regular "steps" to anticipate that bottom.

Another example of a juxtaposed set that can be expressed in a ratio curve is the total transactions in 100-share lots as a percentage of total market volume to the total transactions in 1,000- (and higher) share lots as a percentage of the total volume, the latter representing—in the aggregate—a more sophisticated action than the former. Making comparisons against three different price-action backgrounds—rising, declining and base area—one can construct a simple divergence-analysis curve from this data as follows:

$$\frac{\text{percent of total volume accounted for by 1,000-share-plus lots}}{\text{percent of total volume accounted for by 100-share lots}}$$

To demonstrate how strikingly divergences show up on

mathematical curves prepared from such data, assume the figures are:

All lots of 1,000 shares equal 20 percent

All lots of 100 shares equal 40 percent

Then the curve posting equals 50 percent. But shift the ratio to:

All lots of 1,000 shares equal 40 percent

All lots of 100 shares equal 20 percent

And the curve posting equals 200 percent.

By plotting these ratios against the background of a price-action bar chart, one can make some correlation between price-action and the sophisticated vs. unsophisticated activity as defined in this instance by the percentages of total market volume.

One of my most useful divergence-analysis measurements is what I call a *volume-confirmation curve.* It not only helps to confirm individual divergence analyses but may indicate when there is a sufficient volume of trading in an equity to move its price. Essentially, it measures the *quality* of volume by comparing—against the background of a specific price-action—sophisticated and unsophisticated activity in the individual stock as a relationship of total volume of trading in the issue. Some of the formulae I use may be a bit complicated to explain easily. So here is a simple formula that anyone can use and which illustrates the principle just as well:

Add up all the 100-share transactions in a given stock during a particular period of time—say, a week—and divide the total volume of all such transactions by the total volume of trading in the stock during the same period. This gives the *percentage* of 100-share lots to total volume. Divide this percentage, as a whole number, into the total volume. The resultant relationship can be used as a volume-confirmation curve.

CHART 20. DIVERGENCE ANALYSIS: ODD-LOT SHORT
SELLING COMPARED TO NYSE SPECIALISTS' SHORT
SELLING

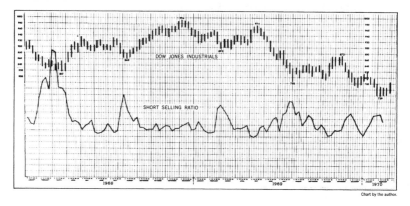

Chart by the author.

The curve is the ratio of odd-lot short selling to short selling by
NYSE specialists (weekly basis). When the curve rises to a peak,
specialists are (relatively) optimistic and odd-lotters are (relatively)
pessimistic; when the curve declines to a valley, specialists are
pessimistic and are distributing stock, while odd-lotters are optimistic.

For example, if the trading in a stock is 20,000 shares
and there are one hundred 100-share transactions, then 50
percent of the trading is from this source. Fifty divided into
20,000 equals 400. Say that a sudden news story breaks on
the stock during the next week and it is difficult to interpret its effect even though the volume in the stock doubles.
If on the doubled volume there are the same number of
100-share transactions, this now represents only 25 percent
of the total volume, which indicates that the increase in
volume may come from sophisticated investors and that
the prevailing trend may continue. Twenty-five divided into
40,000 equals 1,600, a four-times-higher reading of the
curve. If, however, the number of 100-share transactions
jumps from 100 to 300 on the doubled volume, representing
75 percent of the total volume, it indicates that the increase
comes from unsophisticated investors, an unfavorable sign
for trend continuation. Seventy-five divided into 40,000
equals 533.3, higher than 400 but insignificant compared
to 1,600. Related to price-action and the ratio of aggregate
sophisticated to unsophisticated activity, this curve is most

useful, especially in interpreting sophisticated-unsophisticated reaction to sudden news stories.

A similar volume-confirmation curve can be constructed to measure group action—steels, airlines, the glamours or the Industrials. If, for example, the glamours' aggregate volume for a week is 1 million and the total market volume is 50 million, the glamours' volume is 2 percent of the total. Dividing this percentage by the percentage of unsophisticated activity within the group to the total group volume gives the posting for the curve. The *higher* the group-volume percentage of total market volume, and the *lower* the percentage of unsophisticated activity as a percentage of total group volume, the higher is the final answer. A rising curve indicates sophisticated accumulation. When this appears against the background of a sideways trading range, it may be an indication of sophisticated buying in anticipation of an upside move. A rapidly declining curve after a long price rise indicates sophisticated distribution.

There are many other useful divergence-analysis sets that can be constructed from such statistical data as the short interest ratio of a stock and a ratio of its large block-small block volume, relationships between a stock and its group and that of its group with the market, etc. The possibilities are almost limitless.* Chart No. 21 shows three

---

* I have detailed several of these sets but not all of them; space limitations preclude the cataloguing of the dozens of sets that I use, and in any case the mathematical minutiae would be of little interest to most readers. Also, from time to time certain of the sets are modified or even discarded as new models are developed; the sets are not timeless magic formulae. Finally, if the sets were widely disseminated, they would create the very data they seek to measure, which would be self-defeating. I give several examples of divergence-analysis measurements in this chapter, and I have discussed other forecasting indicators for the stock market as a whole which are based on the divergence-analysis concept—for example, the bear-to-bull ratio of investment advisers and the optimism of NYSE specialists vs. odd-lotters in their respective short-selling activities. From these examples, readers can see how divergence analysis works; they even can construct their own models, if they wish—but it is likely that the value of the concept to most readers will be in the insights they gain into the market, into the behavior of investors, into the movement of stock prices and into their own realistic expectations of success.

divergence-analysis curves for El Paso Natural Gas (ELG) from March 1968 to March 1969. The heavy curve represents the percentage of aggregate sophisticated buying to aggregate sophisticated selling; the fine curve represents the percentage of unsophisticated buying to unsophisticated selling; overhead is a volume-confirmation curve. Posted against a daily price-action chart covering the same period of time as the data from which they were derived, these curves show substantial sophisticated accumulation of ELG beginning in late April, while unsophisticated interest in the stock, which had been ascendant in March, turned drastically toward the selling side in April and remained there for months. This sharp divergence in opinion —with sophisticated accumulation contrasting with unsophisticated selling at a time when the stock had declined to a base area that had technically provided support for a period of more than seventeen years and at which price it yielded in excess of 5 percent and sold at less than five times its cash flow—marked this as a low-risk situation indicated to have strong upside potential. During the fourth quarter of 1968 good volume came into the issue— see the volume-confirmation curve—and ELG did break out of its trading range of the previous six months, between 18 and 20, and soared to a year-end high near 26. And, as we can see, after the upmove got under way, the very unsophisticated investor group that sold at the bottom began buying near the top!

As chart No. 21 illustrates, the relationship between the two indicators in a set varies over a period of time. For example, from February to early in April, the curves ran parallel or varied only slightly, indicating that sophisticated and unsophisticated action were fairly well balanced. The degree of variation reveals the extent of the divergence between sophisticated and unsophisticated action. A radical divergence against the background of a particular price-action, as in the period from May to June on the chart, reveals each group's contrary opinion—based on what they are *doing,* not what they are saying—of future price trends, the forecast taking the form of a buying or selling action. This makes possible a tentative forecast of price-action based on the divergence analysis together with fundamental considerations and technical position.

These forecasts are necessarily for the short-term because the prevailing investor psychology can and does change from time to time, making long-term predictions vulnerable. The investor psychology for SCM, for example, was favorable—that is, sophisticated investors were buying the stock—prior to the company's merger with Glidden. But once the merger was announced, sophisticated investors, unwilling to assign to Glidden's mundane paint business the high price-earnings ratio they had accorded to SCM's high-flying business-equipment products, began selling SCM aggressively. At the same time, unsophisticated investors, impressed by what they saw only as desirable expansion of SCM, began buying the stock. The psychology of the market in SCM changed drastically, and the stock, which had been selling in the 80 area, weakened immediately and later dropped to below 20, a development that would have been unforeseeable over the long-term.

Despite the absence of direct correlation between short-term measurements of investor psychology and long-term price-action, I have found such short-term measurements useful in making long-term projections because trends do tend to persist over a period of time. These projections, however, are merely hypotheses, subject to revision dictated by changes in investor psychology, and do not, of course, stand on as firm ground as the short-term forecasts.

There are more divergence-analysis sets for the market than there are for individual stocks because more data is published about the market than about individual stocks. For example, data is published about specialists' purchases, sales and short sales for the stock market as a whole but, unfortunately, not for individual stocks.

In analyzing the various sets, I study not only the diver-

CHART 21. DIVERGENCE ANALYSIS: BUYING IN
ANTICIPATION OF UPSIDE BREAKOUT—EL PASO
NATURAL GAS (ELG)

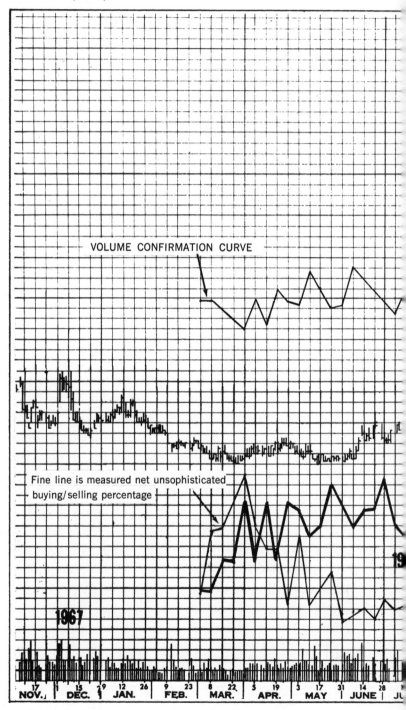

VOLUME CONFIRMATION CURVE

Fine line is measured net unsophisticated
buying/selling percentage

1967

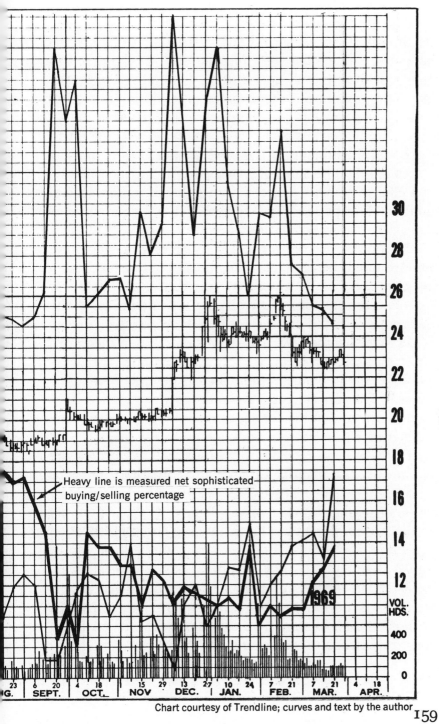

Heavy line is measured net sophisticated buying/selling percentage

1969

gences within each one but the relationships among them. When radical like divergences in several sets show up over a period of time—two, four, six weeks or more—I assume that investor psychology for that particular stock (or for the market) *has* changed and that the price-action *will* change with it in the near future. Generally, the longer and more pronounced the divergence is, the more certain is the subsequent move of the price-action. There is no absolute correlation, however, between the degree of divergence and the amount of the price-change.

A changing divergence-analysis pattern may be followed by a change in price-action within a day or within several months. My experience indicates that it is wise to wait for at least a two-week continuance after a divergence first develops before acting on it. Divergences of lesser duration are much less reliable. This means that sometimes a stock will "get away" before one can act on it, but a few lost opportunities are preferable to sacrificing reliability and consistency. In any case, since there are always more stocks to review than there are funds to invest in them, this is not a serious problem. Of course, sometimes the price-action does not change, despite a clear divergence-analysis reversal. The concept is not foolproof. My experience, however, indicates that in such cases it is rare for any substantial contrary price trend to develop.

In divergence analysis only *statistical aggregates* are significant; the identity of individual investors is of no consequence. The relative sophistication and unsophistication of market transactions is defined by the action, not by the actors. For example, in judging ·the sophistication of a large block transaction read from the tape, it can be argued that both the buyer and the seller are relatively sophisticated—yet one of them is likely to be proven wrong. Actually, it does not necessarily follow that either is "wrong," if their actions are dictated by relevant considerations of portfolio management.

Tape reading by unsophisticated investors, it should be noted, more often than not leads to gross self-deception. More than forty years ago Henry Howard Harper said: "The gyroscopic action of the prices recorded on the tickertape produces a sort of mental intoxication, which foreshortens the vision by involuntary submissiveness to momentary influences." This is still valid.

The important fact in block transactions is not the individual transaction, nor *why*, but *how many*: What is the statistical aggregate of large block transactions? (Even this aggregate means little in the abstract; it must be compared with the aggregate of small block transactions.)

The idea is to assess the *quality* of the buying and selling at any given time. There is always some sophisticated selling with sophisticated buying, always some unsophisticated buying with unsophisticated selling. It is what these groups do *on balance* and in relation to each other that is revealing.

This behavior is significant only against the background of a specific price-action situation: rising, declining or sideways. The action of each group in each price-action situation is important because experience has shown that each group acts from different bases—sophisticates from informed confidence and self-knowledge, unsophisticates from fear or greed—and usually on different information. Indeed, in crisis situations, sophisticated investors often turn the fear of unsophisticated investors to their own advantage.

In short, it is the *divergence* between one group and the other, against the background of a particular type of price-action, which reveals—based on their actual market actions—the opinions of each group with respect to its forecast of price trends, the forecast taking the form of a buying or selling action.

In the application of divergence analysis to the timing of stock selections, three considerations must be kept in mind. First, and foremost, is the general-market environment. No matter how favorable the fundamental, technical and psychological indicators of an individual stock are, the basic direction of the market must be taken into account in any investment decision. Very few stocks can buck a bear market; and in a strong bull market, as we have seen, even the garbage may go up—and come down with a thud. All else being equal, the timing of individual stock selections should be integrated as closely as possible with important market bottoms and tops. This is why the broad market averages are valuable.

Unfortunately, most investors, even professionals, seek action in the market constantly, even though in certain periods they would be far better off to stand aside. The fact is that in 1969 if all mutual funds had withdrawn entirely from the market and placed their money in short-term notes they would have far exceeded their actual performances, and at no risk! This makes it quite clear that there is a "time" to buy, and to buy when it is not the time is always disadvantageous.

The second consideration is the position of an individual stock's group. Chart No. 13 in Chapter Five reveals the enormous variation among group performances. It follows that a stock in a weak group starts out with two strikes against it. George Chestnutt, a highly respected investment adviser, notes that "stocks in the same industry group tend to follow their group average more closely than they follow a general-market average." The chances of success of any stock selection, Chestnutt adds, "are improved through requiring *industry group* confirmation for every selection." I keep divergence-analysis indexes for all key groups—glamours, airlines, computers, chemicals, steels, etc. These indexes essentially are the aggregates of the measurements of the individual stocks that comprise the groups. But I also relate groups to each other and to the market as a whole. This gives me some indication when sophisticated investors aggressively buy or sell a given group. Also some groups, such as the glamours, tend to lead the market; others tend to run counter to it, or lag behind it; and these are valuable indicators in themselves. For example, at market bottoms, the group to be aggressively purchased is the high-risk, quality glamour-growth issues—the fastest horses in the race.

The third consideration, of course, is the individual stock. Indeed, many brokerage houses and fund managers boast that they concentrate only on selecting individual stocks, that they ignore the market. But this is foolhardy. The most consistently successful investment policy is to buy when the market is at an important low and the individual stock's group is relatively strong and the stock itself is favorably positioned.

Another important consideration in stock selection is the fact that high-risk issues as a group move much faster than low-risk issues. The glamours, for example, outperform basic-industry stocks when both are moving up, and they decline at a much greater rate when both are moving down. This volatility is mirrored in the divergence-analysis patterns for the two groups of stocks. Psychological measurements tend to change slowly in low-risk stocks and rapidly in high-risk stocks.

An investor, then, must act quickly when trading in high-risk issues. But since unsophisticated investors, habitually paralyzed by their emotions, are incapable of acting quickly, they tend to make their greatest mistakes in such equities. In these cases, low-risk equities, with their more stable psychological patterns, are perhaps preferable investments, even though their rate of gain is substantially lower than that of high-risk issues. (Actually, low-risk stocks outperform high-risk stocks during those periods after the glamours top out and the basic industry issues show "tail-ending" strength. For example, the GPI topped out in June 1968 while the DJIA didn't make its high until six months later. During that period an investor not only would have avoided substantial losses by staying out of glamour equities but could have made considerable gains in the low-risk issues. This turn-around proves that "performance" at any given point is not necessarily restricted to performers. Indeed, what makes the low-risk stock so appealing in this situation is the fact that it represents the optimum investment prospect: a sharp, short-term gain combined with extremely low risk.)

There are valid reasons for selecting stocks with price-earnings ratios of 50 or 100, but the investor must understand the high risk involved and be prepared to take losses now and then. Conversely, the investor who selects low-risk stocks should not expect them to outpace the high-fliers regularly. This does happen occasionally, as we saw when Western Union, a solid company yielding almost 5 percent, radically changed its policies and rose from below 30 to almost 60; but this is rare. What is important is that the investor realistically match his expectations to his selections.

Divergence analysis reveals one of three situations: net sophisticated buying and unsophisticated selling, or vice versa or ambiguity. If it reveals a definite trend toward sophisticated buying and unsophisticated selling, and

—price-action is sideways, then buy in anticipation of an upside breakout or buy on the breakout;
—price is rising, then buy, but only on a pull-back;
—price is declining, then buy at well-defined technical support areas.

If divergence analysis reveals a definite trend toward sophisticated selling and unsophisticated buying, and

—price-action is sideways, then avoid buying, but do not take a short position;
—price is rising, then sell, and sell short either at well-defined upside price objectives or on violation of a closely drawn uptrend line;

164

—price is declining, then sell, but sell short only on subsequent strength.

The ideal situation for buying is one in which the stock has been in a base area and narrow trading range for some time *and* the divergence-analysis curves have been running parallel, at random or even negative. (Negative in a base area without any further price decline is a good sign because it implies that the stock has been thoroughly sold out at that level.) If and when the divergence-analysis curves turn favorable in this situation, not only is an upward price move probable but the chances of a decline are slight. The illustration of El Paso Natural Gas is an example of this.

I ordinarily recommend buying on weakness only. It is psychologically difficult to buy on weakness, but a favorable divergence-analysis pattern indicates sophisticated buying on that weakness, implying that the stock will find buyers at its technically defined support area. One can slate half a dozen favorably positioned stocks with favorable divergence-analysis patterns for purchase on weakness to certain predetermined price levels. Rarely will all six of them weaken, but at least one almost certainly will, and that will be the right stock at the right time. My most successful selections—in terms of both the amount of gain and the rate of gain—have been those I recommended to buy on a "weakness only" basis (or, where short, on strength).

An important caveat, however, must be noted with respect to this dictum. Buying on weakness means buying at, or following, a major bottom, while the stock is *at the beginning of,* or *within the beginning of,* an important uptrend. To buy on weakness *after* a major top and all the way down is, as pointed out earlier, characteristically unsophisticated. That is why it is important to identify major trends and why stock selections must be integrated with both market and group performance.

In Chapter Five we saw how, given a well-defined technical situation and a favorable divergence analysis, it is sometimes possible to buy on the breakout—that is, on strength. The caveat here is that such breakout purchases usually work out well only in a very bullish market. When the market is uncertain, risky or dull, buying on weakness is the rule. The failure of yesterday's mutual-fund heroes during 1969 is due largely to their slavish adherence to the *relative-strength* concept in which their computers engage in the self-defeating exercise of finding trends once they have become established. This works tolerably well in bull markets but is disastrous at other times, as the funds start whipsawing one another.

In the ideal situation, weakness is at the bottom of a basing area, or at the low side of a trading range. In certain speculative situations, given a favorable divergence-analysis pattern, one may buy the stock just as it is breaking out on the tape from a base area. An example of how this might have been done in 1969 is shown on Chart No. 22 illustrating the price-action on a daily basis of Fairchild Camera for the period April to November. The only divergence-analysis curve used here is a volume-confirmation curve that reveals an extraordinarily favorable burst the week ended August 29. Two weeks later, the week ended September 12, FCI made an upside breakout past its one-third speed resistance line, after which the upside action accelerated. FCI, then, could have been purchased on this resistance-line breakout. The resistance line gave the technical positioning, while the previously bursting volume-confirmation curve provided the clue that a forthcoming upward move was likely to take place.

When such a stock is already in an uptrend, one can buy it on weakness within the up-channel on the probability that the up-channel will not be violated. The Fairchild Camera example also shows that the upside breakout was the beginning of a substantial upmove bounded, indeed, by a well-defined advance channel.

CHART 22. DIVERGENCE ANALYSIS: VOLUME
CONFIRMATION CURVE SIGNAL TO BUY ON
RESISTANCE LINE BREAKOUT—FAIRCHILD CAMERA
AND INSTRUMENT CORPORATION (FCI)

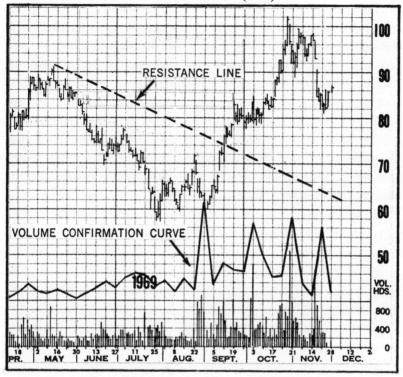

Chart courtesy of Trendline; trendlines, curve and text by the author

The reverse conditions apply for selling situations. Except under special circumstances, stocks always should be
sold on strength when divergence analysis indicates massive distribution by sophisticated investors. This also
applies to short selling near tops. Always bear in mind,
however, that it is much more difficult to pinpoint tops
than bottoms because of the tendency of stocks to "blowoff"
at the top, especially in those instances when the stock has
no "overhead supply."

The phenomenon of overhead supply relates entirely to
unsophisticated investors who hold a stock no matter how
far down it goes, waiting for the time when the stock will
rebound and they can "get even." Refusing to accept a

small loss, they incur an even greater loss, while the delusion that a "paper" loss is not real protects their egos.*
At any rate, stocks approaching their former highs tend to run into a great deal of selling by previous buyers seeking to get out "even." This is overhead supply, which disappears only *after* a stock makes new highs, leaving it "free and clear" from this sort of pressure.

One must take special care with the volatile glamour issues, too. As I noted above, their divergence-analysis patterns change rapidly; in effect, rather than lead the price change, as divergence analysis ideally should, they sometimes change almost concurrently with it. The simplest solution is to avoid the glamour issues when the divergence analysis is almost concurrent with the price-action and concentrate on those instances where it leads the price-action.

To be effective, divergence analysis requires continuous and fresh data. I post monthly, weekly, daily and even hourly data. Most important is the weekly data; all the other data serves primarily to add perspective to the weekly input. The selection of the day on which the weekly data is collected is also a matter of some importance. Most advisory services and brokerage houses use Friday for this purpose so their clients will be able to review their reports over the weekend, together with the Sunday newspaper and news programs. Over the weekend, then, investors are deluged with information, the nature of which, as we have seen, is usually either misleading or outdated. It does

---

* How meaningless is the distinction between "real" and "paper" losses (or profits) can be seen from the hypothetical case of an investor who holds two securities, each of which is presently worth $100. One security originally cost $150, the other originally cost $50. On paper, then, he has lost $50 on one and gained $50 on the other. But in terms of economic power, he is exactly where he was when he made the original purchases: he still holds stocks worth $200. If he sells one security and retains the other, he will have $100 in cash and a stock worth $100. But, depending upon which stock he chooses to sell, he will have a "real" gain or loss of $50, although in reality he is no better nor worse off.

stimulate action, however. Statistics show that unsophisticated investors as a group make a higher percentage of transactions on Monday than on any other day of the week, and sophisticated investors make less. (This undoubtedly accounts for the "Blue Monday" syndrome during down markets. During a fourteen-week period in the spring of 1962 there were twelve "Blue Mondays," a pattern repeated during both the 1966 and 1969 declines.) This exaggerated action makes investor psychology easier to measure, so I collect much of my weekly data on Monday after the close of the market.

Of course, as I noted earlier, this data is neither as complete nor as up-to-date as desirable, so every analysis must be necessarily imperfect. Indeed, well-defined divergence-analysis patterns do not always emerge even for relatively active stocks; the patterns sometimes are indecisive or random. Of every 100 stocks examined, perhaps only two dozen show a well-defined divergence-analysis pattern at any given period of time, and three-quarters of these probably lack desirable fundamental or technical confirmation. The remaining half-dozen are the stocks on which to concentrate, noting also their relative reliability—for example, reliability of *selection* is low among high-risk stocks, and reliability of *timing* is low among low-risk stocks.

Even then, it should be noted, there is no guarantee that these six selections will work out. Divergence analysis is a fallible tool; it has produced failures in the past, and it will produce them again. The nature of sophisticated and unsophisticated investors being what it is, the game that they play is almost always a mismatch, and divergence analysis cannot invariably offset the average investor's handicap. For example, the divergence analysis for SCM indicated sophisticated buying and unsophisticated selling for a considerable period of time and on this basis seemed a good buy. As we have seen, this pattern changed radically with the announcement of the company's merger with

Glidden. So an investor who bought SCM just before the news of the merger lost money even though the divergence-analysis pattern was favorable for buying.

Divergence analysis, then, does not provide an "instant" indicator for all stocks—but that is not its purpose. Its function is to increase the odds in the timing of stock selections in the investor's favor, to bring to light those few stocks likely to outperform the herd. It also helps to keep one out of trouble. In view of the possibilities for disaster generated by inexpert experts and the dissemination of useless information, this is not an inconsiderable accomplishment. Indeed, how unobtrusively the average investor can be led into quicksand is revealed by the record of the price-action of the stock of the Occidental Petroleum Corporation (OXY), shown on Chart No. 23.

For some years OXY has been one of the most widely touted stocks. This optimism was justified for the period from the 1966 crash to June 1968, OXY having risen like a meteor from below 10 to its all-time high of 55⅜. But from June 1968 to June 1969, as OXY declined steadily, the spate of optimism continued unabated. Step by step, as the stock slowly slid from 55 to 35 (and later to below 20), the experts and the financial press recommended its purchase. The following extracts reported in the *Wall Street Transcript* are typical of eighty research reports issued by more than two dozen influential brokerage houses over the twelve-month period of decline. Each extract has been numbered and keyed on the chart, matching the report with the stock's then current price-action. (Note how the stock topped out on November 18, 1968, the day that OXY's management, led by chairman and chief executive officer Dr. Armand Hammer, made a bullish presentation to the New York Society of Security Analysts.) The brokerage houses shall remain anonymous.

1. *July 3, 1968—51⅞*. Since early June OXY has been backing and filling between 50 and 55 while volume has

CHART 23. INEXPERT EXPERTS AND THE
DISSEMINATION OF USELESS AND MISLEADING
INFORMATION—OCCIDENTAL PETROLEUM
CORPORATION (OXY)

Chart courtesy of Current Market Perspectives; curve and text by the author

lightened considerably. This performance suggests the stock is undergoing nothing more than a normal profit taking phase, and that its intermediate to longer term uptrend remains intact. Consequently, we would be inclined to take advantage of the current dip to add to previous commitments. We are raising our short term objective to 63-65.

2. *August 2, 1968—44⅞.* With OXY having fulfilled the downside projection from the minor top pattern traced in June and July, with apparent technical support indicated just below current quotations, and with the stock's price having returned to its major trendline, purchase of OXY is recommended for a trend objective of 69-70.

3. *September 10, 1968—44.* With an aggressive, intelligent management team backed by rapidly rising earnings, Occidental's capacity for further growth remains substantial, and

the stock, we believe, will prove a profitable addition to portfolios geared for appreciation.

4. *November 15, 1968—47⅞. OXY's record of growth
and development during the last decade has been seldom
equalled by any company in the history of American industry.
The common stock appears attractively priced for longer term
enhancement of capital.*

5. *December 9, 1968—47.* The growth of Occidental during the past ten years is almost legendary and illustrates
what is possible when a company follows an aggressive
forward-looking approach to corporate evolution. . . . The
shares are considered to offer potential for above-average
long term capital appreciation.

6. *January 14, 1969—45.* Contrary to some thought now
prevalent that OXY is "through" as an investment, we are
taking this opportunity to re-recommend the stock as a highly
desirable vehicle for inclusion in capital gains-oriented portfolios. . . . Upside price potential can be targeted at 60 plus
over a 6-9 month period.

7. *March 17, 1969—42.* Despite the weakening action of
the market in general, Occidental Pet seems an attractive investment for aggressive individuals seeking appreciation.

These recommendations—and many others like them—
were disseminated among millions of small investors
while, at the same time, the financial press carried bullish
stories about the company's Libyan oil production, planned
refinery complexes, Alaskan holdings and brilliant management. Meanwhile, my own divergence-analysis pattern,
shown on Chart No. 23 above OXY's price-action, clearly
indicated sophisticated selling and unsophisticated buying, except for two brief periods in 1968. Here, then, is a
classic case of sophisticated distribution at the expense of
the uninformed investor, distribution which was made
possible by the experts' brainwashing of the public and,
presumably, of themselves.

1991 ADDENDUM

The 1990s and All That

My approach is what is called *"top down,"* which means I want to be fully invested in a security only when I think the financial market of which it is a part is on my side. This contrasts with the *"bottoms up"* approach which concentrates in the stock market on stock selection and ignores market timing. Most of the disasters I've experienced or observed have invariably been due to neglect of the *top down* approach.

Decennial patterns [pp.140-2] still work, as does the 4-year stock market cycle low [page 142], in my opinion. My confidence that 1990 would witness a 4-year market cycle low was enhanced by the fact that 1990 also was a year ending in "o", as were 1970 and 1950, the last two years that were *both* a "o" year and a 4-year cycle low year. Moreover, 1990 might well have been an *eight year low*, in my opinion, as were 1966, 1974 and 1982—more powerful than the intervening 4-year lows. 1970 was a bear market year, showing the typical decennial pattern for "o" years of middle-third of the year weakness. This is exactly what happened in 1990, as well. Moreover, as shown by the earlier chart of the Value Line Industrials, most stocks have been weak since their 1989 peaks, or earlier. I think this means that once the 4-year market cycle low turns upward there should be a broadly based advance in which most stocks do well.

Not only does almost fifty percent off the Value Lines' 1987 peak and fifty percent off the U.S. Dollar Index 1984 peak seem sufficient by year end 1990 but also the relationship of the 4-year market cycle to presidential elections seems obvious. This relationship is shown in the chart of *Standard & Poors* 400 Industrials Monthly Average on page 172B.

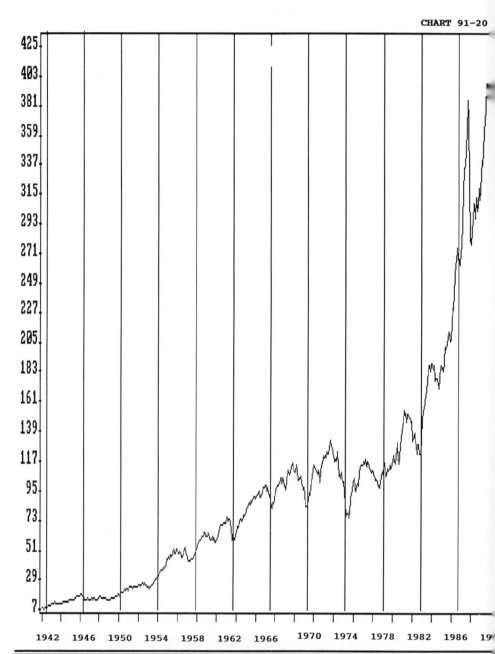

CHART 91-20

S & P 400 INDUSTRIALS MONTHLY AVERAGE: 4-YEAR MARKET CYCLES LOWS 1942 - 1990

172B

The incumbent party wants to be retained in power, so, it gets all of its unpleasant business out of the way early in the presidential term. Thereafter, the party in power takes measures to stimulate the economy so that it is rising prior to the next election. Certainly, this is the way things seem headed at the beginning of 1991, in my opinion: the collapsing economy seems to be setting the stage for *reflation*.

The Years Ending In "1"

Though there are many skeptics about decennial patterns because, unlike the politically-biased 4-year market lows, they seem irrational, I have found them useful. After all, many investment decisions are irrational, that is, based on more than the intellect, alone. Decennial patterns particularly seem helpful when the previous year conformed to its typical pattern. This was the experience in 1990—typical "o" year first-third strength, middle-third weakness, followed by a last-third recovery. Consequently, I thought it would be of interest, now, to examine the decennial possibilities for 1991. The following is based on the *monthly average* of Standard & Poors 400 Industrials, except where otherwise noted.

In 1891 the Dow Jones 12 Stock Average rose 21 percent from a *December* 1890 low to a *September* 1891 high, however there was an intervening 10 percent correction between April and July 1891.

In 1901 the S & P 400 Industrials rose 45 percent from the *June* 1900 low to the *June* 1901 high, then went on to lose 16 percent off the top by December.

In 1911 the stock market rose only 13 percent from the *July* 1910 low to the *June* 1911 peak [but was up 18.3 percent on a daily basis of the DJIA], then fell 16 percent to an *October* low.

In 1921 stocks had a fair year. Even though in 1920 stocks collapsed 33 percent between January and December, the 1921 market was only able to sluggishly advance by little more than 8 percent by year-end.

In 1931 the market did even worse. Having declined 39 percent between April and December 1930, stocks barely managed a 10 percent gain by the *March* 1931 peak. Thereafter stocks plunged 51 percent by year-end! [From that level the market further collapsed another 42 percent by the June 1932 low].

In 1941 there was another poor year. From the November 1940 peak the market fell about 14 percent to a *May* low, rallied 10 percent to a September peak but from that high fell 13 percent by year-end. [Off 14 percent year over year].

In 1951 there was a steadily good year, up about 20 percent year over year. This followed a 1950 which was up 22 percent, notwithstanding the June-July 14 percent DJIA correction as the Korean war began. [1950 was a 4-year market cycle low].

In 1961 there was another terrific year as stocks rose about 26 percent, year over year. In 1960 stocks were flat to down, off about 5 percent for the year.

In 1971 the market rose 15 percent during the first four months, then gave most of it back by November. Year over year, stocks were up 11 percent. In 1970 stocks were down in the first half, up in the second half, flat from year to year. [This was also a 4-year market cycle low].

In 1981 stocks spent the first four months peaking close to the December 1980 level, then fell 13 percent from April to December. Stocks were up a big 26 percent in 1980.

In 1990, stocks rose only 7 percent during the first seven months, then fell 15 percent between July and October. On a year-over-year basis, the S & P Industrials were down only 3.8 percent. However, this understates the case, in my opinion. More representative of the average stock, the Value Line Industrials were off 27 percent in 1990, alone. Together with its 1987 crash, for a 3-year [almost] cut-in-half, it would seem that a lot of bad news had been discounted by the average stock during this particular 4-year election cycle, or 8-year economic cycle.

What about 1991? Even though there was a string of 12 consecutive prior 4-year lows since 1942, at year end 1990, a major problem is that years ending in "1" have had a wide-ranging record, in this century—big downs *and* big ups. 1891 and 1901 *were both strongly up. But barring those very old ups, the only two good "1"* years in this century were 1951 and 1961. 1951 rings a bell for me because the market had a sharp selloff in 1950 when the Korean War broke out, much like 1990's Middle-Eastern war which hadn't materialized by the very beginning of 1991.

In 1971, the market rose 15 percent during the first four months, then gave most of it back by November. Year-over-year, though, stocks were up 11 percent. So, even if 1991 were like 1971, it would be an up year, though rocky along the way. This would also leave open the possibility of a substantial further rise in the next "2" year, 1992. My present conclusion, therefore, is that the technical and cyclical evidence points to the possibility but not the certainty of an up 1991 and even a great year somewhere between 1991 and 1992; this does not rule out at least one good selling opportunity in 1991.

Chapter 10 will be more specific, including what I believe to be the longer term bullish case, notwithstanding America's focus at the beginning of 1991 on the possibility of imminent war with Iraq.

Security Selection Criteria

With these *market timing* considerations in mind, let's summarize what my *stock selection criteria* [pp.142-172] are now, as they have evolved over the past 21 years. First of all, I must understand the fundamentals *and* believe they are *not yet reflected in the price of the stock*. One of the best single overall sources of fundamental information for me is the *Value Line Investment Survey*. I do *not* recommend their investment conclusions, in particular because too much of it is based on over-extended *Relative Strength*. What I do like about it is that on a single page I can very quickly learn about what a company does and the state of its balance sheet. My *check list* follows, some of which I've learned to use after 1970.

01. The fundamental *story*.
02. The balance sheet [*financial condition*].
03. Price pattern. Does the stock appear *high* or *low* *relative to where it's been in the past?*
04. *On-Balance Volume [OBV]*.
05. *Relative Strength* [pp.124,166].
06. Relationship to *resistance lines* [pp.128-30].
07. *Unit measurement* count [pp.130-3].
08. Direction and relationship to 50 and 200-day moving averages.
09. The *Rule of Three* [pp.125-8].
10. *Volume* of shares traded both as an indicator and to determine liquidity, though not as useful as it was prior to the advent of options [pp.116-123].
11. *Momentum*.

---

* On-Balance Volume is constructed like an advance/decline line. Whenever price is up for a trading day, the entire volume for that day is added to a cumulative total, whereas on down days the volume is subtracted.

Keep in mind, it is unlikely any single idea will possess all of the desired characteristics and these rules and tools don't always work. That's where *intuition* and discernment come in to the picture.

Let's start with the *"story"*, first. I am usually not interested in a stock which is reputed to have some special story attached to it because it takes enormous conceit to believe that I am one of the first to hear it. Moreover, how much of the story is already in the stock price *and* what happens if the story changes and I happen not to hear about it, or hear about it *too late*? Consequently, I prefer stocks which are actively traded and which, therefore, reflect *investor psychology* in a more orthodox fashion and are less prone to manipulation. This also eliminates the problem of *illiquidity*. While buying a stock is *always* risky it is important to know *which risks* you are prepared to take. I have found it is better to avoid those companies whose shares are illiquid or have shaky *balance sheets* [item 2].

I've previously shown how to evaluate the price pattern— too high or too low—in the examples of Dow Chemical, U.S. Dollar Index, Blockbuster, Home Federal and I apply this to Intel in chapter 8. Regarding *On-Balance Volume*, MCI Communications' action in 1990 provides an excellent example, I feel, as shown in its chart on page 172H. From an early-1990 low, MCIC, an institutional favorite, rallied strongly but its OBV notably failed. To me this was a sign of potential trouble. Subsequently it got cut-in-half.

Relative Strength is best used, in my opinion, when a stock is in a low area, or even after a move up has begun, but not after an extended rise. This is where I fault the Value Line ranking system. [Refer to my earlier comments on the Growths' Relative Strength.]

The relationship to *resistance lines* was extensively illustrated earlier, as was *unit measurement*.

Ideally, for a stock anticipated to continue up, its 10-week [or 50-day] moving average should rise above and stay above its 40-week [or 200-day] moving average. The reverse for

Divergence Analysis: Timing Stock Selections

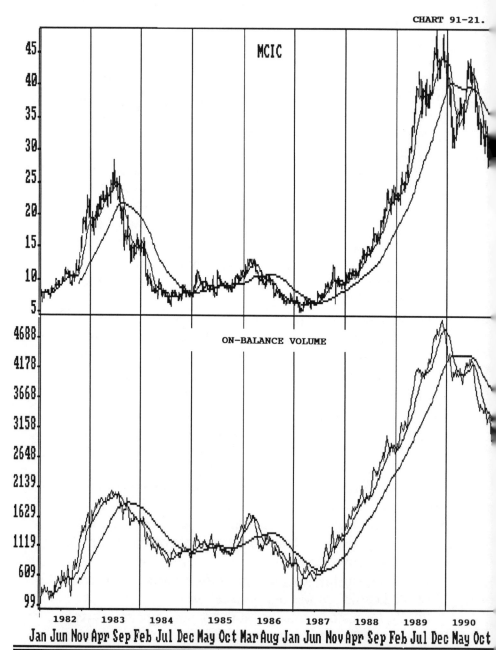

CHART 91-21.

MCIC

ON-BALANCE VOLUME

Jan Jun Nov Apr Sep Feb Jul Dec May Oct Mar Aug Jan Jun Nov Apr Sep Feb Jul Dec May Oct

MCI COMMUNICATIONS WITH ON-BALANCE VOLUME & 10 & 40-WEEK MOVING AVERAGES

172H

stocks presumed to be heading down. This seems well illustrated by the action of *Westmark International* in the chart
on page *172*J. Up from early-1988 and all of 1989, and
down beginning mid-1990. Since the 1990 peak was a *double
top* with the 1989 peak and a *quadruple* of the 1987 low,
these might have been cautionary signs to sell. By late-1990,
however, WMRK had declined four steps in accordance with
the *Rule of Three* and later upside penetrated its declining
2/3 speed resistance line [not illustrated]. So, at the beginning
of 1991 WMRK appeared to be an up stock, I believe.
I also like the idea that this spinoff from Squibb on January
2, 1987 appears to have some potentially exciting ultrasound-
guided biopsy/aspiration systems which could revolutionize
certain fields of medicine, including angioplasty and surgery.
In addition, sales have been growing rapidly and there is
no long-term debt—a simple clean balance sheet.

A different kind of example of the Rule of Three is shown
by the chart of *Dravo* on page *172*K. At the beginning of
1991 DRV appeared to be testing the 8 to 10 area for the
third time since 1982. [8 would be a double cut-in-half—
off 75 percent from an old high]. Dravo is the largest U.S.
lime supplier. Lime may greatly increase in demand in the
1990s due to the Clean Air Act. It is used to help remove
sulfur dioxide from fossil fuel emissions. In brief, I feel that
DRV may represent opportunity at the beginning of 1991,
if bought between 8 and 10].

The role *volume* may play in decisions should be qualified
by the observation that sometimes volume is very high at
both major highs *and* major lows, i.e., at the extremes. A
good 1990 example of rising high volume after a stock had
been cut-in-half was *Calgene*, shown in chart *172*L. After
10-day volume peaked in late-1990, CGNE went on to upside
penetrate its declining 2/3 speed resistance line.

There are many ways to measure *Momentum* but I prefer
a rate of change of the *difference between* the 50 and 200-
day moving averages, as in our evaluation of the Adjusted
St.Louis Monetary Base, or 10 and 25 day [or weeks] moving
averages of RSI.

Divergence Analysis: Timing Stock Selections

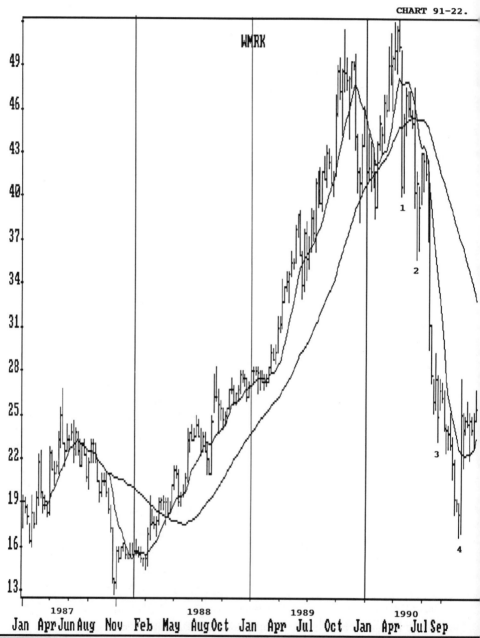

CHART 91-22.

WESTMARK INTERNATIONAL: THE QUADRUPLE, RULE OF THREE + 10 & 40-WEEK MOVING AVS

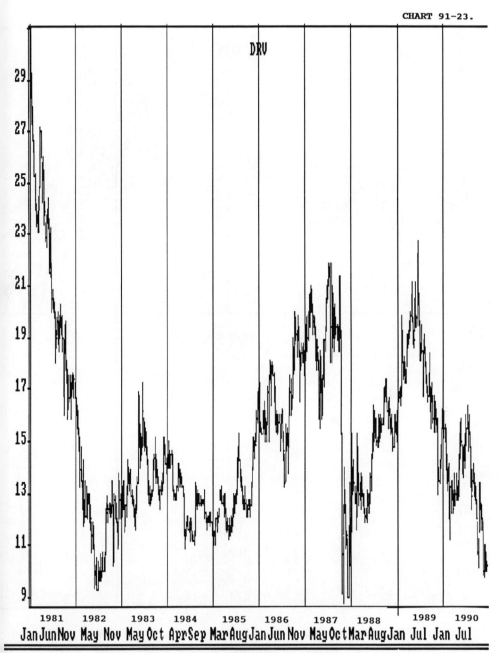

CHART 91-23.

DRV

DRAVO, WEEKLY. LAST 10 YEARS THROUGH DECEMBER 28, 1990

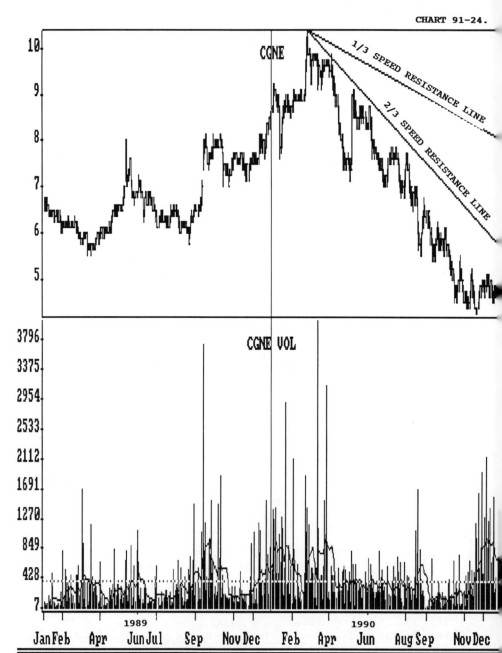

CHART 91-24.

CGNE

1/3 SPEED RESISTANCE LINE

2/3 SPEED RESISTANCE LINE

CGNE VOL

CALGENE. RISING VOLUME PRECEDES RESISTANCE LINE BREAKOUT.

172L

7 / Portfolio Management

It is commonly agreed among professionals that the key to investment success is buying the right stock at the right time. This seems a truism, but in fact it is only half-true. Selection and timing are indeed important; the right stock at the right time gives the investor the opportunity for maximum gain. They do not, however, assure its realization. That requires astute portfolio management as well.

Stock selection and portfolio management, while related, require subtly different skills. There are good selectors who can't manage and capable managers who can't select. The successful investor, of course, can do both. Actually, the best stock selections will always be better than the best portfolio management. The best selections are the best stocks at the best prices. Perfect management means always buying at the bottom and always selling at the top, which is humanly impossible. If one's management cannot be perfected, however, it certainly can be improved.

In managing, one *manages*—that is, one takes the necessary actions at the proper time. Most investors, because they are psychologically insecure, procrastinate most of the time, even when intellectually sure of the right action to take. They simply cannot bring themselves to act when they should. And when they do act, the opportunity often has passed. So most investors penalize themselves twice over: first, by failing to act in time; and second, taking .an action which, by the time it is consummated, often leads to disaster.

There are three broad aspects to successful portfolio management. Organizing knowledge is the first, the aim being to stimulate independent judgment that cuts through the stereotyped thinking churned out by most of the Wall Street establishment. The second is identifying major price reversals—in the market, in industry groups and in particular companies. And the third is acting before recognition by others changes market prices. *The degree of initiative exercised in creating and exploiting opportunities, and in accepting and rejecting specific risks, is the principal determinant of superior portfolio management.*

All this implies that investment success in today's market accrues to those few people who have both insight into investor behavior and the ability to stay in control of their actions. Failure lies on both sides of this narrow course in what Bernard Baruch called "crowd madness"—a madness, incidentally, against which education and accomplishment are no protection.

Almost by definition, then, the successful investor is one of a distinct minority, a loner. Such a person often is thought of as a speculator, the word suggesting the image of a gambler or plunger. But Bernard Baruch, the greatest market speculator of modern times, pointed out that the word "speculator" comes from the Latin *speculari*, which means "to observe and to spy out." He defined a speculator more accurately as "a man who observes the future and acts before it occurs."

As there is no magic formula for selecting stocks, there is no foolproof method for managing them. There are, however, some useful guidelines that at the very least will keep most investors out of serious trouble.

The first step in investment management is to fix a goal consistent with one's basic values, abilities and capital. For example, all other things being equal, high-risk issues outperform those of low-risk; but if the price of success in high-risk investments is a bleeding ulcer, it seems self-defeating to concentrate on such issues.

Of course, everyone's philosophy differs according to his individual needs and background, his temperament, education and so on. There is no single comprehensive dividing line—unless it is age. In the market, as elsewhere, there is a generation gap. The younger managers created it when, eschewing the traditional habits of the older generation, they began agressively turning over their portfolios for maximum profit. Their style, with its initial dramatic successes, opened the way for a reassessment of investment management. Ironically, their recent dramatic failures have kept open the dialogue they inspired.

As elsewhere, the young have drawn the disapproval of the old. This is partly because, as Logan Pearsall Smith said, "the denunciation of the young is a necessary part of the hygiene of older people, and greatly assists the circulation of their blood." Then, too, the older generation seeks to exercise what it considers to be its prerogatives. "I shall go out with the chariots to counsel and command," said Nestor in the *Iliad*, "for that is the privilege of the old; the young must fight in the ranks."

The rub of the controversy, of course, is the meaning of the concept of "performance." We have seen in previous chapters how professional investment managers, both older and younger, interpret it. This is useful as a frame of reference. But an individual investor who doesn't spend full time at management must define performance in terms of his own goals and philosophy and measure it in terms of his ability, over a reasonable period of time, to realize those goals. A high-yielding portfolio, for example, will perform well for an investor who seeks stable income but poorly for one who seeks capital growth.

Having related performance to goals and values, one must then measure it. This implies an understanding of gain—the nature of which appears self-evident but which actually is misunderstood by most investors.

A gain is not simply a percentage advance over cost, as it is usually calculated. It is an advance over cost divided by the time period during which the advance takes place and adjusted for tax obligations. The result is the *rate of gain*. In short, *a gain has no meaning except as it is related to the time it takes to materialize*. If this were not so, all we would have to do is put our money in a savings bank and at compound interest everyone would be a millionaire in a few hundred years.

For anyone who wishes to measure his own rate of gain (or loss) on his investments the method is simple:

At the end of each week, subtract the purchase price from the closing price (vice versa, if a loss) and divide the difference by the purchase price. The result is the absolute percentage gain or loss. Multiply this figure by 365, then divide the product by the number of days the investment has been held. The result is the annualized rate of gain or loss.

Here are three simple examples of such calculations, with the tax factor added:

% ADVANCE OVER COST	TIMES 365	DIVIDED BY NO. OF DAYS HELD	% RATE OF GAIN BE-FORE TAXES	% RATE OF GAIN AFTER TAXES
100	×365	365	100	75*
100	×365	730	50	37½*
10	×365	9	400	120**

* Based upon 25 percent capital-gains tax.
** Based upon *maximum* 70 percent short-term tax rate.

A comparison of these figures is eye-opening. For example, long-term capital gains are not so profitable as they are thought to be by so many investors. There is, of course, no assurance of a 10 percent gain in nine days, but neither is there assurance of a 100 percent gain in 365 days. Indeed, the statistical probabilities of the first may well exceed those of the second. The message is clear: investors who worry excessively about capital gains vs. short-term gains may lose out on far more opportunities for real gain than they save on tax considerations. And in my example I used the maximum 70 percent short-term tax rate, so even those investors in the highest tax brackets cannot afford to overlook the advantages of short-term profits—especially since excessive preoccupation with tax rates tends to distort one's judgment on investments.

The potential for gain is, of course, a major factor in determining basic investment-management strategies, and in this respect short-term trading has the following advantages:

1. Many more short-term than long-term opportunities for gain are available.
2. The profit is nailed down; it doesn't remain "on paper" and subject to decline.
3. The money is available for reinvestment with all the substantial benefits of compounding.
4. Short-term gains can be measured easily. This forces one to come to grips constantly with the success or failure of his investment management; if failure persists, he quickly can take corrective steps. With long-term investments, one tends to sit back and wait, hoping that everything will work out eventually; if it doesn't, one's loss may be substantial.
5. Short-term investments may develop into long-term gains as a result of sudden developments; and, if that happens, one already is in at the right time at the right price. If the stock runs away on the upside, one can always hold it for a capital gain.

This is not to say that long-term investment should be abandoned, only that there is no special virtue in it unless it produces more net gain than an alternative short-term investment. The self-styled "long-term" investor who holds stocks bought years ago may comfort himself with the thought that he will always have a profit in them no matter how much the market goes down, but the fact is that figuring profit based on one's cost twenty years ago is a sheer delusion because it completely fails to take into account either the element of time or alternative investments that could have been made with the tied-up funds. Anyone who loses 25 percent on an investment in a single year and comforts himself that the price is still triple what he bought it at twenty years ago is deluding himself. Unfortunately, many bank-managed trust funds habitually hold stocks with historic profits "built-in" precisely so they can always point to a "profit," one which in fact may have been achieved years ago; this way they can, if they wish, divert attention from the *current* year's performance.

Most individual investors, of course, overlook rate of gain and favor long-term investments for what are essentially psychological reasons. Switching from one investment to another requires constant decision-making, for which most investors lack the necessary self-confidence. Also, if the original investment has been profitable, keeping it reinforces the ego; and if it has been unprofitable, the ego demands staying with it until it becomes profitable and repairs the ego damage. So most investors drift with the long-term, blown along by the winds of their unconscious needs.

In considering the potential for gain, an investor also must consider the other side of the coin—risk of loss. There is an element of risk in every investment, even in government bonds. The only question is one of degree. Generally speaking, high risk goes with high potential, low risk with low potential. But occasionally, as we have seen, one finds a stock with both low risk and high potential. This is the best possible risk-gain ratio.

The element of risk in the market is the Sword of Damocles that hangs over the head of every investor. To ignore it is to court financial disaster. The quality of a portfolio is an important risk factor, and at crucial times may be a vital one. With low-quality issues, an investor runs the risk of being forced out of the game at climactic market lows, when the garbage falls out of sight and no one will touch it. If equivalent performance can be achieved, as we have seen, with high-quality issues that are always marketable, why play Russian roulette?

I believe in concentrating the bulk of one's funds on high-quality stocks, both growth and cyclical. Both show enormous price-action variation, and I have found this action more predictable than that of lower-quality stocks because the blue chips and glamours more intensely reflect investor psychology—or rather, the data that reflects investor psychology is more readily available for them. The absolute gains in individual issues may not always appear to be so dramatic. But on the basis of the rate of gain and consistency, high-quality issues can outperform those of lower quality. And at less risk.

Calculating risk-gain ratios in the market, where mass emotion plays such an important part, is difficult, and the results are certain to be uneven. But it is worth attempting. One way to calculate *general-market risk* is to use the price—that is, the cost—of $1 in dividends as a barometer. By measuring what investors are willing to pay for $1 in dividends we get a profile of investor sentiment toward the market that is especially useful during periods of economic boom and bust.

To calculate the price of $1 in dividends, simply divide stock prices (using the DJIA) by their cash dividends. The result is a better measure of the degree of risk or profit potential of stock purchases than the level of stock prices, which are never absolutely high or low.

Over the past 100 years the market price of $1 in dividends has fluctuated within definite limits. At market highs, when investors are enthusiastic, they are willing to pay more than $30 per dividend dollar; at market lows, when investors are fearful and depressed, the price sinks to under $15 for a dividend dollar.

Since 1900 the market price of a dividend dollar has risen from near $15 to above $30 less than ten times. In 1901, a period of anticipated prosperity under McKinley, the dividend dollar cost rose to $32.79; but by the time of the "rich man's" panic of 1903, it had declined to $12.64. It soared again to $31.75 during the bull market into 1906, then declined to $12.74 by 1907–08, when there was another monetary panic and bear market. When the United States entered the First World War in 1917, the dividend-dollar price declined to an all-time low of $8.71; it did not rise past $30 again until the end of 1928. By 1932 it had declined again to $10.02. For the next twenty years it swung to more than $30 and less than $15 on six occasions during the New and Fair deals. But since the election of Dwight D. Eisenhower in 1952, the market price of a dividend dollar has steadily risen, reaching a peak of $36.28 in 1959; it has never declined to below or even near $15. In the 1962 crash, the low price was $25.73; in 1966, it was $25.77; and during the 1969-70 decline, it dropped to $22.00, the lowest level since 1958.

Stock-price swings are more volatile than those of dividend changes and the two can move in opposite directions. In 1958–59 dividends declined while stock prices rose; in 1962 dividends rose but stock prices fell. Since 1900 stock prices have risen more than 1800 percent, dividends have risen more than 1300 percent. Much of the increase in stock prices can be traced to the rise in dividends. But for the past ten years investors have been willing to pay a higher price for dividends (between $22 and $36 per dividend dollar) than they ever have in any similar period over the past 100 years.

Does this herald a new era, or does it warn of another market decline to the $15 level—which would be equivalent to 500 on the DJIA? In the last chapter I explore the probabilities in this respect; here it is enough to say that the cost of a dividend dollar is one useful measure of investor sentiment which at times may be of far greater importance in determining stock prices than even corporate profits. For example, during 1946–49, when earnings and dividends increased by some 50 percent but the stock market declined 25 percent, the cost of a dividend dollar declined from $30.96 to $14.84.

The historical record indicates that whenever investor sentiment is at the $30-plus level stock prices may be vulnerable to major decline—at best they are high-risk investments—and when the cost declines toward the $15 level, stocks may be on the bargain counter. While this measurement by itself cannot assure success in the market, it does provide us with a simple economic tool with which to estimate *general*-market risk at any given point.

As for calculating the risk involved in buying an individual stock, here is an example of how to use the risk-reward concept. Assume the expectation of a 15-point gain for a stock costing $50 and assume a downside risk estimated at 5 points. This gives a 15-point gain potential compared with a 5-point loss potential, a 3-to-1 favorable ratio. In terms of percentage of cost, the ratio is the same, 30 percent gain potential vs. 10 percent loss potential. But take variations of this example and the results are completely different. If the same 15 points up and 5 points down are applied to a $15 stock, then we have a 100 percent to 33⅓ percent relationship between reward and risk, obviously not good enough despite the 3-to-1 odds—far too much risk-exposure. Or in the case of a $100 stock, using the same 15 and 5 points, while the downside risk is small at 5 percent, the upside potential of only 15 percent is too little to make the game worthwhile.

Here is a rough method—not a definitive formula—of using the same principle to estimate risk of an entire portfolio of stocks:

In comparing two equities, say, the *possibility* of gain in one, *A*, is 100 percent—that is, it might double—and the risk of loss is 25 percent—it might decline by one quarter; and in the other, *B*, the possibility of gain is 25 percent and the risk of loss is 10 percent. Also, assume the *probability* of gain is 1 in 10 with A, 4 in 10 with B; and of loss it is 9 in 10 with A, 6 in 10 with B. If we multiply the possible outcome by the assumed probability of it, we get:

$$A \quad \frac{\text{plus } 100 \times .1 = \quad \text{plus } 10}{\text{minus} \quad 25 \times .9 = \text{minus } 22.5}$$

$$B \quad \frac{\text{plus } 25 \times .4 = \quad \text{plus } 10}{\text{minus } 10 \times .6 = \text{minus} \quad 6}$$

Stock B obviously has a better risk-gain ratio—equal potential with far less risk. A portfolio of B-type stocks, then, would be a safer investment than a portfolio of A-type stocks—and just as profitable, even though any single A stock has the potential of increasing in value four times as much as any B stock.

The problem, of course, is defining the gain and risk possibilities of individual stocks. One can estimate the risk factor in a stock by relating the company's dividend yield, the projected growth rate of per-share earnings and the alternate use of his funds in the form of the bank interest rate.

"For instance," explains economist Charles H. Jones, research partner of Wood, Struthers & Winthrop, "a company whose common stock provides a 4-percent cash return and whose anticipated growth rate is 7 percent would have a combined return of 11 percent and hence would be more favorably priced than another company with a 5-percent return and a 5-percent growth factor." The implication of this is quite clear. A stock selling at 10 times earnings with a growth rate of 3 percent annually must be considered *expensive* while a stock selling at a 25 times PE multiple but growing at a 40-percent annual rate must be considered cheap.

"It is also common practice, however," concludes Jones, "to impose some mental discounting on the future growth rate, since the cash return is a known factor whereas the anticipated growth is subject to considerable adjustment."

He suggests a simple formula that takes this adjustment into account:

$$\text{Interest} + \text{Risk} - \text{Growth} = \text{Yield}$$

Which simply expresses the fact that a stock's yield is a function of the interest and risk rates less the growth.

Even this method, however, is not definitive. Investor psychology and the alternate uses of money *outside* the market must also be taken into account. And so must the rate of inflation. In 1969 consumer prices rose at an annual rate near 6 percent, so even those people playing it safe with 5 percent at the savings bank lost money!

Risk, then, involves consideration of a range of factors: the risk of principal if a company goes bankrupt; interest-rate risk—the rise and fall of money costs can increase or decrease the value of a portfolio relative to current yield; the inflation risk just noted; the psychological risk of the general market—how much optimism or pessimism is reflected in prevailing market prices; and specific market risk of buying a stock at too high a price.

An investor should first determine what his risks are, then take only such risks as are not excessive—and even then, only when they are justified by the realistic hope of sufficient gain.

The average investor's portfolio reflects his approach to the market, so it is not surprising that most are a combination of the most conservative investments and a collection of cats and dogs—in other words, a mixed bag collected without direction. They are marked by one other debility: far too many positions to facilitate the following of any one of them with care. Investment funds must be concentrated in a handful of issues to be effective. An investor with $50,000 should concentrate it *in equal dollar amounts* (not equal amounts of shares) in four or five issues or positions; with $500,000 to invest, six to eight issues or positions are enough; with $10,000, perhaps two or three.

Even with a $100-million fund, I doubt that more than a dozen positions are desirable or necessary. While the number of positions will vary depending upon the total amount of funds and the prevailing market climate, the principle remains the same: to avoid putting all one's eggs in one basket or spreading one's money around so thinly it will have no impact. Concentration in a limited number of issues allows one to maintain control of a portfolio, to take profits as issues work out and/or to switch to more attractive alternative opportunities that may arise.

Diversification protects against disaster, but over-diversification reduces profit potential. No one's stock selection can be perfect; if it were, every investor could pick one stock and put all his money into it. Hence the need for diversification. But it follows that the better one's stock selection, the less diversification is needed.

The investor who limits himself to a handful of securities that he knows well stands a much better chance to make money than one who has a superficial knowledge of many stocks and jumps all over the board. As John R. Hayes has said, people are incapable of making effective decisions when they have more than a limited amount of data to work with.

Yet most investors deliberately load up on decision-making on the theory that the harder they work and the longer they agonize, the more superior their decisions will be. Well, it isn't so; in fact, the reverse is true. Decisions produced under the harassment of daily pressures are usually inferior. What are needed are not more decisions but better decisions, decisions to which one can commit significant amounts of capital. Not the least value of divergence analysis is that it allows one to concentrate on selected stocks and groups that offer the potential for substantial gain at modest risk.

In decision-making one should strive to control one's own investment fate rather than be a prisoner of the crowd. The surest way to do this is to position oneself for whatever may come. I suggested earlier that one should try to select stocks in base areas before the price-action has changed. If the selection is poor, the risk is minimized; if it is good, one is better positioned for future price-action, either for the short- or the long-term. Indeed, we can conclude that one's original positioning in an equity bears considerably on all subsequent decisions touching on that stock; and the more advantageous the original positioning, the easier it is to decide among later alternatives.

For example, when trading on the market is uncertain and within a narrow range, a *hedged* position—short-selling some stocks and holding others long—is the only sensible strategy for those seeking action. Others may do better to stand aside at such times. Even shorting stocks like Xerox and IBM, which may have temporarily overrun themselves, can carry relatively little risk in an uncertain market if their technical positioning is such that their upside potential is perhaps only 5 to 10 percent, while their downside potential may be 10 to 25 percent. Buying on weakness in other stocks that are thoroughly depressed but have good prospects presents the other side of the same risk-gain situation in an uncertain market.

As I have noted earlier, the individual investor has the maneuverability to position himself, which the large institutions, with their red tape and immense capital, lack. "The difference in big money and small money is the degree of flexibility," says the manager of a large fund. "You must anticipate more and guard against the loss of maneuverability. By employing more decision-makers, we hope to provide more flexibility. Now the hang-up in this method is the communication—with small money, a one-man band can play all the instruments."

Even the individual with several million dollars in the market has no real problem. Indeed, one of the most sophisticated investment managers I know, who operates a small $5-million private hedge fund, gets himself all or almost all invested or liquidated with no more than three telephone calls.

As I noted earlier, position in the market is crucial. Yet it is generally ignored by the unsophisticated. For example, in their transactions, most investors buy and sell their entire position in a single block, which implies knowledge of the best buying and selling prices—a most unrealistic implication. The basis of this practice is unclear. It may reflect an unconscious desire to be perfect—in at the bottom, out at the top; probably it is simply ignorance. In any case, purchases and sales ordinarily should be made on a scaled basis. This usually results not only in favorable average prices but, more important, creates the positioning—with all the leverage inherent in that posture—for further profitable actions.

In buying, once the buy target area is decided upon, an initial position—say, half—should be taken on minor weakness, with the understanding that if the stock weakens further—perhaps up to 10 percent—the original judgment will be corroborated by taking the balance of the position on the new weakness. With this half-and-half tactic, if the stock goes up at once, one has only half as much gain, but the position is favorable and one can invest the balance elsewhere. If the stock does weaken further, one can act on that weakness out of opportunity rather than out of disappointment that one's original judgment has been faulty; psychologically, one is an opportunist rather than a victim. After the full position has been taken, one ends up with a lower average cost or, if the stock has weakened further—say, 10 percent below the *average* price —with a clear indication that the original judgment *was* poor and that the issue should be closed out and a limited loss taken. In either case, the risk is minimized. Needless to say, *chasing* stocks is almost always a foolish policy.

In selling, once a reasonable if small gain has been realized, it is often wise to take half of it to assure that whatever happens subsequently the overall position will be profitable. The balance of the position covers the possibility of further gain, and a stop-loss cover protects against a substantial reversal. In his little book, *Confusion de Confusiones*—note the title—published in Amsterdam in 1688, Joseph de la Vega advised investors to "take every gain without showing remorse about missed profits because an eel can escape sooner than you think."

One of the most frequently recurring problems in investment management is how to react to unanticipated news breaks. Most news is "discounted in advance" by sophisticated investors and reflected in current prices. But some news genuinely surprises the investment community and triggers drastic price changes, sometimes overnight. The problem is judging which is which and knowing how to act.

Spot news ordinarily is affected also by the general-market environment. In a bear market good news usually is shrugged off, bad news may lead to precipitous spilloffs; and in a bull market the reverse applies. This implies that the reaction to spot news is also psychologically influenced; it is, and news must be judged for its psychological as well as its fundamental effect. More important, to cope with this effect one must be psychologically able to make quick decisions.

Each situation, of course, must be judged on its own merits, but here are a few typical developments that broke in July 1969:

On July 22, Sperry Rand announced that its earnings per share for the second quarter had dropped from 47¢ to 46¢. The stock, which had been trading at above 52, promptly fell off more than 7 points as 150,000 shares were traded. A widely circulated estimate had placed Sperry's earnings at 50¢, so when the statement was released it came as a surprise to the Street. The earnings decline was slight, but the possibility that it might be the beginning of a reversal in Sperry's fortunes, and the fact that the market was in a down phase, prompted immediate institutional selling. During the remaining three trading days of that week another 500,000 shares of the stock were traded; by the end of the week Sperry was selling near 40, off 12 points. So those investors who sold immediately after the announcement suffered less than those who waited a few days to think over the situation.

Earlier that same week the tobacco industry had announced it would discontinue network advertising after its contracts expired in 1970. Examining all aspects of the situation, one would have concluded that it would not adversely affect tobacco stocks. The industry's troubles had been widely reported, so the news was no surprise; the stocks were high-yielding and selling at low price-earnings ratios; and the cigarette companies were rapidly and successfully diversifying. Indeed, there were no adverse effects. But, assuming a slightly different viewpoint, one could have concluded that the announcement would adversely affect the network stocks because a significant portion of their revenues came from cigarette advertising. It did, and the network stocks dropped sharply almost immediately.

At about the same time, Pan American Airways passed its dividend, triggering a precipitous decline in its stock. Interestingly, the other airlines, which already were depressed, also drastically declined further, demonstrating that when an industry leader falters the entire industry is tarnished. The thinking is clear: if industry conditions are so negative that one of the leaders suffers, then it is only a matter of time before the rest of the industry will suffer. A huge volume of institutional selling of airline issues followed the Pan Am announcement, TWA dropping 50 percent within a few days, to 21, down from the previous month's high of 43.

The above examples are fairly commonplace; but every now and then a spectacular public event occurs that may affect the market in unsuspected ways. Such an occurrence was the assassination of Robert F. Kennedy in June 1968. The killing of such a public figure, upon whose future rode the hopes of so many millions of people, especially in the vital area of race conciliation, might have been expected to depress the market, as it depressed most people. Instead, the market rose. How are we to interpret this? One theory is that a substantial segment of the monied class hated RFK with vigor; like Franklin D. Roosevelt, he was considered a "traitor to his class." The people of this persuasion feel strongly that an inheritor of vast wealth should strive to preserve, not—as they see it—destroy, property values. So, to the extent that these people are sophisticated investors—and I don't doubt that the majority of them are—they may have regarded the shooting as a buying rather than a selling opportunity.

Perhaps this interpretation is too cynical. Perhaps the tragedy, like a classic Greek drama, stimulated a catharsis from which emerged a bullish rededication to redress grievous wrongs and to fashion a more just society. I hope so.

Earlier that year the market had acted unsuspectedly to another, but less dramatic, piece of news, the raising of the discount rate by the Federal Reserve Board. This, too, ordinarily might have been expected to depress the market, but it didn't. At the time, my own divergence-analysis measurements showed sophisticated investors buying and unsophisticated investors selling, a bullish sign. Indeed, it seemed clear to me that Lyndon Johnson's famous speech of March 31, in which he announced the halting of the bombing of North Vietnam, turning the nation toward peace, had fostered among sophisticated investors a bullish psychology that would overcome a piece of negative fundamental news like the Board's action. And it did.

Spot news that concerns an individual company is easier to evaluate than news of wide-ranging consequence. But one must look beyond the obvious. For example, when Xerox Corporation announced its proposed merger with CIT Financial, unsophisticated investors looked upon the move as a boon for Xerox—expansion will make the company bigger, so it must be good. But sophisticated investors, viewing the merger as a dilution of Xerox quality (see Chapter Three), began distributing Xerox stock, forcing the company to call off the merger. Not, however, before the stock had plunged almost 60 points. A similar merger, but one that went through, SCM-Glidden, left SCM's stock more than 75 percent lower.

Merger announcements must be evaluated in terms of respective price-earnings ratios and the *nature* of the business being merged. While it is management's job to convert "blue sky" into solid assets, blue sky, not solid assets, is usually the stuff of which high stock prices are made. So what may look good for a company over the long-term may be disastrous for its present stock price. This is why sophisticated investors unloaded Xerox (and SCM) almost immediately, while their unsophisticated brethren were thinking how marvelous the news was.

"What the news is," analyst Joseph Mindell said twenty-five years ago, "may be of less importance than how the market responds to it. News flowing with the trend presents no problem. It becomes deceptive when it reaches a turning point and when it runs against the trend."

Various scholarly studies have indicated that perhaps half of all price-changes in individual stocks may be attributed to fluctuations in the market as a whole; the remaining amount of price-change in an individual stock—residual fluctuation—relates uniquely to the particular company's specific prospects: current and expected earnings, dividends, growth rate and industry (group) action. So, as Mindell cautioned, an investor must beware of magnifying the news and of attributing too much causal effect to it; indeed, one should not grant a statement authority just because it appears in print.

The authors of a study on determining risk-gain probabilities make some astute observations on the effect of news events upon general-market variability. Even though these events may seem unique, they say, they share a character that "demonstrates some continuity over time."

"Labor unions," they explain, "will continue to strike; countries will continue to declare war or to make undeclared war; the Fed will continue by turns to tighten up and loosen the money supply; and so forth."*

Some stocks, however—those of a few companies and industries—react to the impact of events to an additional degree not traceable to the events' effect upon general-market variability. Residual fluctuation, say the authors, "tends to be larger for companies in which technological changes in products or processes are taking place very rapidly. It also tends to be larger for one-product companies, companies for which style is an important factor and for companies whose fortunes depend upon a single executive." Obviously, widely diversified companies with balanced management will show less residual variability than others.

What does it take to manage a portfolio astutely? Good judgment, of course, but also a necessary *balance* between boldness and caution, skepticism and gullibility. These qualities must be applied to ten basic considerations involved in portfolio management: the *return* expected; the *risk* assumed in pursuit of the return; *diversification* (concentration); *liquidity,* the percentage of one's portfolio invested or in cash at any given time; stock *selection;* how to *sell; timing* of buying and selling; *volatility; time horizon,* the period of time in which one expects his investment objectives to be achieved; and *sub-strategies,* such as emphasis on high technology issues, or on cyclical stocks when the cycle is about to reverse, or on vogue stocks reflecting current market fads, etc. These elements are deeply interrelated and it is difficult—at times impossible—to discuss one without reference to another. At any time one of

* Jack L. Treynor, William W. Priest, Jr., Lawrence Fisher and Catherine A. Higgins, writing in *Financial Analysts Journal.*

these considerations might be more important than the others, but none can be ignored if one is to be mostly right most of the time.

With respect to risks, too often the wrong ones are taken at the wrong time. One should assume fullest risk at major market bottoms, with 100-percent invested positions in volatile quality glamour stocks that have favorable risk-gain ratios. As major topping or uncertain areas develop, one should switch from higher- to lower-risk equities and cut back from 100-percent investment in long positions to include a percentage in short positions and cash or its equivalent.

Diversification, as I have said, should always be limited to a few equities concentrated in a few selected groups, and these should be studied and watched carefully.

Liquidity should be virtually nil at major market bottoms; and from 50 to 100 percent at major topping areas, or a substantial percentage in short positions, consistent with a hedged strategy, which I discuss in the next chapter.

1991 ADDENDUM

The computer has enormously speeded up the collecting and processing of financial data to the extent that some academics have sought to elevate security analysis to a science [pp.134-6]. However, I agree with Joe McNay who, in the earlier interview, also stated, "I think one of the real trouble areas for investors right now is that some people think it is a science and they can do it through a computer. I call it 'Two Quants* and a Computer'". He was referring to the newest institutional vogue of *indexing*, trying to match the stock averages, particularly the S & P 500 Composite. How pathetic that so many professionals no longer believe they should try to excel and beat the averages!

Another friend, Bob Farrell of Merrill Lynch, recently made a wise comment about the use of indicators. In the June 1990 journal of the Market Technicians Association, Bob said, "...what we are trying to do with a computer is to quantify things that, over the years, we've made subjective judgments about. Still, there is not a single formula that works all the time. *A sense of proportion and degree must come into play* [emphasis mine]. The parameters on indicators will change, and not every indicator will fit together at an extreme. Yet, some action should be taken. I think it is an intuitive business, and always will be..."

Successful money-management is much like playing winning tennis. 70 years ago Bill Tilden transformed himself from a good but ordinary player to become master of the tennis court. I agree with a recent review by Alexander McNab of Tilden's 1925 classic, *Match Play and the Spin of the Ball* [New York Times-June 11, 1990], when he said Tilden was, "...also arguably...the greatest author of tennis instruction books." This was the third of his four instruction books, all of which are out of print. Among Tilden's rules I pick *four* which I think are veritable gems when applied to managing investments. I quote:

---

* Quantitative analysts.

" . *Never play any stroke in tennis without a definite idea of what you are trying to do with it.*

. *A great match player is always one stroke ahead of the one he is making.*

. *No matter what the score may be against a player, if he is still master of himself, he has a chance.*

. *Nothing destroys a man's confidence, breaks up his game and ruins his fighting spirit like errors. The more shots he misses, the more he worries and, ultimately, the worse he plays."*

Three ending points about investment management:

First, there are times during the life of a given investment, or the market of which it is a part, that the wisest thing to do is nothing. This also applies to the ability to refuse ideas of others, no matter how persuasively argued. As the Chinese philosophers have taught us for thousands of years, *avoiding error* is important in and of itself.

Second, we all have experienced luck in our lives, sometimes good and sometimes bad. This raises an aspect of investing that should be faced squarely, namely that sometimes investments are entered into, not objectively, but in the pursuit of *Lady Luck*. As Freud enlightened us about many years ago, gambling and sometimes investing are often concealed efforts to find the love our parents never gave us. However, since the stock market is a jealous mistress, the pursuit of parental love in the market is almost always doomed to failure. This is why often the almost perfect investment, the one in which we plunge too heavily, is also usually the greatest failure.

Finally, I am also indebted to Freud for his articulation of the psychological phenomenon of, *"Those Wrecked By*

Success"*. While it isn't difficult to agree with Freud that, "privation, frustration of a real satisfaction, is the first condition for the outbreak of a neurosis", it is, "so much the more surprising, indeed bewildering...when...one makes the discovery that people occasionally fall ill precisely because a deeply-rooted and long cherished wish has come to fulfillment."

He then cites a number of his own cases as well as that of Shakespeare's Lady Macbeth, concluding that in each of these instances, "analytic work soon shows us that it is forces of conscience which forbid the person to gain the long-hoped-for enjoyment from the fortunate change in reality."

This seems to be a psychologically devastating explanation of why some of those who made enormous fortunes in the Eighties then went on to undermine themselves. Et tu, Mike Milken. This, in effect, was also the explanation given by Cincinnati Bengals safety David Fulcher to explain their last minute loss to the San Francisco 49ers, "It goes the same way again. We beat them and then we give it up. We've got to do something to stop people from doing what they do to us late in the ball-game." [*New York Times*— December 10, 1990]. Those wrecked by success on Wall Street have much to learn from this.

* From Freud's 1915 essay first published in *Imago*, entitled *Some Character-Types Met With In Psycho-Analytic Work.*

This page intentionally left blank.

8 / Selling Strategies

> It is not a custom with me to
> keep money to look at.
> —GEORGE WASHINGTON

Just as nobody talks about a poor relation, so nobody discusses selling. The fact is, most investors don't like to think about selling; and, as we observed in Chapter Two, the orientation of brokers toward buy recommendations aids and abets this evasion.

Even when a stock soars, most investors are loath to sell and take profits. Why? Bernard Baruch said: "Whatever men attempt, they seem driven to over-do. When hopes are soaring I always repeat to myself, 'Two and two still make four.'"

Whatever the reason, it seems that there are few things more unbalancing to the mind than the act of suddenly winning a large sum of money. Yet *knowing how and when to sell may be the single most important factor in investment success.*

In Chapter One I said that the psychology of selling is completely different from the psychology of buying. To learn how and when to sell, it is necessary to comprehend what those differences are and why they exist. This leads to the examination of two basic aspects of our society and of human nature: the propensity toward ownership and the ever-present need to protect one's ego.

For example, does an investor, after he buys a stock, unconsciously seek to confirm the correctness of his purchase decision? Psychologist Leon Festinger, discussing his "Theory of Cognitive Dissonance," suggests an experiment that throws some light on this:

> Buy two presents for your wife . . . choosing things you are reasonably sure she will find about equally attractive. Find some plausible excuse for having both of them in your possession, show them to your wife and ask her to tell you how attractive each one is to her. After you have obtained a good measurement of attractiveness, tell her she can have only one of them, whichever she chooses. The other you will return to the store. After she has made her choice, ask her once more to evaluate the attractiveness of each of them. If you compare the evaluation of attractiveness before and after the choice, you will probably find that the chosen present has increased in attractiveness and the rejected one decreased.

Festinger here illustrates the basic psychological considerations that underlie many sales practices, particularly mail-order advertising, which stresses "trial" periods and "money back" guarantees. After an individual buys something, he exhibits pride of ownership and seeks, *and finds,* justification for his purchase.

Most investors, when they buy a stock, make not only a financial but an emotional and intellectual commitment to the purchase; and all their subsequent behavior, from following the company's fortunes to recommending the stock to their friends, often serves principally to justify the original purchase. The combination of pride-of-ownership, ego-justification and procrastination is what lies behind the striking inability of most investors to make and implement objective selling decisions. It is why unsophisticated investors, unlike their sophisticated brethren, decline to accept profits and limit losses. But every silver lining has a cloud, and a profit may turn to a loss and small losses may become large ones.

Taking profits and limiting losses are obvious considerations in selling. A more subtle consideration, and one usually overlooked by most investors, is how selling affects a portfolio overall. Since all investors have limited capital, one's failure in timely selling limits one's subsequent ability to buy. An investor may know what to buy at a market bottom, but if he didn't sell at a topping area, and so has no cash available, he cannot capitalize on his knowledge. So an investor, in evaluating whether or not to sell a particular issue at a particular time, must not only consider taking profits or limiting losses but also what effect selling will have on his ability to buy later. Without the ability to buy, one can't play the game.

The simplest criterion for selling a stock is: *if it isn't worth buying at that very moment, it isn't worth keeping.* What this amounts to is placing a value on the stock one owns: is it worth the current market price?

"Valuation of common stocks," says the manager of one performance fund, "is the whole point of money management." He adds: "Valuing stock is hard work. It requires a historical study of price-earnings relationships under different conditions. It requires a feel of price-earnings multiple changes. It requires an understanding of the psychological impact on certain multiples. It requires conceptualizing what the price relationship *might be,* not what it is. It requires integrity. It requires common sense."

In appraising individual stocks, I rely essentially on the integration of psychological measurements, technical positioning and fundamental data, as I have explained in previous chapters. But I also consider other factors. These can be placed under two general headings: one, developments relating to the security but independent of the market generally; and, two, market developments unrelated to the security itself. The first is fairly easy to detect, partly because it is an isolated phenomenon. For example, a stock suddenly begins to falter, or the company pursues a course that dilutes the stock's market value, as SCM did when it merged with Glidden. The second encompasses a broad spectrum of possibilities. For example, in a declining market, such as those of 1962, 1966 and 1969, an investor will want to reduce his exposure and increase his cash position. In this case, he will look to sell those issues that have the least attractive short-term prospects and the greatest marketability and which historically have shown the least resistance to bear markets.

Another possible market development that must affect stock valuation is a distinct change in the general-market attitude toward a group of stocks, such as the decline in airline issues in 1967, and the decline in automotive stocks in 1968–69. "Such a major change in investor attitude," says the head of one fund, "may or may not be accompanied by a change in the fundamentals, but . . . whether [it] is or not, aggressive capital, once recognizing the situation, must seek more attractive alternatives."

A good example of this is the major loss experienced by many institutions in recent years by their efforts to play it safe through buying utility stocks with well-defined earnings and dividend growth trends. Indeed, utility earnings and dividends did grow as the institutions had projected, yet their *stocks* declined, despite the realized growth rate. What happened was that the utilities' growth proved to be slower than that of other groups. As a result, utility PE multiples declined as more astute investors realized that in terms of *relative* value other groups were more attractive.

Before buying a stock, I always formulate a selling strategy. Before? Yes. This requires me, in advance of the action, to set goals—price objectives—so that if my selection is a success I know where and how to accept profits, and if my selection is a failure, I know in advance exactly where to get off, and how much my loss will be.

Assuming that one buys the right stock at the right time, the classic advice of minimizing losses and letting profits run is still sound. Profits should be allowed to run even when divergence analysis shows sophisticated selling, or distribution, of the stock. This can be done because sophisticated distribution, like accumulation, takes time—except in those instances of extraordinarily unfavorable spot news, when the action is fast.

In my view it is no accident that during periods of sophisticated distribution, many brokerage houses and advisory services recommend issues that already have had major upward moves. This is less because of any deliberate intent to mislead than because, as we have seen in Chapter Two, average expert opinion is no better nor worse than average opinion. Occidental Petroleum, it may be recalled, topped out the day its chairman delivered a bullish speech before a large group of security analysts.

Under cover of strength that is stimulated by such recommendations and by unsophisticated enthusiasm generated by the higher prices, the sophisticated sell as the unsophisticated buy. But sometimes the recommendations are so glowing—if U.S. Garbage was a buy at 70, it's a steal at 60—that, fueled by a squeeze on unsophisticated short sellers, a stock will overrun.

In formulating a selling strategy, one must take into account this possibility, which sometimes results in profits greater than otherwise could be anticipated. One way to deal with this situation is through a combination of a trend-line defining the up-channel of the advance and/or by setting a stop-loss point (SLP)* at a certain percentage below the stock's high as it makes those new highs. This percentage should not be too close, to leave sufficient rein for action. Ordinarily it might approximate 10 percent, but this should not be taken as a rigid formula because, once substantial profits have accrued on paper, portfolio, tax and other factors should be considered. For example, as

* I use a *mental* stop-loss and take action after the stock reaches the price because I find that when the specialist on the floor of the Exchange has a succession of stop-losses on his book the stock often comes down to them—if it already is nearby—the stops are set off and the stock immediately reverses. By using a mental stop, I avoid being the victim of such tactics and retain an element of judgment. But for most investors, who may not wish to assume the burden of keeping track of mental stops, the standard practice of entering a stop-loss in advance with one's broker may be best.

Control Data rose to 170 in 1968, a short-term buyer of it at 140 might have set an SLP of 155; a long-term buyer who purchased the stock at 30 might have stopped it at 135. Both actions would have made sense.

Up-channel trendlines (preferably resistance lines) are more precise: the rule is to sell upon decisive penetration of the up-channel. Until that happens, one can ride with the trend, regardless of the tenor of the divergence-analysis data. Subject to the prudent acceptance of part profits, there is no more point in selling sooner than there is in fighting the tape. The tape tells its own story; analysis can only help us to ride it, not control it. Not understanding this difference can be costly.

But since stocks do not always overrun, and since many stocks do reach well-defined upside objectives and then suddenly reverse trend—as we illustrated in Chapter Five in the case of Xerox "working off" precisely three bull units—the soundest method I have found of managing selling is combining those tactics just discussed with the half-and-half tactic discussed in Chapter Seven, as applied to selling on strength.

It works quite simply. Taking the Xerox case as an illustration, when the stock worked off its third unit at 115, one half of the position should have been sold on the strength approaching that target area and the balance stop protected at 10 percent below 115, or on the breaking of the up trendline. This means that half would have been sold, say, at 114, the other half at 103, when XRX subsequently nosedived. The average selling price would have been 108½—not precisely at the top, but close enough to lock in substantial profits. If XRX had overrun to 150 and then precipitously declined, the first half still would have been sold at 114, the balance, 10 percent below 150 (or on breaking the uptrend), at 135 for an average sale price of 124½.

In every case, by selling half on strength and allowing the balance to run subject to loss protection, you never ride a stock up only to ride it down, in deep despair, later on.

Furthermore, this kind of selling strategy leaves one *positioned* for whatever may come. Baruch believed in selling stocks on strength, while they were still rising, observing that even if he missed the last 10 or 20 percent he would always avoid being caught when prices collapsed. Philosophically sound, but I think there is no question that the half-and-half tactic produces greater profits and superior mobility.

The question of taking profits must be dealt with in each case on the basis of psychological, technical and fundamental considerations and in terms of the overall portfolio and tax situations. Of course, an investor who relies upon divergence analysis must understand that, since the data underlying the analysis is short-term in nature, selling decisions based upon tax considerations may differ from those based upon forecasts of price-action. But as I have noted in discussing what really constitutes a gain, tax considerations are not as important as they commonly are thought to be.

This does not mean that divergence analysis has no application for long-term investors. In my own experience stocks selected on the basis of divergence analysis often have moved up for periods of many months. And, of course, every long-term investor wants to take his position at the lowest possible price, which divergence analysis helps him to do.

Together with divergence analysis technical projections and tools are useful in suggesting selling targets on strength, especially where there is overhead supply, because price-action then tends to conform more readily to the projection. And don't forget that the doubling in price of a stock from a previous major base often is a selling target for sophisticated investors.

Up to this point we have looked at selling principally in terms of taking profits. We now shall explore the dark side of the moon, *losses.*

The beginning of wisdom with respect to losses is that

they are inevitable. And the corollary to this is that they
can be limited. A rule observed by Baruch—after an unfor-
tunate youthful experience—was that the first loss is usually the smallest. Most investors, however, refuse to accept
the fact of losses and so, with this attitude, are unable to
limit them. Out of an unconscious need to be proven
"right," they hold on to a small loss until it becomes a large
one. This, says one fund manager, "is about the same as refusing to get off a train that you find is going in the wrong
direction just because you do not want to waste the ticket."

In portfolio management, the refusal to accept losses is
disastrous. The basic principal in modern business management is to allocate resources to exploit new opportunities, not waste them in solving old problems. But an investor who rides down with a poor stock, refusing to sell and
take a small loss, cannot take advantage of new opportunities because his cash is tied up with old problems. Inevitably, he becomes a steady, if not a big, loser. This is
what wears down many investors. As one observer has
pointed out: "It is more important in the stock market
game not to be a big loser than it is to be a big winner.
Putting it another way, it doesn't matter how many winners
you don't buy; what hurts is the number of losing stocks
you do buy."

Well said, and good advice. But, unfortunately, I have
found that, where selling to accept a loss is involved, even
the best advice is seldom heeded. The typical reaction of
most investors to such advice is to ignore it, then to come
back for it a second and third time and to ignore it again,
while the stock goes down. Even otherwise sophisticated
investors often behave like this when it comes to selling. I
have a friend, a shrewd investor, who on his own initiative
bought Anaconda at 48. Within several weeks it soared to
a high of 66, and my friend asked me what to do. My own
work did not show any favorable prospects for the stock,
and Anaconda's historic chart indicated a major top in the
65-67 area, so I suggested selling at least half and placing

a stoploss on the balance at 10 to 15 percent below the high. "But," my friend said, "my broker tells me that the mutuals are buying it aggressively, and he expects it to run up into the 70's." So despite the fact that, even if his broker was right, the stock's biggest play already was over, my friend sat tight.

Within sixty days Anaconda declined to the low 50's, and my friend again asked me what to do. "You still have a small profit," I told him. "Sell. My psychological measurements are most unfavorable." But still he held it. Sixty days later the stock was down to the 40's, and for the third time my friend asked my advice. Delicately I pointed out that my advice in the 60's and 50's had been ignored but that, for what it was worth, I thought he still should sell because, while the bulk of the decline was over, Anaconda had the potential to decline to the 20-to-30 area. That, too, was ignored. A month or so later Chile forced Anaconda to sell its mining interests there and the stock plunged to the 30 area, where it showed strong technical support. My friend, disgusted with himself for riding a quick profit down to a substantial loss, finally sold out at 30, which turned out to be near the bottom. When I asked him why he had sold out at that point, he replied: "I'm so disgusted with that stock I don't want anything further to do with it!" A perfect example of what Freud described as "voluntary sacrifices" that "serve the impulses of spite or self-punishment."

My friend, however, has plenty of company—and some of it surprisingly distinguished, as we have seen in the case of Occidental Petroleum, when the experts recommended Occidental even as it slid downward. What can be done? At what point should one cut his losses? Assuming that one has bought at a sensible level and has used the half-and-half tactic described earlier, a reasonable loss would be 10 percent of the average purchase price. But this is not a hard-and-fast rule. Sometimes technical considerations warrant marginally increasing or reducing this percentage.

The point is that when a stock is purchased a selling strategy should be devised that takes into account the possibility that the stock may not work out. In this way losses may be limited.

By keeping the matter of losses in perspective, one gains flexibility in portfolio management. For example, if a portfolio consists of, say, five positions, each representing 20 percent of the total assets, then a 10-percent loss on a single position is only 2 percent of the total—surely a small enough price to pay for avoiding disaster and giving the other four positions a chance to work out.

Some stocks don't decline but they also don't work out as originally anticipated. This is almost as undesirable as an actual decline. As I suggested in the last chapter, a "time horizon" should be established before buying; if the purchase fails to work out within the period allotted, then obviously the assumptions for buying were wrong, and the stock should be sold, releasing funds for more active use. The *rate of gain* yardstick discussed in the last chapter is useful here.

Tax selling is another area in which losses can be minimized with more astute management. More investors delay tax loss sales as long as they can. They realize that selling a stock in which they have a loss gives them a tax advantage; at the same time, the cost of doing so is a blow to their egos. So they procrastinate, and in the process play into the hands of sophisticated investors each December. "Errors," said Freud, "are *compromise*-formations," and this is precisely what most investors fall into: they make the tax sale, but they wait until the last minute to do it— that is, as close as possible to December 31, all the while hoping that the stock will go up so they will not have to make the sale at all! The stock, of course, usually continues to go down because sophisticated investors, having excellent insight into the psychology of the situation, stand aside until the price becomes abnormally low.

By making tax sales early, one can avoid a deeper loss.

Sophisticated investors sell stocks whenever they think they should, without hesitation, even early in the year. They avoid tax selling in December—many avoid it even in November—because they know it will be indulged in by the unsophisticated. The later in the year one waits to make a tax sale, the greater one's loss is likely to be. Furthermore, by waiting too long, a seller penalizes himself twice over: the original loss is magnified and the reinvestment of the proceeds after December 31 is likely to cost considerably more as the combination of tax-sale-pressure relief and new-year-reinvestment demand bolsters prices—at least temporarily.

If there is any aspect of selling that is less understood than selling itself, it is *short* selling. It has been called immoral, antisocial and dangerously speculative; but in fact, when used as the tool it is, it is basically protective and conservative, a hedge against the vagaries of the market.

Short selling is a method aimed at making money when the market declines. Three parties are involved: short seller, buyer and lender. Essentially an investor sells a stock he doesn't own to an ordinary buyer (who doesn't even know he's buying "short" stock). Since a stock that is sold must be delivered to the buyer, the seller's broker arranges to borrow it, perhaps from another customer, perhaps from another broker.

The buyer of the stock pays the short seller's broker, who *credits* his account *but* hands the money over—temporarily—to the lender of the stock as collateral for the loan, with the lender having interest-free use of the money as a consideration. In addition, the short seller must deposit with his broker an amount of money equal to the value of the stock. When the short sale is "closed out"—that is, when the short seller "covers" his position—he buys the stock in the open market with the money deposited with his broker and delivers the replacement stock to the lender, who in turn pays back the collateral deposited. If the short seller has "bought in" the stock at a lower price than he sold it short for—the object of a short sale—then his profit is the difference; if he buys it at a higher price, the difference is his loss.

What distinguishes a short sale from the sale of an owned stock is the fact that the sale of an owned stock *completes* that circle of transactions and can be forgotten, while a short sale *begins* what in effect is a reverse cycle of transactions that must be followed through to completion. If one's original judgment proves wrong and the price of the stock goes up instead of down, the seller must cover the short position to limit losses; this risk exposure ordinarily should be confined to no more than 10 percent above the average selling price just as one would limit any other loss.

The short sale should be initiated exactly as the sale of an owned stock: ideally on strength, utilizing the half-and-half tactic. Short selling almost always should be done on strength, especially where high-fliers blowing off are concerned. It follows also that the considerations that pertain to selecting buying points for longs (purchases) apply as well to selecting buying points to cover short sales. Indeed, the considerations in shorting are the same as in buying and selling but in reverse order—that is, instead of looking to buy low and sell high one looks to sell high and buy low. To be able to sell short successfully, one must be as objective in finding reasons to sell as in finding reasons to buy; more important, one must be psychologically capable of going short in a relatively big way at major market tops when the crowd is caught up in the usual euphoria that characterizes tops.

This psychological capability is difficult to attain, for there probably are more popular misconceptions about short selling than about any other market activity. Selling short, for example, is supposed to be more dangerous than buying because theoretically a stock can go up to infinity but down only to zero. I can only say that no stock has ever risen to infinity, though a number have dropped to zero. Many people also think that a short sale must be terminated within a specific time. But this is not so; a short position can be maintained so long as the stock can be borrowed, and this seldom presents a problem—unless the stock begins to soar upward.

There are some real disadvantages to selling short as compared with buying long. All profits on short sales, no matter how long the position has been held, are taxed as short-term capital gains. The seller also pays any dividends that fall due on borrowed stock; and he receives no interest on any credit balance achieved by selling short.

Since the market invariably declines more rapidly than it advances (it advances almost three-fourths of the time and declines the other fourth at a more rapid rate), one can make a great deal of money quickly selling short. The principal purpose of short selling, however, is to protect the predominantly long portion of a portfolio as well as to make money in an uneven market. By selling short, an investor can employ his money in a down market rather than stand aside with cash or take a chance on finding those rare long positions that may go up even in a major bear market. Finding such stocks is almost impossible, and even standing with cash is no bargain since the recent inflation rate has been running in excess of the 5 percent paid by most savings banks. Short selling, as part of a hedged investment posture, makes one an investor for all seasons, able to watch the market go down with no less equanimity than if it were rising to new highs.

Hedging, the holding of both long and short positions simultaneously, helps an investor control the risk factor in the market. The idea of hedging long has been recognized as sound business practice. A flour miller, for example, may sell wheat futures short to protect himself against inventory loss between the time the wheat is purchased and the flour is sold. Businessmen invariably adjust their inventory levels not only to the level of customer demand but also to reflect their estimates of future cost and availability. The consumer who buys a car before he really needs it because he anticipates higher prices in the future also is hedging.

In the market one can hedge in various degrees. These positions are called *fully hedged, net-long* and *net-short*. To be fully hedged is to be invested equally long and short. We saw in the last chapter that there are two broad categories of market risk: general-market risk, which involves all stocks as a group, and specific risk, which relates to the particular stock. By being fully hedged one theoretically eliminates general-market risk. That is, the investor who buys $50,000 worth of stocks is "risking his money in the stock market" as well as exposing himself to the specific risks of owning each stock. But another man with $50,000 who buys $25,000 in stocks and shorts $25,000 worth has not "risked" any money in the market as such (of course, the specific risks remain) because he is—theoretically— not subject to the ups and downs of the market as a whole.

For example, if an investor buys Rainbow Industries long at 50 and sells U.S. Garbage short at 50, in a fairly neutral market he may hope to sell Rainbow at 60 and close out Garbage at 40, for a net gain of 20 points. In a rising market he would hope to sell Rainbow at 80 and cover Garbage at 60, for a net gain of 20 points. And in a declining market he would hope to sell Rainbow at 45 and close out Garbage at 25, for a 20-point gain.

The possibility exists, of course, of the long stocks going down and the short stocks going up, and this can happen, as mistakes are inevitable; but assuming one's *selection* of stocks is above average, is diversified and is managed prudently, the fully hedged position theoretically eliminates the general-market risk factor.

An investor with reasonable judgment and experience, however, need not be fully hedged all the time but net-long when the market trend is up and a greater proportion of short, if not net-short, when the market trend is down.

Hedging (and diversification and moving with the

trends) often is combined with "leveraging"—operating "on margin" with money borrowed from banks and brokers. With leveraging, an investor can augment his original capital by as much as margin regulations allow—during noninflationary times usually an amount equal to his original capital. We can see how this works by comparing two theoretical $50,000 portfolios, call them Ordinary and Margin. The manager of Ordinary invests $40,000 in the best stocks he can select and puts the balance into safe bonds or keeps it in cash. The manager of Margin is more conservative; he buys $30,000 of the same stocks as Ordinary's manager bought, leaving him $20,000, and an additonal borrowed $50,000 to invest. This he divides into two equal parts. With $35,000 he buys more good stocks; with the other $35,000 he sells short those stocks he thinks are most likely to go down. His portfolio now consists of $65,000 in long positions, of which $35,000 is hedged.

If the market goes up 20 percent, assuming that the long stocks of Ordinary and Margin have been well selected, they will rise 30 percent, and Margin's short positions will rise only 10 percent. The balance sheet then will read:

ORDINARY	MARGIN
Gain on $40,000 long at 30 percent = $12,000	Gain on $65,000 long at 30 percent = $19,500
	Loss on $35,000 short at 10 percent = $ 3,500
Net Gain = $12,000	Net Gain = $16,000

If the market goes down 20 percent, again assuming good selection, the shorts will decline 30 percent and the longs will decline only 10 percent. The balance sheet then will look like this:

ORDINARY	MARGIN
Loss on $40,000 long at 10 percent = $4,000	Gain on $35,000 short at 30 percent = $10,500
	Loss on $65,000 long at 10 percent = $6,500
Net loss = $4,000	Net gain = $4,000

The hedged, leveraged portfolio is more profitable—by 33 percent in a rising market *despite* decreased risk; and reverses a loss into an equivalent profit in a declining market *because of* decreased risk.

Since all profits on short sales are taxed as short-term capital gains, it is advisable to keep a modest proportion of short positions in one's portfolio, even in a down market. Long-term capital gains in a major bear market sometimes may be earned by buying highest-quality, long-maturing bonds, which may increase in price after the first phase of a major down market in stocks. For example, from the end of 1929 until 1932, one could have made substantial capital gains in bonds while at the same time profiting handsomely from a net-short position in stocks. This observation may be particularly relevant, as 1969 ended with bonds at their lowest prices in more than 100 years.

Stocks and good bonds, however, are not necessarily inversely related, and one should strictly limit one's bond purchases unless the following conditions exist: One, bond prices are down and bond yields are unusually high. Two, bonds are being accumulated by sophisticated investors. Three, the leading economic indicators clearly point to a future downturn in business. Four, the Federal Reserve Board recognizes this downturn and acts to ease the money market by an action such as lowering the rediscount rate.

Under these conditions I would use 25 percent of my funds to purchase highest-grade bonds on margin—with the maximum margin available, provided, of course, that bond prices hadn't already moved up. But I would cut back accordingly in the absence of any of the essential conditions, for bonds should be no more than an adjunct to an investment program, attractive at such times as 1929–32, and—who knows?—perhaps again in the early 1970's in view of the fantastically soaring interest rates of 1969.

The best-known exponents of short selling as part of a hedged investment strategy are the managers of the proliferating hedge funds. "In the argot of the now generation, hedge funds are what is happening in Wall Street," says Peter Landau, the author of a perceptive study of the phenomenon. Hedge funds, he adds, are "the logical extension of the current cult of success."

Hedge funds originally were private pools of capital to which each member might bring $100,000 or more. Some hedge funds are now offered to mutual-fund buyers. But the most respected funds are still the private ones, which attract sophisticated, well-heeled investors. Some of these funds, in fact, won't touch anyone with less than a quarter of a million dollars.

The hedge funds leverage their assets to the hilt and trade freely and aggressively, both long and short. Their strategy of selling short in a falling market gives them an advantage over mutual funds, whose usual course under such circumstances is to increase their cash position, placing themselves in danger of being "redempted out." Finally, since they are private partnerships, hedge funds legally are not subject to the proliferating red tape of SEC regulations—a loophole the Commission has been trying to close.

The dean of hedge-fund managers is Alfred Winslow Jones, whose own fund, A. W. Jones and Company, has gained more than 1,000 percent in a recent ten-year period, even after deducting the standard 20 percent management fee. Jones, a former editor for *Fortune* magazine, was one of the first students of the market to see short selling as a speculative means that could be used for conservative ends. With his success the word got around and now there are estimated to be more than 300 private hedge funds with assets of perhaps $2 billion, many of the top ones managed by former Jones associates.

There are as many techniques for using shorting in the management of hedge funds as there are managers, but they all can be reduced to two basic approaches. The first is called *defensive shorting*. This technique acknowledges that even the best managers are sometimes wrong. Without it, Jones once said, "I would not have been able to sleep so well at night." A defensive short usually is of the same nature as the long stocks in the portfolio. For example, if a fund is long on a high-flier, it will short another high-flier, not a stock like AT&T. Or, a fund in blue chips long in a rising market would choose a solid but sluggish stock as a defensive short. U.S. Steel, whose price has eroded steadily over the past few years, is a good example of this kind of defensive short. It is not the kind of stock to snap back overnight and force a hurried cover. "You might not make as much money in a rising market," says one fund manager of defensive shorting, "but you don't get crushed when the market turns around."

The second technique is known as *aggressive shorting.* "An aggressive short," says Landau, "usually isn't related to anything in a fund's portfolio. It is a stock selected because the managers really feel they can make money in selling it short."

Most hedge-fund managers, whether they short defensively or aggressively—and they often do both at different times—wait until a prospective short stock begins to slide before selling it. They do not try to pinpoint precise turning points—though I believe this can and should be done. They also avoid ailing companies that may be ripe for a takeover, stocks that have a small float (they may not be available to cover the position quickly in an emergency), stocks that sell at low prices (minimal downside potential) and institutional favorites. Add to these precautions the need for tactical mobility. "We're either right," explains one fund manager, "or else we've got to cover and get the hell out. You can't let a short idea sit and mold. You can come back to it and find you've been crushed." This mobility accounts for the rapid turnover of most hedge-funds' short positions.

The supreme test of a hedge fund, of course, is how well it performs in a bad market. By this criterion most of the public funds were a failure in 1969, showing typical declines of from 20 to 30 percent. It is difficult to measure the performance of the private funds since they are not required to open their books to the public; but a few of the smaller private funds are reported to have declined even more severely—40 to 50 percent. These declines can be traced partially to the funds' failure to build up their short positions before the market collapsed. In addition, the public funds are hampered by the law that restricts their short positions to 25 percent of their portfolios. But, from observing the stocks that many hedge funds have sold short, and from actual experience in advising hedge funds, I am quite convinced that the principal reason for their failure in 1969 lies in their unrealistic selection of short-sale candidates. It is a rare hedge-fund manager I've talked to who isn't principally interested in shorting fad stocks that have run up to unrealistic levels, sometimes selling at 100 times earnings and more. On the face of it this sounds like an intelligent approach, but as we've learned earlier, what is logical does not necessarily follow in the market. Such vogue stocks invariably are thinly capitalized and for the very same reason that they run up to 100 times earnings they just as easily can run up substantially further. It is true that eventually such stocks collapse, but the hyped-up trading conditions in them together with a short squeeze cause them to act more "irregularly" than other, more widely capitalized, issues; consequently, they don't lend themselves to very precise technical measurement, and investors shorting them are usually left to guess at tops. More often than not these short sellers get squeezed (scared) out of their positions with huge losses.

Why they seek the highest-risk stocks of all to short is beyond my comprehension, especially when there are so many well-defined shorts, with large capitalizations, that truly serve the purpose of hedging. These include: cyclical stocks, when the cycle is about to reverse—Chrysler and Johns-Manville are good examples of this type; blue-chip glamour stocks whose movements are "regular," such as

Xerox (see Chapter Five); and vogue stocks, *when the fad is fading.*

The oils in 1969 were a classic example of the last type, and my own experience with them illustrates exactly how selling targets may be determined, in practice, both for selling *per se* and for the taking up of short positions.

In January 1968, Atlantic Richfield (AFI) announced it had drilled a successful oil well in the Prudhoe Bay area on Alaska's North Slope. The company announced a second discovery well a few months later. Then, in July 1968, it astounded the oil industry with a report that tests of the discovery area indicated that it held reserves of 5 to 10 billion barrels of oil. The North Slope thus represented the largest oil strike on United States territory since the discovery of the huge East Texas field in 1930.

Discovery of oil riches—especially in a faraway, exotic spot—is rarely lost upon the market. AFI almost tripled in price by the end of 1968, and after a 2-for-1 stock split, rose to near 130. It later "corrected" to the low 90's, then soared again to a new all-time high, this time near 140, by June 1969. The stocks of other companies with North Slope interests soared as well; but the whole group began to falter after mid-year, together with the rest of the market. Excitement was rekindled, however, when Alaska announced the sale of drilling rights on state-owned lands on the Arctic Slope. The sale was set for September 10, 1969.

Bullish stories had been headlined throughout the world during the preceding weeks. A $500-per-year computer-programmed advisory service had issued a "Special Study" in which it had enthusiastically recommended buying oil stocks. Many other services had followed suit. I myself had been asked to advise certain institutions holding large positions in Atlantic Richfield, Standard Oil of Ohio, Phillips Petroleum and a half-dozen other participants in the North Slope play on two particular questions: Should the stocks be held or sold? If they should be sold, should this be done *before* or *after* the winning bids were announced?

Remembering Occidental Petroleum, and after examining both the divergence-analysis patterns and technical measurements of these stocks, as well as giving consideration to the abnormally high PE multiples to which they had soared, I was forced to conclude that this appeared to be a classic example of sophisticated distribution taking place during a period of temporary strength engendered by all the hoopla. Below is the full report I prepared for institutions on Phillips Petroleum just five days before the bids were opened. Typical of the other studies I did on similar oil stocks during this period, it demonstrates how technical, psychological and fundamental considerations can be integrated into the formulation of sensible selling decisions.

PHILLIPS PETROLEUM *(P)—September 5, 1969 Close @ 33⅝*

HISTORIC POINT & FIGURE CHART: (See Chart No. 24)
Note how the recent rally to 36 stopped cold at the major overhead downtrend line projected through the series of declining tops from the December all-time high near 39. Also, note how the recent decline to almost 24 reversed at the base trendline projected through the 1962 and 1966 crash lows.

HISTORIC MONTHLY BASIS LINE CHART: (See Chart No. 25)
Note how the December and February double tops at 38+ met the major overhead trendline projected through the 1956 and 1961 highs. This suggests any renewed strength in *P* would likely have a maximum potential of 40, *i.e.*, marginal all-time highs. Major base support is indicated at the 23-24 area.

Following the stock split of 1956, made during a period of major topping action, the stock declined in two major waves over a period of more than a year. The stock split this year was announced during a period of major topping

CHART 24. HISTORIC POINT-AND-FIGURE CHART: PHILLIPS PETROLEUM COMPANY

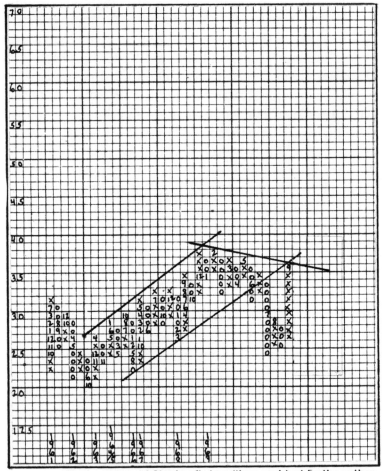

Chart courtesy of Chartcraft; trendlines and text by the author

action, also, and, as our psychological measurements below reveal, sophisticated distribution took place from mid-February to early June of this year, before *P* made its major break.

INTERMEDIATE-TERM DAILY-BASIS LINE CHART / *With Divergence-Analysis Curves:* (See Chart No. 26)

The major uptrend from the 1966 low of 22 terminated at the late 1968 high near 39. From January to May of this year the price-action etched a broad topping area from

CHART 25. HISTORIC MONTHLY-BASIS LINE CHART: PHILLIPS PETROLEUM COMPANY

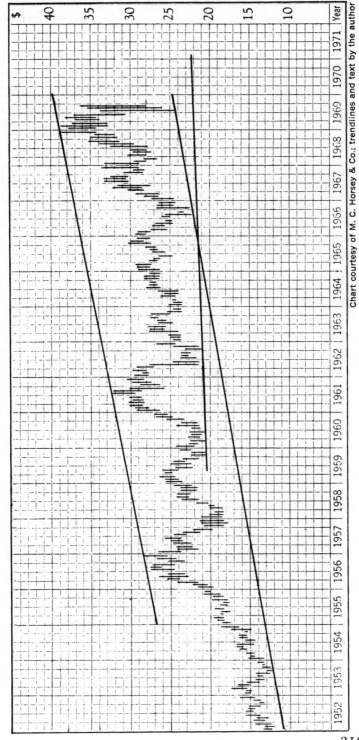

Chart courtesy of M. C. Horsey & Co.; trendlines and text by the author

215

which a major downside breakout took place in June, declining from a May high of almost 38 to a July low of almost 24. Since then, there has been a sharp recovery rally to last week's high of 36. This raises the question whether P is now at the beginning stages of a major upmove, or the recent sharp rise (50 percent in five weeks) is no more than a recovery rally of a technical nature. Our psychological measurements suggest the latter to be the case.

Our *ratio curve* shows quite clearly that the favorable pattern of predominantly sophisticated accumulation which had prevailed throughout most of 1967–68 decisively reversed to unfavorable by mid-February. (Note how the reversal took place exactly at the overhead trendline on the *historic chart.*) This provided an excellent selling signal throughout March–April–May, which was decisively confirmed by the mid-May to early-June drop of the *volume-confirmation curve.* During the recent rise from 24 to 36 both the ratio and volume-confirmation curves remain in low ground, providing us with evidence that this move can be characterized as no more than a recovery action, and *not* the beginning of a major upmove, *i.e.,* the buying quality has—on balance—been of unsophisticated character. Our conclusion as of this date, therefore, is that current strength should not be followed and should be used as a major selling opportunity.

On the initial move from the July bottom of 24.375, a "unit" of 4.875 points was formed. A 2⅓ unit contra-trend workoff yielded an upside target of 35¾, which was reached by last week's move to 36¼. A three-unit workoff yields 39, which would again bring it to the·major historic overhead trendline from where it turned down in February of this year.

Conclusion:

P should be sold on strength in the mid-to-upper 30's as the upside potential appears to be no more than 36 to 39, while the downside potential (which our work indicates more likely) appears to be 23 to 24.

CHART 26. INTERMEDIATE-TERM DAILY-BASIS LINE
CHART WITH DIVERGENCE ANALYSIS MEASUREMENTS
OF INVESTOR BEHAVIOR: PHILLIPS PETROLEUM
COMPANY

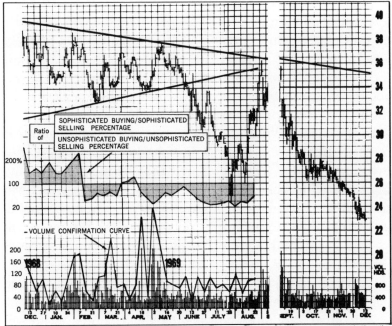

Chart courtesy of Trendline; trendlines, curves and text by the author

One fund manager holding a position of 100,000 shares
of Phillips called me the day before the bid openings and
we discussed Phillips at some length. The Phillips management had given him an impressive story (over and above
the North Slope play) of sharply increased expected earnings from 1970 forward, marking P as a turnaround situation. The fundamental data sounded impressive, and, of
course, there was the added "kicker" of the North Slope
play. Also, this manager is one of the most astute stock
selectors I know. Nevertheless, I strongly urged him to sell
while there was still time—*before* the announcements of
the winning bids. My reasons were essentially those in the
memorandum quoted above plus the psychological insight
that even if all the fundamental facts and conclusions were
100 percent correct, the stock still was a sale because the
price-action that already had taken place had discounted

217

the good news completely; indeed, once the news was out, the stock price was likely to "kamikaze."

This is precisely what happened. On September 10, Phillips traded as high as 35¾. The bids were opened after the market closed. On September 11, Phillips opened sharply lower, trading as low as 31½ that day—off 12 percent from the prior day's high. A few weeks later it sagged to 26, about 30 percent below the Arctic play-excited peak; before the end of the year it had declined below 23.

In the case of Phillips, divergence analysis and technical measurements were helpful, but the key was *insight* into investor behavior. The fact is, whether selling short or buying and selling, the individual with insight can outperform the performance-minded institutions. He has more mobility. A thin float, for example, does not affect him as much as it does the managers of many millions. The individual can reverse his field more easily at such times as the day in 1968 when Lyndon Johnson announced the bombing halt, turning a down market into an up one.

Of course, one must be psychologically prepared to sell short. This was one of the problems with some of the public hedge-fund managers; they were geared for the upside of the market and uncomfortable on the short side.

It has been said regarding the hedged concept that a person may become so preoccupied with selling short that he will miss buying opportunities. Jones shrugs off that suggestion. "Men who learn to sell short," he says, "seem to have better judgment on what stocks to buy."

1991 ADDENDUM

Since selling is the opposite of buying, all of the tools and yardsticks discussed earlier are also useful in coming to conclusions about when to sell. Obviously the time frame of your decision-making should be an important component of whether and when to sell. Nonetheless, all stocks should be purchased with the idea of selling at price parameters established prior to the purchase. Without such a "forecast" the concept of potential risk and reward too often gets lost. Moreover, *most* stocks reach a point where they get overvalued, often oscillating between "too" high or "too" low, as in the extreme example of Blockbuster. With this background in mind, let's examine the very actively traded stock of a great company, *Intel,* which in recent years has demonstrated a number of technically well-defined points at which to buy and sell, short-term and long-term.

Referring to the chart on page 218B, I observe that *INTC's* low in January 1982 was near 7. This suggested to me early in 1990 that the *outer limit* for some time might be near 49, since that *squared* the 1982 low. The first high earlier in 1990 was just below 49, whereas the final high was 52. Both of those highs were not too far above the trend projected through the 1983 and 1987 peaks, i.e., 49 was a potential triple top, in accordance with the Rule of Three.

I also note that each of the 1983 and 1987 peaks was characterized by a typical burst of investor over-enthusiasm as the stock was *split*. As mentioned on pp. 224-5, stock splits often, not always, are ending signs for a stock—all the good news is out!

Further, I observe that in 1987, 1988 and 1990 each of Intel's bear moves down closely approximated the cut-in-half rule. What about the possible outcomes on the way up from the 1990 low of 28 [INTC at 38 in early January 1991]? The 1990 high was 52; triple the 1987 low is 54; quintuple the 1986 low is 55; triple the 1988 low is 57; double the 1990 low is 56.

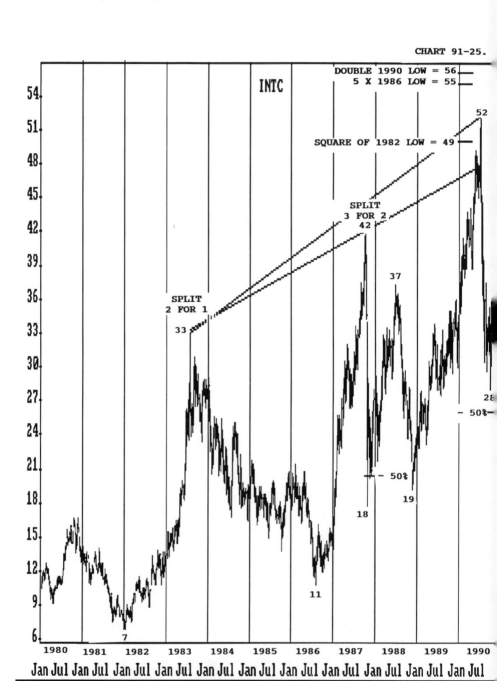

CHART 91-25.

INTEL WITH CUTS-IN-HALF AND MULTIPLES OF LOWS FROM 1980 TO 1990

218B

Additionally, unit measurement on a daily chart [not shown] counts to 47 for a 2-1/3 bull unit contratrend advance, 52-3/8 for three bull units and 60-1/2 for four of them. All of these yardsticks, then, suggest to me in early 1991 that—if I am right that INTC is an up stock—it will probably be an excellent sale within the 50-60 zone, in my opinion.

After a potential fall from that zone, Intel, being a great company, may ultimately go as high as 121, which squares the 1986 low, though the lower "magic" number of 100 may prove irresistible. And, naturally, whatever subsequent decision is to be made about Intel should also depend on one's market overview. Having said that, however, I must also point out that *semiconductor* stocks typically, but not always, lead the stock market on the way up. Hence, it has usually paid to be early vis-a-vis the stock market on the buy side of Intel, as I believe the chart illustrates.

This page intentionally left blank.

9 / Measuring Performance

The first measure of performance must be objective self-analysis. It is not enough to be told what to do; psychologists have shown that little is achieved by absorbing advice. What a person needs, said Jung, is "authentic knowledge" of his own "psychic inventory," for without it, "the underestimation of the psychological factor is likely to take a bitter revenge."

Self-knowledge is an important factor in investment success. The individual, said Jung, learns about himself only when he is willing to "fulfill the demands of rigorous self-examination. . . . If he follows through his intention, he will not only discover some important truths about himself, but will also have gained a psychological advantage." This is the advantage of the sophisticated investor.

Sophisticated investors, for example, know that investment mistakes are inevitable but can be limited; that success in the market comes not to the investor who makes the most killings but to the one who makes the least damaging mistakes.

Measuring Performance

Many investors are generally able but lack one or two key abilities that they may be able to acquire once they are aware of their need. After a series of consecutive performance evaluations, one's abilities and failures become more obvious. Some investors, however, may conclude that their circumstances or their temperament make future failures inevitable. Such a person would be wise to avoid "doing it himself" and either withdraw from the market or entrust his investments to a professional.

But one must understand the client-broker relationship. "There is an interaction between client and broker that can mean the difference between success and failure," say Albert Haas, Jr., and Don D. Jackson, M.D., in their book, *Bulls, Bears and Dr. Freud.* "The reason why an individual chooses a particular broker may contain elements beyond those usually thought of in normal business transactions."

For many years customers gave their brokerage business to the various member firms of the exchanges and demanded little in return. Since the advent of vastly increased institutional activity, however, large investors, both individual and institutional, have used the substantial commissions they generate as leverage to secure professional services from the brokerage houses. The larger the account, the greater the leverage for obtaining investment-management services without paying any fee beyond the brokerage commissions.

As we have seen, however, there are few good investment managers and relatively few enlightened brokers. Those very few who are the best charge high fees and won't handle small accounts. This puts the average investor looking for help in the position of a baseball manager looking for a .350 hitter. The man he wants is somewhere, but where? This book cannot help in the search, but hopefully it has provided some guidelines with which an investor may evaluate candidates. An investor who finds a capable professional should apprise him of his investment goals, then give him complete discretion. To do otherwise is to invite both practical and psychological problems. On the practical side, instant decisions often must be made, and a professional manager simply doesn't have the time to call a long list of clients before he acts. And, psychologically, the withholding of complete discretion creates the problems of split responsibility and second-guessing, which almost always lead to unsatisfactory performance and misunderstanding. Of course, the investor must measure the performance of the professional even more stringently than he would measure his own. And if the professional fails to deliver the goods—that is, make money—then the investor must go elsewhere. It doesn't matter how prestigious the bank, investment-management service or brokerage firm may be. "What's important," says one broker, "is, how good is the guy handling your account? How is his judgment, how is he under pressure? Does he have a feel for the market, a real rapport with the investment climate? Does he have an investment philosophy that he can articulate from time to time? If he isn't this kind of person all the fancy trappings won't do you much good."

Whether an investor measures his own performance or a professional's, the measurement must cover a specific and limited period of time and take into account the risk factor. For example, different stocks habitually rise and fall at different rates of speed, and hedging $1,000 worth of a stodgy issue against $1,000 worth of a fast mover would give no true value of risk. One must therefore estimate such things as the volatility of every holding.

The test of any measuring system is how much it contributes to the decision-making process. To make an effective contribution the measuring system must be incorporated into the decision-making process, otherwise it becomes simply an intellectual exercise. Ideally, the system periodically should measure not only the performance of every individual stock and that of the portfolio as a whole, including their respective annual rates of gain (or loss), it should also compare the returns with those of alternate investment possibilities.

The investment manager of a large insurance company suggests seven capabilities a measuring system should have:

1. A means of comparing companies in terms of risk-return relationships.
2. A means of compiling an overall risk measurement for a portfolio.
3. A means of testing the manager's own assumptions—that is, how much change in a particular factor's rating or weight would be needed to change his attitude toward a stock, an industry or the whole market?
4. A means of putting the manager on the line to weigh his comprehension of what the objectives of his particular portfolio are.
5. A means of isolating reasons for past mistakes by clearly pinpointing wrong assumptions.
6. A kind of early-warning system to determine in which areas research resources should be concentrated.
7. Consistent uniqueness to the investor's environment and outlook, so that the system does not become outdated or less effective because everyone else uses it.

This sophisticated system probably demands more time and effort than most individual investors can afford to give to it. So for individual investors I have devised a simpler technique to measure performance. This requires equipment no more sophisticated than a pencil and paper (even though an adding machine or calculator would reduce the time needed) and probably takes less time than an hour a week. The formula for calculating percentage gain and rate of gain, which I explained in Chapter Seven, is probably adequate for measuring individual holdings and the portfolio as a whole. This measure can be applied at any time, but the more significant deviations after making a purchase may not show up before several weeks have elapsed.

Assuming a hypothetical portfolio of four stocks, Oil,

Computer, Airline and Steel, with equal dollar amounts invested in each security, the record might look like this:

	OIL	COM-PUTER	AIR-LINE	STEEL	AVERAGE ENTIRE PORTFOLIO
Selling Price (or Current Market Price)	75	60	50	50	58.8
Cost	50	30	40	80	50
Gain in Points Absolute	25	30	10	−30	8.8
Percentage Gain or Loss	50	100	25	−37.5	17.6
No. of Days Held	180	90	365	30	166.2
Annual Rate of Gain Percentage*	101.4	405.5	25	−456.2	38.7

* As outlined in Chapter Seven, rate of gain is obtained by multiplying absolute percentage gain by 365 and dividing the total by the number of days the stock is owned. (Dividends and commissions, of course, are omitted from these calculations.)

Performing these calculations each week forces one to come to grips with reality. Not only does this system indicate the real performance of each stock, it also clearly shows those stocks that perform better or worse than the overall portfolio, and their impact upon the portfolio.

These calculations do not provide an absolute standard against which to measure comparative alternative investments. But this is not crucial since, as I noted in Chapter Seven, each invester should set his own goals based on his needs and philosophy, then determine whether or not he has met them. Anyone who wishes to measure his performance against a broad market average can use Standard & Poor's 500 Index. The S & P 500 Index is broadly representative of the total market and the data is readily available and is produced by a respected independent source. Since we assume equal dollar investments in each position, all we need do is compare equal dollar investments in the S & P average over the same period of time.

Of course, no method of continuous monitoring and measurement can ever make up for poor stock selections. But what it will do is force the investor to come to grips with those investments that haven't worked out, and if he eliminates those, he then can concentrate his money where the action is likely to be.

At this point it may be helpful to look more closely at a well-known but little understood market phenomenon, stock splits. Most investors see stock splits as favorable; but, measured in terms of subsequent price-action of the stocks, splits are not favorable—except to sophisticated investors who know their meaning. Under cover of the strength which has been generated by the enthusiasm of unsophisticated investors upon the announcement or implementation of a split, sophisticated investors—barring overriding reasons to the contrary—often use this as an opportunity to massively distribute the stock.

Splits are usually announced after the end of a long rise in price. The news of the split frequently adds a final climactic burst of strength to the stock, and after trading in the split stock begins, unsophisticated investors start buying it in droves. In effect, of course, they are buying at a topping area.

Stock splits not only change nothing (what they amount to is the changing of a $10 bill into two $5 bills) but in most cases they play on the emotions of unsophisticated investors, providing sophisticated investors with an opportunity to sell on strength. After the split, the price of the stock frequently goes down. Some typical examples: American Machine & Foundry split 2-for-1 at its peak near 64 in 1961 and subsequently declined to about 15; American Airlines split 2-for-1 in 1967 and fell from 50 to 24; IBM split 2-for-1 in 1968 and dropped from 380 to 290. And the trend continues. In 1969 Johns-Manville split 2-for-1 and fell from above 40 to near 30 within 90 days; Pitney-Bowes split 2-for-1 and declined from 40 to 30 within 60 days; Teledyne split 2-for-1 and dropped from 45 to below 30 between March and July, and so on. (All prices are adjusted for the split.)

Mutual funds sometimes split their shares, giving their owners a false sense of gain. How false the sense of gain is can be seen with the help of a little arithmetic. If a fund has assets of $300 million and there are 10 million shares outstanding, each share is worth $30. A 3-for-1 split in shares would create 30 million shares but would not increase the net assets of the fund, so each share would then be worth $10. An owner of 1 share at $30 then would own 3 shares at $10—no net change in value.

Split stock doesn't always decline; but, all other factors being equal, it generally attracts the poorest quality of buying and should be avoided. And an investor who holds a stock that has had a substantial rise and then shoots up further upon news of a split should think about selling.

Another delusion under which many investors labor is the presumed advantage of low-price stocks. Unsophisticated investors have an ingrained belief that they can "afford" to buy low-price stocks but cannot afford to buy high-price stocks. Any objective examination of this notion must clearly show that: One, the price of the stock *per se* makes absolutely no difference whatever with respect to what one can or cannot afford; and two, high-price stocks can be bought more advantageously than low-price stocks. This does not mean that a particular low-price stock may not be worthy of buying. After all IBM, Control Data and others once sold at only a few dollars per share. But on the whole, there is absolutely no question that the above two statements are thoroughly sound. With respect to whether or not one can afford to buy a particular stock, the only relevant factor is the amount of dollars one has available, the price of the stock itself being almost irrelevant. With respect to the advantages of high-price over low-price stocks, as we noted in Chapter Five, commissions on high-price stocks are substantially lower than on low-price stocks.

Low-price situations with long odds and a big payoff occasionally arise—usually when a company unveils a revolutionary process or product. If, after considered judgment, an investor wants to *gamble* a small portion of his total funds and has sufficient profits available with which to offset a possible loss, he might put perhaps 5 or as much as 10 percent of his total investment capital into such a situation, with the idea of holding it for a long period of time. Sometimes, even when these situations don't work out, speculative enthusiasm moves the stock price up sharply, perhaps for only a brief period. If such a stock doubles from its original cost, then a sensible tactic is to sell half, recovering the entire investment, and keep the balance for a free ride.

I noted earlier that any measure of performance must take into account the risk factor. We have seen how to evaluate risk in Chapter Seven. One risk, however, which is not even seen as a risk and which, therefore, is usually overlooked, is the ordinary summer vacation. For most investors, this may be the biggest risk of all, made more hazardous because it is overlooked.

It is no accident that major market changes often occur during the summer months, when most Americans vacation. Stock prices often peak in July or August, then turn downward, reaching the nadir in October. One reason, I believe, is that sophisticated investors, who never neglect their investments, take advantage of unsophisticated investors, who are on vacation and out of touch with their brokers.

Bernard Baruch called investing "continuous work." Market trends tend to continue, but they break eventually, and one must be on top of the situation to take advantage of it. A buy or a short sale, no matter how astutely conceived, is of little value unless it is followed up continuously until the position is closed out. One sometimes must sell an issue the same day one buys it. The decision depends upon the market conditions as they unfold daily. As Goethe once said: "The right man is the one who seizes the moment." Failure to follow one's investments continuously is analogous to leaving one's money in a public place for safekeeping and hoping it will still be there when one returns.

What, then, does an investor do at vacation time? There are two alternatives. He can leave his investments in the care of a professional with specific instructions or with the leeway to act as he sees fit. Or he can liquidate his holdings altogether and take a real vacation from the market. I recommend the latter.

There is much to be said for taking periodic vacations from the stock market. First, as I pointed out earlier, in investing, a few quality decisions are better than a lot of mediocre ones. Since making decisions all year must inevitably lead to deterioration of one's judgment, a vacation should produce fewer but better decisions. Second, since everyone needs a vacation, why not make it a real one, without market worries? Third, there comes a time in the market, as it approaches a major-topping, high-risk area, when it is especially difficult to make money, even with hedging. One must beat the averages just to say even, and what is the point of that? Much better to liquidate and get away from it all for a while.

Barton M. Biggs, a successful hedge-fund manager, noted recently that new hedge funds often perform better in their first year than in following years. "The money manager or investor who starts a year with nothing but cash and builds a fresh portfolio from scratch," he explained, "has a significant advantage over the manager who goes into the year fully invested. When you begin with cash, it makes you focus on opportunity, and you buy the ten or twenty most attractive stocks you can find at the time."

Every investor can give reasons for keeping stagnant stocks: tax considerations, past performance, a new product that will come through any day now, prescience that the market has not yet caught up with them and so on. The real reasons, of course, lie in a reluctance to admit error and in the fact that it is easier to do nothing than to sell. As Biggs pointed out, however, "it is the 'holds' that are too cheap to sell but not attractive enough to buy that clog and clutter up your portfolio and retard your performance." Periodic liquidation is one way to get rid of such deadwood.

With savings banks paying 5 percent, and inflation running at 5 percent, what is a reasonable stock market investment goal? I believe anything less than 10 percent would be self-defeating; but even 10 percent is not enough because of the element of risk. Adding another 5 percent for risk makes the total 15 percent, which is a realistic goal for any institution (other than those, like pension funds, which have a special fiduciary obligation).

The individual, however, with his greater mobility, can aim a little higher. For a fairly active and moderately sophisticated investor who starts out with a modest nestegg—say, $25,000—and who can manage to be mostly right most of the time, a gain of 20 percent annually is not an unreasonable goal. Compounded annually, this equals $1 million in twenty years. An investor who implements this concept can look forward to a more-than-comfortable retirement.

Of course, even moderate success in the market may exact too high a price. Each investor must decide how much stress he can tolerate. My friend, former Ambassador to the United States Burudi Nabwera of Kenya, put this problem into perspective so well when he told me not long ago that he wished me never to have so little money that I couldn't enjoy a comfortable life, but that he would not want me to have so much money that the weight of it became a burden.

10 / The Age of Aquarius: Bull or Bear?

October. This is one of the
peculiarly dangerous months
to speculate in stocks. The
others are July, January,
September, April, November,
May, March, June, December,
August and February.

—MARK TWAIN

Speculation on the future is as old as man. Jacob, in buying
the birthright from Esau, was a "bull" and Esau a "bear."
The Greek philosopher Thales, famous for his speculations
on the nature of matter, also speculated on olive presses,
buying them all one year on the prospect of a bountiful
olive harvest, then selling them to the growers at a fat
profit when the crop ripened. But it remained for the seven-
teenth-century Dutch traders to establish the first active
stock market.

Their most curious market, however, was not in shares
but in tulip bulbs. Bulbs became a form of currency, like
American cigarettes in postwar Germany. "Businessmen
would obtain loans on their property," notes Robert Sobel
in his excellent book, *The Big Board*,* "in order to purchase
a handful of very ordinary bulbs, whose only value lay in
the fact that within a fortnight someone else would be willing to pay a higher price for them." In 1635 the most desirable varieties of bulbs sold for 2,500 florins on the

* Macmillan Company, New York, 1968.

Amsterdam exchange, ten times more than the price of a yoke of oxen and thirty times more than a suit of clothes. Then, in November of that year, a visiting sailor picked up a bulb in the Amsterdam exchange and, thinking it was an onion, casually ate it. Everyone suddenly saw the ludicrousness of the bulb market and within a week tulip bulbs were almost worthless. Sophisticated investors, having sensed that the bulbs were overpriced, had sold short, so they reaped fortunes at the expense of the amateurs, who, as usual, had bought in near the top. Who knows? Perhaps the visiting sailor was in the pay of the short sellers.

In the New World, auction markets were established both in Philadelphia, the banking center of colonial America, and New York, where the speculative action was. In March 1792 a group of auctioneer-brokers established a regular meeting place "for the accommodation of the dealers in Stock" in a small room at 22 Wall Street. Thus was born the New York Stock Exchange, the nation's largest securities market.

The NYSE in its present form is like nothing so much as a private club in which its members—after paying a small fortune for a seat—may trade without paying commissions. Since 1931 the number of regular memberships has been held to 1,366. Of these, some 650 are held in the names of partners or stockholders of member-firm brokerage houses; the rest are held by individuals. About 100 of these are "two-dollar brokers," people who handle transactions for brokerage houses whose own floor brokers are too busy. Another 120 handle odd-lot transactions; about twenty trade primarily for themselves; and perhaps 350 are specialists. A specialist, according to the Exchange's rules, has two functions: "He must effectively execute orders which are entrusted to him by other members of the Exchange. He must maintain, insofar as reasonably practicable, fair and orderly markets on the Exchange in the stocks which he services by dealing for his own account."

In maintaining a "fair and orderly" market, a specialist must be prepared to buy or sell for his own account when there are no public buyers or sellers. This function of "making the market," a vague responsibility and one for which it is difficult to appraise performance, became a center of controversy on the Street in 1969. The hub of the controversy is the specialist's role in block trading. Buying a few hundred or even a few thousand shares of a stock is one matter; absorbing blocks of 50,000 or 150,000 is another. Many specialists refuse to do it. "The specialist accepts the fact that he is a fiduciary," complains one block trader. "If he will not commit as much or more than I do—when he's got that greater leverage—then he shouldn't be a specialist."

But the specialists insist that their job is to protect the public, not their fellow professionals. "It is not our function to provide the institution with total liquidity," says one of the most respected specialists of the NYSE. "A guy who has to sell . . . shares to meet his mortgage payment has to be able to sell very close to the market. But if a guy owns half a company, it's not our job to buy it from him."

Amex chairman Frank C. Graham believes that portfolio managers must bear part of the responsibility for moving large blocks—especially of thin issues. "It takes them a long time to get into a thin stock," he says, "so why should they expect to get out overnight?"

Can the specialist system of making the market survive such strain? It is already evident that those specialists who do not have the skill, courage or capital to trade blocks are going the way of the dinosaur. But the problem goes deeper than the measure of the abilities of the specialists. At its heart is the increasing influence upon the market of the institutions and the commissions their activity generates on the NYSE. Enterprising non-member brokers, realizing that the fixed commission structure of the NYSE provides an umbrella under which they can offer NYSE stocks to institutions on more favorable terms, have created a "third market," where NYSE listed stocks are traded over-the-counter. This growing third market is in effect a stock exchange, but it operates in a gray area unregulated by the SEC.

Certain member firms of the NYSE and of the Amex, (all of whom by the rules of their exchanges are required to conduct all transactions in listed stocks on the Exchange floor), have entered the struggle for the big blocks by assuming major positions in certain issues for later resale; these brokers, referred to as "positioning" firms, must commit huge sums of capital to such operations.

These positioning firms both compete with and perform the function of the specialists. The result is that today the specialist and the block house together make the markets in all the institutionally favored stocks. "We are all specialists now," says the floor partner of a major positioning firm. "There are only nine or ten of us, but I'll bet one of us participates in every major print on the tape."

This joining of interests may partly relieve the crisis of the specialist system, but it is unlikely to provide a permanent answer, for a "fourth market" already has developed where institutions trade directly with one another through private computer systems. The systems differ in details of operation, but each seeks to help institutions find a ready trade through time-shared computers. Describing two of the principal systems, Instinet and Autex, one observer said recently they both "have the potential to make the central auction-market concept obsolete." But only through a central auction market, where transactions are reported instantly, can the individual investor know the true value of securities. The SEC, prodded by the NYSE, recently moved to assert its jurisdiction over the fourth market.

The exchanges have been struggling with other internal difficulties for the past several years. Rising volume and backed-up paperwork have raised the specter of brokerage houses failing—perhaps in a chain reaction. Even now an estimated $100 million a year is being laid out by brokerage houses to compensate for errors in orders.

Not only the operations but the very structure of the industry is changing. The NYSE in September 1969 amended its constitution to allow its members to go public. The idea, of course, is to raise money to finance both larger volume and necessary operational changes. But the ramifications of the Exchange's move go far beyond the raising of capital. They have the potential to alter radically many of the traditional relationships in the industry.

How these changes will affect the individual investor remains to be seen; but whatever happens, he certainly will have to bring to bear upon the market's activities increasingly scientific measurements. Divergence analysis, as I hope I have shown, is a step in that direction. Another effort directed to that end is the work of the University of Chicago's Center for Research in Security Prices (CRISP).

Since 1960 CRISP has been studying the investment decision-making processes and evaluating the historical record of investments in common stocks. The director, James Lorie, sees the Center's work as part of a trend toward more scientific analysis of investments. "Looking at the trade journals and the business school textbooks," he says, "you find a general movement toward rigorous empirical work, coherently related to some underlying theory, and carried out with modern statistical knowledge."

The Center's research is designed to answer three basic questions: How are securities valued? How does the market function? How should portfolio managers select securities? Its first study showed that if an investor had picked a purchase date at random between January 1926 and December 1960, and if he had picked at random any later sales date within the same period, the median return, assuming reinvestment of all dividends and payment of brokerage commissions on purchase and sale, would have been 9.8 percent per annum compounded annually.

Such lumped statistical analysis of stock prices, however, has its limitations in terms of practical application for the individual investor. It would have been very interesting, for example, if CRISP had taken 1,000 actual Investors and measured how they had done. We might well have discovered that, as the old Wall Street axiom says, 90 percent of the people lost money every year. A statistic indicating that the market makes almost 10 percent a year might be very misleading.

Some of the experts have seized upon this study as a portent of what the future may be expected to hold, especially in view of the fact that the 9.8 percent return was achieved despite the inclusion of the period of the Great Depression and that without that disastrous decade the return averaged 11 to 12 percent. "Perhaps," says John M. Hartwell of J. M. Hartwell & Company, "the bad old days will return . . . but it has not been a fruitful premise for investing to assume that the 1928–37 decade experience will return and I doubt that it is a useful premise today."

Such an assumption, however, carries very real risks. In the 1920's, for example, the apparent stability of the economy and the booming market created a euphoric consensus outlook on the future. Only a few dissenters envisioned the collapse of the 1930's. Today once again, the consensus envisages sustained prosperity after perhaps a brief pause. "This raises the question," Henry Kaufman of Salomon Brothers & Hutzler noted recently, "of whether the long-term forecaster is again trapped by the immediate environmental forces."

The experts tell us that the Great Depression cannot happen again. We were safe, they insisted at the end of 1968, from a recurrence of even the 1966 crash, when the DJIA plunged 265 points. Yet 1969 can hardly be called a picnic. Eliminating part of the spectrum from future possibilities fails the test of history. As Aldous Huxley said: "The horror no less than the charm of real life consists precisely in the recurrent actualization of the inconceivable."

The fact is that not only 1966 but *1929* could happen again. They were both financial panics, and the recent monetary and market situations are the tinder that since 1792 has fueled American financial panics; it needs only a psychological spark to set it off. The outward manifestations of a new panic probably would be different from those of 1929—that is, we would not have mass unemployment, bread lines and apple vendors—but the same despair would ripple throughout the nation.

Panic has been called an irrational wave of emotion and apprehension superinduced upon a crisis that is real. A study of the dozen or so Wall Street panics in our history shows that they usually occur during periods of heavy speculation spurred by great optimism. Most panics have been set up by loose banking and market practices, illiquidity and tight money. Most banking and market practices are now regulated, so these two factors no longer are significant; but illiquidity and tight money still are very much in evidence. Anyway, says Barton M. Biggs, "a weak financial structure never was the cause of panics; rather, it merely made them possible. People, speculation, the desire to get something for nothing create panics, and there is still a full quotient of those elements."

The 1929 crash, in which prices on the NYSE declined almost 90 percent, left the nation with mass unemployment for a decade. With the safeguards of the New Economics, this double disaster is unlikely to recur. But suppose, in a new panic, stock prices declined one-third from their 1966 all-time high (to DJIA 667) or one-half (to DJIA 500), and certain individual stocks dropped 90 percent or more; who is to say that the hardship would not be as great for the individual investor?

It could happen. All it would take is a further loss of confidence in our business and financial institutions and in our political leadership. With money tight, inflation intolerable and the dollar under pressure, the stage is set. As John Kenneth Galbraith said recently: "What is necessary for a new disaster is only for memories of the last one to fade, and no one knows how long that takes."

It is impossible to predict what might trigger a new panic, but the Trojan Horse that could do it stands even now in the middle of Wall Street: the mutual fund.

The funds' first serious scandal, overindulgence in letter stocks, was described in Chapter Two. The next blow could strike those funds—and there are plenty of them—holding thinly capitalized issues that they quietly accumulated over a period of time—the funds themselves pushing up the prices and absorbing most of the float—but which they now cannot dispose of except at a huge discount. In the summer of 1969 one fund with about $1 billion in assets held many issues with markets so thin that it could not even get quotes on them, let alone sell them!

We have seen how poorly the funds performed in 1969. This has not helped fund sales, and it has increased even more the ratio of redemptions to assets under management, which has been rising for some years. And the worst may be yet to come. "We haven't seen anything yet," one observer said recently. "The industry that rarely has a cash reserve of more than 7 percent is going to be caught short. Fund managers are going to get a crisp note from the head-man: 'Raise your cash reserves by 10 percent effective immediately. No exceptions.'"

But how will the fund managers raise the cash? Who will buy the letter stocks, the thin issues, the nursing homes, the short-order franchisers? There won't be any block buyers for many of such issues, so the funds would have to dump issues that are liquid—the Xeroxes, Polaroids, AT&Ts and IBMs—leading to a full-scale break in confidence. Should that happen, we may see a fund-redemption holiday similar to the bank holiday Franklin Roosevelt declared in 1933. Indeed, one banking authority asserted that "it is quite possible that enough damage has already been done to ignite a financial panic of some magnitude. Increasingly, there are rumors and stories of borrowers pleading with lenders for funds while at the same time bank liquidity has already sunk to hazardous levels, levels which are worse than in 1966 and 1929."

Panic, of course, represents opportunity to the sophisticated investor; in fact, the greater the panic, the greater the opportunity. Merely standing aside with cash would enable one to pick up bargains at the bottom. With a well-conceived short posture in stocks and a long posture in bonds as part of one's portfolio, the profit could be enormous. So the direction the market takes is not that important to the investor; what is important is that he be prepared for it to go in either direction, then act accordingly.

In short, one cannot accept blindly the experts' assumptions regarding the future. Hartwell himself, for example, after assuming a 9-percent or better return on stocks, notes that this assumption will incite investors, especially institutional investors, to aim for this return, and that "the effort to achieve this objective will necessarily funnel substantial funds from bonds and mortgages and other fixed investments into common stocks, and in the process change the historical pricing of all investments."

This will further depress a bond market already severely strained by the pressures of inflation. And with the rising influx of institutional funds into the stock market at the expense of investment in bonds, the question arises of who will finance the expanding volume of debt instruments.

Henry Kaufman recently predicted:

If these financial trends are extrapolated into the future, it is hard to see how rapid economic growth could be financed and therefore achieved. Real demand for goods and services will be increasingly distorted by inflationary considerations. In the financial markets, the flight from currency will accelerate as investors switch from bonds to stocks, and from institutional savings and investments to inflation hedges, making it increasingly difficult to finance socially desirable programs and other demands contributing to economic growth.

237

Sidney Homer, another partner of Salomon Brothers & Hutzler, pointed out recently that our economy over the past ten years has been financed 97 percent by debt instruments and only 3 percent by the net sale of equities, and that a drying up of these sources of long-term credit must impair economic growth. "Large corporations can finance with equities," Homer explained, "but home owners cannot, nor can governments, nor many small businesses."

It is generally agreed that inflation has been the chief cause in the sharp increase in American bond yields (which, of course, has caused the decline in bond prices) since 1965. A look at the historical record shows just four periods of exceptionally high bond yields: 1813 to 1818, 1860 to 1865, 1917 to 1922 and 1965 to 1970 at least. Each period coincided with war-bred inflation and lasted approximately *five* years. Whether or not the current period will end in 1970 remains to be seen. We now have in America not only inflation but, more dangerous, an inflationary psychology. Inflation is expected, so we buy more, save less; avoid bonds and savings accounts; demand higher wages, higher prices for our products and higher rents. We also demand a higher rate of return on our investments—one reason why in recent years blue chips have been ignored in favor of growth stocks, distorting the market. "If inflationary trends and inflationary expectations are sustained over the next few years," Homer predicted recently, "these market distortions will grow and spread, thus forcing basic and unfavorable changes in the structure of our capital markets and of our economy."

The assumption, then, that the market will continue to yield high returns is an obstacle to its realization, especially in an inflationary economy. And inflation may well continue, for, as Pierre Rinfret points out, the United States economy is not business but *politically* oriented. In discussing tight money, a deflationary measure that can lead to increased unemployment, Rinfret says: "The politicians will opt for inflation over employment any day in the week." He predicts an annual rate of inflation of 3.5 percent, a rate that in five years will make the current dollar worth only 80¢.

An examination of the last major inflationary period, however, 1957 to 1959, suggests that inflation can be brought under control and that, indeed, 1970 may be the year of decision in this regard. Since 1951, when the era of pegged bond prices ended, the average yields of long-term Treasury bonds have increased a total of about 400 basis points. William B. Hummer, a partner of Wayne, Hummer & Company, recently pointed out that almost three-fifths of this gross rise occurred in two inflationary periods, 1957 to 1959 and 1966 to 1969. In the early 1950's and 1960's consumer prices remained relatively stable, rising at annual rates of only 1.04 and 1.36 percent, respectively. But during the inflationary periods consumer prices rose at an average annual rate of more than 3.5 percent. "Over-expansionary federal government fiscal and monetary policies during much of both three year periods," Hummer believes, "were the ultimate source of mounting inflationary pressures and resultant accelerated increases in bond yields." These policies were reversed in 1959, producing a budget surplus of $240 million in fiscal 1960 (a shift of $13.1 billion from the previous deficit of $12.9 billion) and the mini-recession of 1960. Under the Nixon Administration, restrictive fiscal and monetary policies once again have been instituted, and if they are adhered to, the economic situation of 1970 may resemble that of 1960.

If this happens, we can expect a recession in 1970 similar to—perhaps far more severe than—that of 1960. The signs in 1969 already were strong that the credit crunch was braking the economy: business activity had slowed, and the consumer was feeling the pinch of high prices and high taxes. "In any other year," one observer of the market noted, "a slowdown in business would probably have been bearish. But this year the circumstances are

239

different. The stock market could label a mini-recession as bullish. That's because the sooner we get the pause in economic expansion, the quicker we will see a relaxation of the cruel crunch, and a trend toward somewhat lower interest rates." But this assumption suggesting all will be rosy after a brief pause is a bit too convenient.

The hard question is, can the Administration bring inflation under control without precipitating a financial disaster? The authorities are trying to let the air out of the balloon slowly, an exercise never before tried. The attempt in 1966 to bring inflation under control was abandoned as soon as it appeared to be working because the economy then was on the brink of a debacle. The monetary bailout operation of 1966–67 that followed probably encouraged even more speculative excesses than were present in 1966. As 1969 ended, the alternatives were to continue the attempt to deflate without serious pain—an accomplishment never achieved before throughout modern history—or to reflate, blowing up the balloon once again.

Most economic prognosticators assume that the credit crunch will ease. They predict that the next ten years will fulfill itself as the "Spectacular 70's." With more people, a larger work force, more jobs and more buying power and a GNP of nearly $2 *trillion* ($2,000,000,000,000), "the projected image," said the editors of *U.S. News & World Report* in a recent report, "is that of a land in which the affluent society of the present day is to become more affluent than ever, as . . . more of the nation's potentials are fused into the biggest boom yet."

"As in the past," the report noted, "the chief factor in the increased economic potential will be a rise in productivity. . . . Better education, additions to capital stock by industry, improved public facilities and more efficient management have been the main ingredients in the formula for ever-higher productivity. In all of these areas, the trends continue to be upward."

Of course, we saw in Chapter Three how reliable are economists' forecasts, and how economists tend to overlook basic sociological factors that deeply affect our society. So we should not be too surprised if the economy fails to live up to their expectations. Almost all of their prognostications are based upon the dubious assumption that the Vietnam War will be closed out by mid-1970, and few of them even mention the volatile racial crisis, which shows every sign of heating up further under the Nixon Administration. Indeed, Wilbur Cohen, former Secretary of HEW, sees the next ten years as the "Scary 70's," and Sterling E. Soderlind, writing in the *Wall Street Journal,* sees them as the "Vexing 70's," the vexation arising from "accelerating aspirations" that cannot be met even with a trillion-dollar economy. We have put men on the moon and are now planning to put men on Mars; meanwhile, poverty and prejudice are threatening to tear apart our society, if pollution doesn't poison it first; and on a global scale, overpopulation and famine loom on the horizon. The fact that we have committed ourselves to space exploration rather than to the pressing social problems at home points out the failure of our political leaders to set realistic national priorities.

Despite these ominous signs, most market projections are bullish for the long-term—that is, to the end of the 1970's. Some of these projections are based on fundamental considerations, others on technical references. One reason advanced for rising stock prices is an anticipated shortage of stock in the face of increased institutional demand for it. Another is the speculation on technology, which one observer predicts could propel "a takeoff from the highest stage of development so far witnessed in the economies of the world." In the past I have tried my own hand at long-term hypothesizing, and it might be useful now, in estimating longer-term-stock price swings in the 1970's, to examine these hypotheses within the context of the bull market that began in 1949.

The Age of Aquarius: Bull or Bear?

In Chapter Six we saw how decade patterns might be helpful in evaluating overall market timing. Now we shall see how we were able to formulate some hypotheses that have been useful as a framework in which to estimate terminal points of major market tops and bottoms over the long term. These hypotheses are based partly upon decade patterns, partly upon observations of mass behavior and partly upon technical and fundamental considerations. All chart references are to Chart No. 27, which illustrates the grand expanding triangle of the bull market advance from 1949 to 1970.

To illustrate the application of these hypotheses to actual market conditions, I have excerpted liberally from an article I wrote for the March 17, 1969, *Barron's*. In the article, titled "Nineteen Sixty-Six and All That," I projected a major and precipitous decline in 1969 similar to that of 1966. The excerpts follow:

We hypothesized more than 18 months ago (August 1967) the likelihood of the stock market (as measured by the DJIA) declining some 300 points to slightly below the DJIA 700 area. . . . The theoretical basis of this hypothesis may be found in the price-action of the DJIA itself. This has been in the form of a grand expanding triangle that has contained the entire bull market advance which began in 1949 (see Chart). The key reference points [are] "A" and "A-1," "B" and "B-1," [and] "C" and "C-1," with "C-1" being the hypothesized downside target which may be realized . . . in the DJIA 700 area. One can readily observe that every time the price-action touched the grand overhead trendline, it subsequently (within a few years) declined to the grand bottom trendline before resuming a major advance movement. In other words, all further advance attempts proved to be abortive until there was, first, a subsequent decline to the grand bottom trendline.

It was this observation that suggested . . . that the intermediate advance movements of 1967 and 1968 were likely to be abortive. They were. It may be asked why we should seriously consider the possibility of such an enormous decline, based on what may be construed essentially as a mere technical projection. The reason may lie in the very nature of stock market activity itself, namely, that in order for the dominant

CHART 27. GRAND EXPANDING TRIANGLE OF THE BULL MARKET ADVANCE FROM 1949 TO 1970

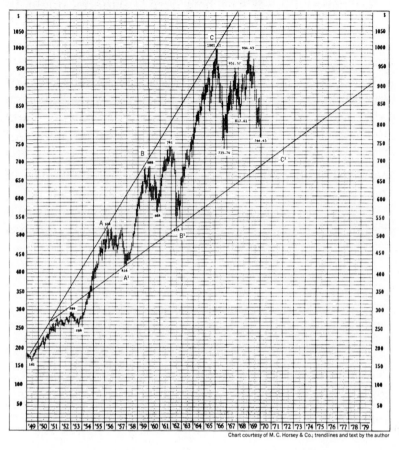

Chart courtesy of M. C. Horsey & Co.; trendlines and text by the author

leadership group of sophisticated investors to drive stock prices up, there must first be created a condition of panic and fear among the larger group of unsophisticated investors to the point where stocks are dumped promiscuously. Then, at crash lows, sophisticated investors have a chance to accumulate sufficiently massive amounts of stock to make the game worthwhile.

In any serious effort to forecast stock prices, the conceptualization of the results of one's work should be one of the primary outputs of it. Furthermore, the form of this conceptualization should be useful to intelligent investors who seek insight into investor behavior—their own and that of others. Even though it is rare that the hypothesis is realized in full, nonetheless it

243

may prove a useful tool, inasmuch as it provides a standard against which relatively short-term market action may be gauged. When the market conforms to the hypothesis with reasonable constancy, it provides useful guides from which to project future price-action.

Based on the theory outlined above . . . we were able (January 13, 1969), in a private advisory service publication, to further hypothesize more specific details of a projected decline in 1969. It should be specifically noted, however, that each stage of the projection is subject to verification based on measurements of investor psychology such as prevail at those times. Since the stock market's action since our January 13 projection has conformed almost precisely to the hypothesis, with a complete first-step decline and subsequent recovery movement —and with the second-step decline now under way—it will be useful at this point to continue and update the projection. . . .

The overall 1966 decline may provide some useful lessons for projecting the DJIA price-action for 1969. From December 1968's high of 994.65, the market declined 79 points to January 8's low at 915.53. This constitutes a complete first-step of the projected overall 1969 decline. The recovery from the first decline was then completed by the move to the February 14 high at 959.16, retracing 44 points, or 55 percent. (This is weaker than, but still approximates, the 1966 retracement of that first-step decline, which equaled 59 percent.)

Using the 1966 second-step decline as a yardstick, we can project the present decline movement (constituting 1969's second-step) to terminate at about DJIA 874.20, a drop of 84.96 points from the February 14, 1969, high at 959.16. This uses the same percentage as the 1966 second-step-to-first-step decline. One should not, of course, expect these projections to work out with mathematical precision; nonetheless, the 874 area does approximate the technically indicated area of major resistance—880. . . .

The four 1966 decline and recovery steps did not develop in a straight line but are part of broadened price formations etched by interim rallies and declines within each step. We believe this to be the present case. While shorter-term psychological measurements have turned more favorable (or less unfavorable) for the latest week, there is no change in their major trend. Hence we must assume that the present rally falls within the framework of an overall down movement. . . .

If the 1966 precedents are followed through the rest of this year, we may then anticipate the possibility, following the completion of the second-step decline, of a subsequent:

A. Second-step recovery rally of about 50 percent, back up to DJIA 916.54.

B. A third-step decline of 124.68 points (this longest drop being 147 percent of the second-step), yielding a downside target of DJIA 791.86.

C. A sharp third-step recovery rally of 52.36 points (42 percent) to DJIA 844.23.

D. A climactic fourth-step drop of 72.07 points to the DJIA 772.16, which would be the hypothesized terminal point of the overall four-step decline.

Whether or not the 1966 precedents will be followed remains to be seen; but the first phases of the 1969 decline have traced a strikingly similar pattern.

Indeed, the second decline step terminated at 895.39, a little more than 2 percent above my hypothesized 874.20; and the second-step recovery rally soared to 974.92, some 6 percent above my projected 916.54; while my third-step decline target of 791.86 was practically on the button, as the 187-point May-to-July decline terminated at 788.07. Then the fourth-step decline terminated in December at 764.45, within 1 percent of the projection. What was important, however, was not so much the precision of the exact high or low points of each step but whether or not the precipitous major decline occurred as anticipated. It did.

We can see, then, that long-term patterns of market activity can be useful in obtaining perspective regarding the possible general direction and reversal points of the market, even though the precise working out of these hypotheses will necessarily always be inexact. In formulating these hypotheses, certain observations concerning the action of the market from 1949 to 1970 appear relevant, if not completely explainable. For example, as we have seen, the bull-market advance that began at DJIA 160.6 in 1949 assumes the shape of a grand expanding triangle.

The Age of Aquarius: Bull or Bear?

The grand trendlines A—C and A1—C1 are the upper and lower limits of the advance. Within the framework of the twenty-year bull market as defined by the triangle, the stock market reached the upper grand trendline A–C on three occasions: 1956, 1959 and 1966. Each of the 1956 and 1959 grand highs were followed by grand lows. As a psychological precondition for the market now to make a grand upmove to the A–C grand upper trendline, it first may have to decline (for the third time) from the 1966 top to a bottom touching the grand bottom trendline A1–C1. This third whipsawing shakeout of unsophisticated investors at the bottom grand trendline may be necessary to induce sufficient unsophisticated investor pessimism that will provide the psychological basis for the market to make a major bull move into the 1970's.

A close study of the triangle reveals the following patterns:

1. The major advance from 416.15 that began at the grand bottom trendline in 1957 rose to a 741.30 high in 1961. The 325.15-point rise was retraced exactly two-thirds by the subsequent decline to 524.55 in 1962, also at the grand bottom trendline. The advance from the 1962 low rose 476.55 points to the February 1966 high of 1001.11. If the 1962-66 advance were corrected by two-thirds, this would imply a downside target of 683.72.

2. The 1957 low at 416.15 touching the grand bottom trendline was followed by the 524.55 grand low in 1962, which is 25 percent higher. A third grand low 25 percent higher up would call for a decline to the 650 area.

3. If we add five years and three months in time and a 78-percent advance to the 1960 bottom of 564.23, we get a February 1966 high of 1004.33, very close to the actual 1001.11 high. And, if we add five years and three months time and an 81-percent advance to the 1962 bottom of 524.55, we get a September 1967 high of 949.44, within 1 percent of the actual high of 951.57. History then repeated itself by following this high with another precipitous decline.

4. Another interesting pattern emerges in a comparison of recent five-year periods. The 1955 high of 489.94 was followed

by a 7-percent higher 1956 high of 524.37. In 1957 the market made another attempt to move upward to new highs, failed, then precipitously declined starting in midsummer.

Five years later a similar series of developments took place. In 1960 the market made a high of 688.21, followed in 1961 by an 8-percent higher high of 741.30. In 1962 the market made another attempt to move upward to new highs, failed, then precipitously declined in the spring-summer months. Five years *later* the same pattern emerged. In 1965 the market made a high of 944.82, followed in 1966 by a 6-percent higher high of 1001.11. In 1967 the market made another attempt to move upward to new highs—also in the summer months. This attempt was also abortive, as were those of 1962 and 1957, and was also followed by a precipitous decline to new lows.

5. The 1955 October low of 433.19 was followed by a 4-percent lower low two years later in 1957 at 416.15, also in October. The 1960 October low 564.23 was also followed two years later in 1962 by a 3-percent lower low, again in October. Although the 1966 October low of 735.74 was not followed by the same two-year pattern, this does suggest a later lower low near the 700 area. The fact that major lows were established in the month of October also is of more than passing interest.

In a second *Barron's* article (February 9, 1970) I extended the 1969 projection to the end of 1970:

It is now exactly four years since the Dow Jones Industrial Average made an all-time intra day high of 1,001.11. Ever since the bull market started in 1949, each major decline was followed by new all-time highs within a period of approximately one year, except for the last (1966) peak. Since time is an important element in investor psychology, this indicates that since February 1966 the entire advance movement since 1949 has been in a broad correctionary phase.

Whenever the stock market begins such a phase it usually consists of three definable moves. The first is a major decline, the second is a substantial recovery, and the last is a final decline which completes the total correction. Inasmuch as the precipitous 1962 decline was followed by a major three-year advance, it is not surprising that most investors assumed that the 1966 drop would be followed by another major bull move. However, whereas the advance from 1949 to 1966 was fueled by an environment characterized as one of growth and/or inflation, the current environment is the first time in two decades when a classic deflationary situation prevails.

Evidence that today's market weakness is different from those of prior periods, and that the ultimate low may be even lower than generally expected, can be found in many market indicators. For example, during the 1957, 1962 and 1966 declines, the advance-decline ratio bottomed at or above its 1953 low; in 1969, however, it made a decisive downside penetration. Indeed, within recent weeks, the DJIA has decisively penetrated a point-and-figure uptrend line which has contained the entire market advance of the past 40 years! . . .

Following a year-end rally into early January, the market has declined once again and is now approaching the originally envisaged DJIA 700 target area. Since our long-standing hypothesis has, so far, been realized, step-by-step, the question of obvious interest now is: Will the market in fact establish a major bottom at or near DJIA 700?

To answer this question meaningfully, one must explain why the past year's market weakness is different in character from all other major declines of the past 20 years. . . .

The broadest difference between present and past declines is that current fiscal and monetary actions are an attempt to correct the excesses not of a few years but of two decades. Indeed, the deflationary measures now being pursued so vigorously by the Administration and the Federal Reserve represent an exercise being tried for the very first time. Neither the authorities nor the professors really know what will result. This is part of the market's problem, because if there is anything to which it reacts negatively, it is the unknown.

Using various techniques, such as unit measurement, I then projected a possible downside target area for 1970:

On the decline from the December 1968 high of 994.65 to the February 1969 low of 895.39, a large bear unit of 99.26 points was formed. A two-unit workoff yielded a downside target of 796.13, within 1 percent of the actual July low of 788.07. A three-unit workoff—the normal expectation in an overall down market—targets at 696.87, thus approximating DJIA 700.

We can reasonably conclude, then, that the market is likely to rally sharply from near the 700 area, but this does not necessarily mean that the past year's decline must reach an

248

end at 700. As we've noted above, sometimes there is a climactic fourth workoff. On the assumption of a sharp rally from near the 700 area, the possibility exists of a final move down toward a four-unit workoff at 597.61.

Whatever the final bottom of the 1968-70 decline may be, it appears that a substantial wipeout of most, if not all, of the gains since the October 1966 bottom may be a necessary precondition for a new long-term bull market. This in turn would set the basis for an important grand-advance movement into the 1970's.

One final note of caution, however: Even though our early 1969 hypothesis proved most useful throughout 1969, no investor should assume that the hypothesis of possible 1970 price-action outlined above is a suitable basis on which to make investments. Hypotheses and forecasts are two different things: divergence-analysis forecasts are based on the continuous, week to week, measurements of investor behavior in the stock market and are a basis for taking action; hypotheses are *assumptions* made in order to draw out and test creative thinking.

A study of the stock fashions of the last twenty-five years made by Paul F. Miller, Jr., president of Drexel Harriman Ripley, in *Institutional Investor* shows that investors periodically changed their goals. From 1947–53, for example, remembrances of things past, like the Great Depression, drew investors to stocks of "sound value" with emphasis on dividends. During the 1953–56 market rise, long-term growth became fashionable, with such stocks as IBM, Alcoa, 3-M and Scott Paper leading the way. The period of 1956–59, with its recession, led to a search for "consistency of earnings increases." This search, combined with the technological boom launched by the orbiting of Sputnik I, led to an emphasis upon "smaller market capitalizations" and tobaccos, food, services, utilities, textbooks and electronics. The period from 1959–61 featured a speculative boom with an appetite for high "compound annual growth rates" and new issues. Semiconductors, bowling, vending and leisure-time issues were all the rage, and "performance-consciousness" appeared for the first time. From 1962–66, following the 1962 abortion, there was a boom in corporate profits; the growth favorites of the past were ignored for airline and auto stocks. Since 1966 performance has been the fashion, with smaller market capitalizations comprising the bulk of the speculative issues. But, as performance has become harder to achieve, there has been a deterioration in marketability, quality of earnings and reasonable price-earnings ratios.

We see, then, that the stars of tomorrow's market are not necessarily those of yesterday's. With this thought in mind, we may now consider some *possible* stars of tomorrow, remembering that *there is no assurance that they will live up to expectations or, even if they do, that their success will be reflected in tomorrow's stock prices.*

One money manager, the veteran T. Rowe Price, who believes that inflation cannot be halted and will shape the next fashion in stocks, said recently: "I am trying to convince my young men here that there's another way to look at investments than through earnings growth. They have to learn to predict trends in *value*. They have to understand that in runaway inflation investors *will* pay more for assets even if those assets are not producing current earnings."

Price suggests four broad areas in which tomorrow's stars may be found. The first includes companies that can help reduce labor costs, companies in electronics, automation and data-processing machines. Service companies, cosmetics and toiletries manufacturers and other beneficiaries of increased leisure-time activities make up the second area. The third area includes the technologically oriented companies. High-risk investments, they are hard to find at a reasonable price. And the fourth area centers on natural resources—companies that own land, minerals, timber and other basic commodities.

These and many other similar suggestions have a

common denominator that implies rapid and predictable earnings growth, the anticipation of trends—economic, sociological and technological—and the capability to change.

Perhaps no field is more widely touted for its rapid-growth potential than that of data processing. It is estimated that the computing-systems market will reach $20 billion in 1975, more than double the dollar volume of the 1969 market. But the biggest growth is expected to be in the specific services and proprietary products that complement the computers. While the market for general-purpose digital computers is expected to rise 178 percent by 1975, that for independent peripheral equipment is expected to increase 400 percent, and that for contract and package software is expected to expand 450 to 640 percent.

To me, one of the most promising areas for future investment is that which deals with communication between man and machine. A research group in Great Britain recently cracked one of the barriers to communicating in English with computers, producing a way for machines to analyze ordinary statements of command or request. Of course, computers even now can read human languages. But a directly addressable computer is something else and should prove to be one of the milestones in human progress.

Presently, the most widely used equipment for communicating with computers is the information-display system that utilizes a cathode-ray tube (CRT) similar to a TV-set picture tube. This provides instantaneous read-out of desired information. Some observers believe that the market for CRT data-display equipment can grow from $140 *million* in 1969 to $5 *billion* by 1975.

The optical character (OCR) is another man-to-machine communicating device with a future. OCRs use rapid optical techniques (as opposed to slower mechanical techniques like manual keypunching) to translate input data into machine-readable form. Of approximately 75,000 computers now in use, less than 1 percent are estimated to utilize OCR techniques; by 1975, of the 150,000 computers expected to be in operation, perhaps 20 percent of them will use OCR equipment.

According to research analyst Don Sinsabaugh of a NYSE member firm, computer time-sharing is another development in the field with a bright future. Time-sharing, or RAIR (Remote Access-Immediate Response) computing, an acronym coined by EDP *Industry Reports,* provides a number of users with direct access to a single computer simultaneously and remotely so that each has the illusion of having exclusive machine time. Like a chess master playing many opponents simultaneously, the computer switches from one user to the next, though at intervals measured in milliseconds. And since the time is shared, so is the cost, which puts an expensive computer within reach of a modest budget. Conceived in the late 1950's, RAIR computing is still in its early commercial development. But Sinsabaugh predicts that it should grow from a market of roughly $70 million in 1968 to almost $1 billion by 1973. The real significance of the development of RAIR, says Sinsabaugh, is that "the computer is now at the fingertips of Peter Drucker's 'knowledge worker,' much as the industrial laborer had electrical or mechanical energy at his side in the Industrial Revolution."

A final thought on the stars of the future. The major bottleneck affecting the data-processing industry (and all the rest of us) is the telephone company. The deplorable telephone service of recent years makes it apparent that data-processing firms and their customers, who are dependent on the telephone lines for data transmission, desperately need another communications vehicle. And one exists: Comsat—Communications Satellite Corporation (CQ). Its present authority is restricted to the international field, but CQ management has been pressing for authority to create a domestic satellite system. If this authority is granted, CQ has an almost unlimited growth potential.

But before an investor rushes out to buy Comsat or

equities in any of these specialized aspects of man-to-machine communication, he should remember what was said earlier about stock selection and market timing. One must select the right stocks at the right price—ideally when glamour equities are at a major bottoming area. Under these conditions—and barring obsoleting technological changes in the future—investments in this field may outperform those in most others.

A word of caution, however: Conventional financial analysis cannot be relied upon for the appraisal of companies in a newly emerging technology. Such criteria as sales trends, costs, earnings, returns on capital, capital turnover, liquidity, quality of assets and capital structure are only marginally applicable in evaluating the prospects of these companies. There simply is not enough of a track record on which to base judgments; and glowing statistics, as we saw in Chapter Three, can easily be manufactured for the balance sheet.

An even more fundamental reason why conventional financial analysis of these companies is inadequate, notes Joseph H. Spigelman, research director of Basic Economic Appraisals, Inc., "is the fact that the main assets of most of the companies . . . are ideas and the brain power to generate them. These defy quantification." So in evaluating these companies, one must ultimately evaluate their management.

In this book I have tried to show that whether the market goes up or down, specific investment opportunities exist in specific stocks, both long and short; and that implementation of successful investment policies requires the riding of the ebb and flow of investor sentiment rather than acting on the misplaced assumption that one can control it or ignore it. Since the market tells its own story, our job is to listen to it, then act on it, buying when we see the opportunity and selling when the opportunity matures, whether it be a day or a year later.

I have tried to show that investing requires as much aggressiveness and caution and acumen as any other moneymaking enterprise, plus some knowledge of the psychological handicaps and a mastery over one's emotions. The great investors, men like Bernard Baruch and Joseph Kennedy, achieved their success by utilizing a psychological approach to the market. Their market moves were trades against their psychological insights into crowd behavior. Divergence analysis is designed to help the average investor, who lacks the brilliant insights of the masters, to move in that direction.

Success, of course, cannot be guaranteed—it can never be where risk is involved. But if we can gain some insight into the present and future price-action of some stocks and of the market as a whole, insight that will enable us to make considered judgments before acting, we will be ahead of most investors. As Oliver Wendell Holmes once said: "A moment's insight is sometimes worth a life's experience."

The point is that in addition to absolute right and wrong there also are degrees of relative right and wrong; and while we may strive to be absolutely right all of the time, we must realize that this is humanly impossible. Our principal concern, then, must be to try to be relatively right most of the time. In the market, as in life, that is quite enough.

1991 ADDENDUM

In describing a recent workshop on *Cassandra Revisioned,* the C.G. Jung Foundation of New York said, "There is an upsurge of interest in divination in our culture, as people seek the answers to life's questions through reading the stars, cards and other sources of ancient wisdom. One can also learn to consult the 'inner oracle' by cultivating one's own medial intuition. Cassandra is a mythic image of an afflicted medium; she had the oracular gift, but no one would believe her."

Hedge fund manager Jim Birmingham of Lincoln, Massachusetts not only scoffs at such notions but adds that, "No one can predict the stock market." However, over the past two decades he has outperformed the market averages, year after year, and doing so with rarely a down year. Furthermore, since he is a voracious consumer of investment research, most of which he laughs at, how else to explain his consistent performance without accepting the notion that day after day and cumulatively he is making a constant series of forecasts?

I feel the basic reasoning why investment forecasts are necessary, despite their inherent lack of perfection, was best described some years ago by theorist, A.M. Clifford:

> "A carefully devised plan to meet an unknown future, to be continuously checked for modification as the future unfolds, is essential to intelligent investment management; and such a plan is utterly impossible without an estimate of what the future probably holds in store— and that calculation is a forecast. Consequently, all investors who wisely plan for the future are compelled to forecast whether they like it or not, and regardless of the risks involved."

With this background in mind, let's see how far we can look ahead in terms of potential risk and reward.

The Age of Aquarius: Bull or Bear?

First, I think it important to provide some anecdotal evidence of what I believe to be prevailing investor sentiment at year-end 1990, early-1991. What was expert opinion as America was on the verge of war in the Middle East? I think this is a fair sampling:

A. The departing leader of the New York Stock Exchange, John J. Phelan Jr. [who stepped down December 31,1990 after six years as chairman], said he expects the downturn in the nation's financial markets to last another six to eighteen months. [*Investors Daily*— December 21, 1990].

B. The *Institutional Investor*'s December 1990 cover of a special Money Management Forum issue was, "HOW TO WIN IN A BEAR MARKET".

C. Consumers' confidence, as measured by the University of Michigan, at December 1990 was 65.5 percent, down from 88.2 percent in July. This was only a few percentage points higher than the low in 1982. The Conference Board's Consumer Confidence index was cut-in-half from its 1989 peak, near 120, by December.

D. *Barron's* front-page of December 24, 1990 headlined, "The Stock Market in '91", featured interviews of four of the most widely known technicians and strategists. These four are people I respect. All four were bearish.

My perception of the sentiment environment, then, is that it was one of almost universal gloom. With this background in mind, let's go for it—what might lie ahead? In 1969 I used the concepts of the *whipsaw* [page 134-5] and the *grand expanding triangle of the bull market advance from 1949 to 1970* [pp.242-9] to make a long term forecast.

In recent years the stock market has etched new triangles*
which seem to me to be just as important as those of more
than 20 years ago. Outlined in the *weekly* chart of *Standard
& Poors 500* Stocks Composite on page 254D are the *grand
expanding triangle* of 1982-1991, the *ascending triangle* of
1987-1991 and the *inverted triangle* of 1989-1991. Let's
explore them.

The bottom of the *grand expanding triangle* is the trend
projected through the lows of 1982,1984 and 1987 which
came close to being tested—for the fourth time—at the
October 1990 low of 294.51. At January 9, 1991, the current
position of this trend approximated the 290 level, a level
also defined by the 4-bear unit count based on the initial
July 1990 decline [see page 136G]. In other words, this level
clearly seems to be the stock market's major risk parameter,
at this juncture. With the stock market at 311.49, this means
I think risk in the stock market approximates slightly less
than 7 percent. Assuming I am correct about the risk and
that either the October 1990 low or an early-1991 low will
constitute a failed fourth "now or never" attempt, to break
the trend, this means that I also feel that the potential of
a new bull market is substantial. The bottom of the *ascending
triangle* is defined by the trend projected through the 1987
and 1990 lows and that implies a higher support, nearer
the 300 level. The top of this triangle which originates at
the 1987 peak, was instrumental in defining the stock market's
July 1990 peak inasmuch as that represented a failed fourth
attempt to exceed it [also recognized the 3-bull unit level
on the daily chart; see page 136G]. The two parameters [above
and below] of this triangle are also marked by the facts
that whereas three times the 1982 low equals the 300 level,
six times the 1974 low equals the 360 level. This implies
confirmation that the yardsticks defining these levels are
significant.

* Edwards and Magee have dozens of illustrations of triangles in their stock market classic,
Technical Analysis of Stock Trends.

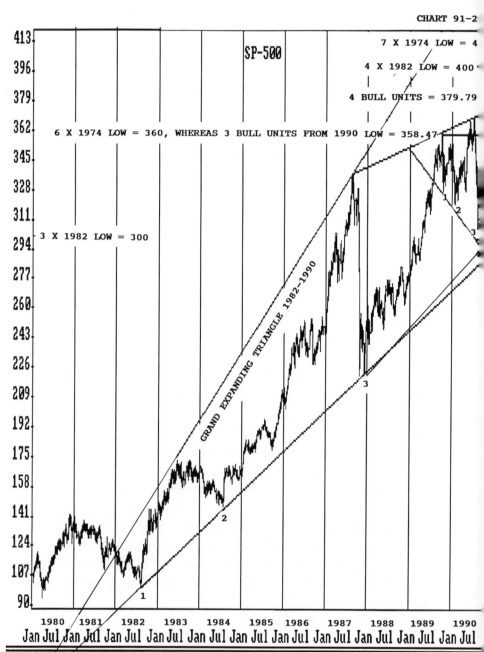

CHART 91-2

SP-500

7 X 1974 LOW = 4

4 X 1982 LOW = 400

4 BULL UNITS = 379.79

6 X 1974 LOW = 360, WHEREAS 3 BULL UNITS FROM 1990 LOW = 358.47

3 X 1982 LOW = 300

GRAND EXPANDING TRIANGLE 1982-1990

413
396
379
362
345
328
311
294
277
260
243
226
209
192
175
158
141
124
107
90

1980 1981 1982 1983 1984 1985 1986 1987 1988 1989 1990
Jan Jul Jan Jul Jan Jul Jan Jul Jan Jul Jan Jul Jan Jul Jan Jul Jan Jul Jan Jul Jan Jul

S & P 500 STOCKS, WEEKLY + INVERTED, RISING AND GRAND EXPANDING TRIANGLES

254D

The *inverted triangle*, which was etched during 1989 and 1990, shares the same overhead parameter as the ascending triangle. The declining side of it seems to me like an almost textbook illustration of the Rule of Three, including the fourth and last climactic gasp. With these three triangles helping to define the stock market's major levels of risk and reward, what upside potential is there?

The 3-bull unit count on the daily chart [page 136G] estimates a target of 358.47, which would be back toward the 1990 peak. A workoff of four of these bull units would be a new all-time high to 379.79. That level might be reached, yet stay within the top of the two smaller triangles, between 1991 and 1992. After hitting one of these levels, I assume the market would then experience another reaction, or bear phase, yet not break the bottoms of the two rising triangles.

Thereafter, the upside price objectives seem fairly clear cut. First, the 400 level since that would *quadruple* the 1982 low, whereas 420 would *septuple* the 1974 low. Eight times would be a target of 480. Moreover, since the rising side of the grand expanding triangle has been touched *only twice*, in 1983 and 1987, I believe a *third attempt* is in the cards. By 1992 the 480 level would hit the top of the grand triangle. That's as distant a point as I can see for now.

Even as America faced war in the Middle East, a financial crisis and a recession—or worse—at home, in early-January 1991, the long-term bullish case seems to be shaping up. The closest parallel between the potential U.S.-Iraq war is the Korean War, in my opinion. In 1950 the stock market also sold off sharply as the war started, then moved much higher. The fundamental bullish potential then was created by the end of World War II, as resources were diverted from war to peace. In other words, the end of the larger war was a more important factor than the beginning of a new and smaller war. I believe that same situation exists today with the recent end of the Cold War.

The Age of Aquarius: Bull or Bear?

Growing poverty in the world—in America as well—and the heightened awareness of the contrast between affluence and poverty, which is broadcast through television to the most remote places, create the circumstances for the potential of new advances in political freedom and wealth on a scale that may well dwarf the industrial revolution.

APPENDIX

APPENDIX

I. Stock Market Data [All data daily unless otherwise noted]

The Big Picture

01. Standard & Poors 500 Stocks, Composite—Weekly
02. Standard & Poors 400 Industrials, Monthly Average

The Broad Stock Market

03. Dow Jones Industrials
04. Standard & Poors 500 Stocks Composite
05. New York Stock Exchange Composite
06. Value Line Composite
07. Value Line Industrials, Weekly [1]
08. Russell 2000 Index
09. New York Stock Exchange Unweighted [QCHA cumulated]

Bellwethers

10. Dow Jones Transportations
11. Value Line Rails [1]
12. Dow Jones Utilities
13. Value Line Utilities [1]
14. New York Stock Exchange Financials
15. Hambrecht & Quist Technology Stock Index [2]
16. Hambrecht & Quist Growth Stock Index [2]
17. American Stock Exchange Index
18. NASDAQ Composite
19. Dow Jones 65 Stocks Composite, Weekly
20. Wilshire 5000 Index, Weekly
21. London Financial Times 30 Index
22. Tokyo Nikkei Index
23. Taiwan Fund *and* Taiwan ROC Fund

24. Hong Kong Index
25. Malaysia Fund
26. Thai Fund

The Internal Stock Market

27. Advances and Declines, Daily and Weekly
28. Advancing & Declining Volume, Daily & Weekly
29. New Highs and New Lows, Daily and Weekly
30. Daily 10-Most Actives
31. Weekly 20-Most Actives
32. Total Market Volume
33. Unchanged Issues
34. Total Issues Traded

Investor Sentiment

35. Odd Lot Shorts, Sales and Purchases
36. CBOE Put and Call Volumes, Daily and Weekly
37. CBOE Put and Call Premiums [3]
38. OEX Open Interests
39. Bullish, Bearish and Consolidation/Correction, Weekly [4]
40. Corporate Insider Sales/Purchases Ratio, Weekly [5]
41. Public and Specialists Short Sales, Weekly

II. Fixed Income [All data daily unless otherwise noted]

Short Term Interest Rates

01. Federal Funds Rate, Weekly [6]
02. 3-Month Treasury Bill Auction Yields, Weekly
03. 3-Month Eurodollar Deposit Rate Futures, Daily and Weekly
04. Treasury Bill Futures, Daily and Weekly

Intermediate Term Yields

05. 5-Year Treasury Notes, Weekly [6]

Appendix

Long Term Bonds

06. Treasury Bond Futures, Daily and Weekly
07. 20-Year Constant Maturity Treasury Yields, Monthly [6]
08. Cash U.S. Treasury 10s of 2005-2010
09. Dow Jones 20 Bonds Index, Daily and Weekly
10. Yields on Moody's AAA Corporate Bonds, Weekly [6]
11. U.S. Treasury Zero Coupons of 2015

Money

12. Adjusted St. Louis Monetary Base, Weekly [7]
13. M2, Monthly

Inflation/Deflation

14. Gold Bullion. Daily and Weekly
15. Commodity Research Bureau's Futures Price Index,
    Weekly [8]
16. CRB Spot Market Index Raw Industrials, Weekly [8]
17. Crude Oil, Daily and Weekly

Currencies

18. U.S. Dollar Index, Daily and Weekly
19. Japan Yen, Daily and Weekly
20. German Deutschemark, Daily and Weekly
21. Swiss Franc, Daily and Weekly
22. British Pound, Daily and Weekly

III. Once a Month Review of Standard & Poor's Weekly-Basis
Industry Groups [9]

IV. Individual Stocks

Appendix

Data for all of the above are available from the <u>Wall Street Journal</u> or <u>Barron's</u> with the exceptions footnoted above for these additional sources:

[1] Value Line, New York City

[2] Hambrecht & Quist, San Francisco

[3] Chicago Board of Options

[4] Chartcraft, Inc., Larchmont, New York

[5] Vickers Stock Research Corp., Brookside, New Jersey

[6] Federal Reserve Bank of St. Louis, <u>U.S. Financial Data</u>

[7] Federal Reserve Bank of St. Louis [telephone each Thursday]

[8] Commodity Research Bureau, New York City

[9] Standard & Poors, New York City

Index

Index

263

Index

Vietnam War, 63-65
  budget deficit caused by, 82
  inflation and, 83, 84
Volume-confirmation curve,
    153-56
  chart of, 167
Volume of trading, 116-23

Wall Street Journal
    (newspaper), 39, 41,
    95, 122, 241
Wall Street Transcript, The
    (periodical), 41, 170
Wallich, Henry C., 31-32
Warburg, James P., 38, 103
Washington, George, 193
Wayne, Hummer & Company,
    239
Wellington Electronics, 23

Westergaard, John, 58-59
Western Union Telegraph
    Company, 61-62, 164
Williams, Edward F., 57-58
Wojdak, Joseph F., 56
Wolfe & Company, 68
World trade, 89
World War I, 65, 68
World War II, 63, 65, 68

Xerox Corporation, 4, 59-60,
    123, 133, 198
  chart of unit measurement
    of, 132
  proposed CIT Financial
    merger of, 189-90

*Zolar's Stock Market
    Horoscope*, 16n